ISIS

THE ETERNAL GODDESS OF EGYPT AND ROME

ISIS

THE ETERNAL GODDESS OF EGYPT AND ROME

LESLEY JACKSON

Published by Avalonia

www.avaloniabooks.co.uk

Published by Avalonia
BM Avalonia, London, WC1N 3XX, England, UK
www.avaloniabooks.co.uk

ISIS - THE ETERNAL GODDESS OF EGYPT AND ROME
© Lesley Jackson, 2016
All rights reserved.

First Published by Avalonia, December 2016
ISBN 978-1-910191-02-6

Typeset and design by Satori

Cover image: Winged Isis, Brian Andrews © 2016 and Photo Lui, Tat
Mun/Shutterstock.com

Illustrations by Brian Andrews © 2016.

British Library Cataloguing in Publication Data. A catalogue record for this book is
available from the British Library.

DEDICATION

This book is dedicated to the Two Sisters, Isis and Nephthys,
and also to Sue and Mia.

BIOGRAPHY

Lesley Jackson has always had an interest in, and a yearning for, the mysterious geographical, be it lost worlds, otherworlds or the sacred places of this world. A career in IT was merely a logical façade. Many years of involvement in the local archaeological society deepened her interest in ancient cultures and their religions.

Since being blessed with early retirement, Lesley has devoted much of her time to researching and writing about early religion and mythology. Ancient Egypt is an enduring passion, but other paths are always beckoning from around the misty hills. She is the author of *Thoth: The History of the Ancient Egyptian God of Wisdom* (Avalonia, 2011) and *Hathor: A Reintroduction to an Ancient Egyptian Goddess* (Avalonia, 2013).

She lives in the remote East Riding with a tolerant husband and an ever increasing volume of books and rocks. Any remaining spare time is spent travelling or baking and making chocolates.

ACKNOWLEDGEMENTS

No study of Egyptian religion would be possible without access to their writings. I am indebted to all of those who have studied these ancient languages and have provided translations for the rest of us to use.

I would like to thank the British Library, the Egyptian Exploration Society, and the University of Hull for the use of their libraries.

Quotes are included with permission of the following:

J F Borghouts *Ancient Egyptian Magical Texts* E J Brill 1978. © Koninklijke Brill N.V.

R O Faulkner *The Ancient Egyptian Coffin Texts* Aris & Phillips 2007.

TABLE OF CONTENTS

Isis

CHAPTER 1

INTRODUCING ISIS

"'Who are you?' they say to me. 'What is your name?' they say to me."[1]

Defining the Indefinable

Isis is one of the best known of the Egyptian goddesses and so is quite hard to introduce. How do you summarise an All-Goddess? I originally titled this chapter 'Defining Isis' but quickly realised that was somewhat optimistic. There are a number of questions and themes running through this book but before we can attempt to understand Isis we need to get to know her in more depth. The worship of Isis spans many millennia and Isis in the Old Kingdom was very different to Isis at the end of the Greco-Roman Period; in what follows, I have tried to illustrate how she changes.

When we are getting to know someone there tends to be a standard set of questions we ask directly or try to ascertain; what is your name, where are you from, what do you do, what is your status and how do you relate to other people? Most of us define ourselves in the same way. As with anyone, it is possible to define Isis both by her attributes (such as Magician) and by her relationships (as the wife of Osiris).

Isis was originally significant because of her relationships with others, namely Osiris and Horus, and she is probably most revered as

---

[1] *The Ancient Egyptian Book of the Dead*, Faulkner, 1989:33 Spell 125

a loving wife and devoted mother. She also has a very close bond with her sister Nephthys but these are not her only partnerships. Relationships are very important to Isis and this may be why it was so easy for her to absorb other goddesses as she began to grow into the All-Goddess of the Greco-Roman Period. One of the questions that I am interested in is whether Isis is still the same Isis that came from the Old Kingdom or whether Isis has become the Great Mother Goddess who was with us in the very beginning. The interconnectedness of all life is central to the concept of the Great Mother and Isis becomes increasingly connected through her relationships with the other deities and her assimilation of other goddesses.

Many deities are strongly associated with specific aspects of life or the personification of places or concepts. It is too clumsy to classify a major deity by reference to one of their many aspects but looking at attributes is a way of getting to appreciate them and understand them a bit more. I will investigate the various aspects of Isis and these change considerably over time. Originally Isis was connected with royalty and not with any part of the cosmos but her role in the Osiris myths linked her to events which were of cosmic significance. As the cult of Isis and Osiris grew so did her importance and her aspects started to diversify. The Greco-Roman Isis kept all of her Egyptian powers and added more from the strong Greek influence in Egypt, particularly in the Delta region. She eventually becomes a beneficial Goddess of nature, a Saviour and, to many, the sole Goddess. There is a danger of being 'all things to all men' and through that losing uniqueness and individuality. Did this happen to Isis? Have we lost the character and essence of Isis as she transforms into the generic All-Goddess? How much of the Egyptian Isis was present for her followers in the Classical Period? From about 500 BCE Isis develops from an Egyptian Goddess into a pan-Mediterranean Goddess that virtually everyone could find a connection to. What was behind this meteoric rise? Was it Isis or the aspects attached to her which were so important and how much was manufactured for political reasons?

The Sources

We have two sources of information about Isis; the texts of the Ancient Egyptians and those of the Classical writers.

– Egyptian Literature and Other Documentation

Most of the literature comes from funerary texts and these are discussed in detail in chapter 14. We have no version of the myths of Isis, Osiris and Horus from the Pharaonic Period. Small amounts of information come from inscriptions in temples or with offerings and on documents. All the hymns to Isis come from the Greco-Roman Period, composed by both native Egyptians and Greeks. Many of the Greek hymns are *aretalogies*, a form in which the Goddess herself speaks saying "*I am Isis*" then stating her powers. The hymns to Isis are discussed in detail in chapter 21.

– Plutarch

Most of our understanding of the Osiris myth comes from Plutarch and it must be remembered that he was a Greek applying his cultural interpretation upon a very old Egyptian myth: he was writing 2,500 years after the *Pyramid Texts* were composed. There were many parallel versions of the myth so he will have based his interpretation on those from his local area. For example, in one Middle Kingdom version it is Sobek (the Crocodile-headed God) rather than Isis who crosses the sea in search of Osiris. It is thought that various traditional oral sources of the Osiris myths existed alongside the texts used by the priesthood. Plutarch tried to present a version of the myth that eliminated or reconciled all the inconsistencies that he was aware of. He was also unsure of the accuracy and authenticity of his sources and sometimes included the different elements. His objective wasn't to produce a literary version of popular myth, rather, an academic work designed as a guide for contemplation and study, a commentary on the myth rather than an official version of it. Plutarch believed that Isis and Demeter were the same Goddess so this will have influenced his interpretation of the mythology. He was a priest of the temple of the Oracle at Delphi and his mistress was a priestess of Isis.

– Other Classical Writers

There are many references to Egypt and the Isis cult by Greek and Roman writers such as Herodotus and Diodorus and these are listed in the bibliography. They have to be read with caution though: many of the authors had never been to Egypt, some were not involved in the cult and others were hostile to Isis so will be heavily biassed.

Isis in Classical Fiction

Isis was incorporated into fiction written in the Classical Period. Apuleius is considered to give a reasonably accurate description of the cult and initiation.

– *The Golden Ass*: Apuleius

Apuleius was born in the 120's CE in Algeria and was educated in Carthage and Athens, eventually becoming a lecturer at Carthage. He was a well-known writer and his novel *The Golden Ass* tells of the adventures of Lucius who was turned into a donkey through meddling in magic which he didn't understand. After much misery he is saved by Isis who restores him to his proper form. The story then becomes a serious, and almost personal, testament about initiation into the Isis cult. There are a number of translations of this novel which are given in the bibliography.

– *Ephesiaca*: Xenophon of Ephesus

Nothing is known about Xenophon of Ephesus, though his novel is thought to have been written in the 2nd century CE. The plot has a religious basis where the heroine Anthia has adventures similar to those of Isis. He assumes that Artemis and Isis are interchangeable, sometimes treating them as separate aspects of a single Goddess. Anthia was a priestess of Artemis at Ephesus, her father dedicated her to Isis until her wedding day. In the novel Isis and Artemis are upholders of chastity. The marriage was solemnised at the festival of Artemis-Isis. An oracle tells the couple to make offerings to Isis on the banks of the Nile and to visit the cult centres of Rhodes, Tarsus and Alexandria. Obviously they encounter dangers but Isis and Artemis are their saviours who rescue them when all else has failed. Anthia goes to the temple of Isis at Memphis and begs *"Mistress of Egypt who have helped me often, save me yet again"*. The pair is united to live happily ever after and say to Isis *"To you, greatest goddess, we owe thanks for our safety; it is you, the goddess we honour most of all, who have restored us"*.[2] Witt discusses this novel in detail.[3]

---

[2] *Ephesian Tale of Anthia and Habrocomes*, Xenophon of Ephesus & Anderson, 1986: 59 & 62
[3] *Isis in the Ancient World*, Witt, 1997:243-254

CHAPTER 2

THE ORIGIN OF ISIS AND HER MANY NAMES

"Behold I am come as the Mother from Chemmis."[4]

In the Beginning

Isis has drawn a veil over her origins. The fact that no place in Pharaonic Egypt claimed to be her place of origin suggests that the Egyptians faced a similar problem. Some of the anonymous Pre-dynastic deities who foreshadowed the ancient Dynastic deities can be glimpsed, such as the prehistoric Cow Goddess who we now know as Hathor, but there is nothing for Isis, no-one before her who was in any way comparable. Each *nome*, or province, of Egypt had its own deities. Isis is not a major deity in any *nome* of Lower Egypt, not even in the Delta region which later became her cult centre. She is a *nome* goddess in the 1st *nome* of Upper Egypt which is in the First Cataract region but she shares this with five other deities.[5] Was she always a Goddess of this *nome* or was she added as she became more important? We do not know. Although the southern region of Egypt was strongly associated with Isis in the Greco-Roman Period it is interesting that this is the only *nome* associated with her in the country's early history but it

---

[4] *The Myth of Horus at Edfu: II. C. The Triumph of Horus over His Enemies a Sacred Drama (Concluded)*, Blackman & Fairman, 1944:5-22
[5] *The Complete Gods and Goddesses of Ancient Egypt*, Wilkinson, 2003:86

never claims to be her place of birth. This is one indication that she was not an initially a very important Goddess nor a Pre-dynastic one.

In the Greco-Roman Period both Behbeit el-Hagar and Dendera claimed to be her place of birth. Dendera was a cult centre of Hathor since the 4th Dynasty and when Isis assimilated Hathor she could well have adopted Hathor's legendary place of origin.

One suggestion is that Isis was originally a local Goddess from the Delta region. She was always closely aligned with Osiris and his oldest cult centre is in the Delta, near Busiris, but unfortunately the origins of Osiris are as obscure as those of Isis. Osiris and Isis have very similar names leading some to suggest that they were originally a pair of deities. These ideas are covered in detail in chapter 5. If Isis originated as a local Delta Goddess then the claim of Behbeit el-Hagar may be more accurate. Cult competition and local pride are the more likely basis for these claims.

The Delta is the area of Egypt most open to foreign influences so it is fair to ask whether Isis was originally an Egyptian Goddess or one heavily influenced by, or even from, Libya or the Near East. There does not seem to be any evidence to support this theory so we can assume that Isis is a true Egyptian.

The Throne

Isis' name might give a clue to her origins. The Egyptians knew her as Aset and the hieroglyph used to write her name is a stylised throne. The core of her name "set" is the word for throne or seat. This same symbol was her original crown, a double emphasis on her importance in kingship. A Throne Goddess is only needed when there is a kingdom and a ruler. The early cattle herders and agriculturalists certainly wouldn't have had one and the Pre-dynastic tribes would have started out with tribal chiefs rather than with the notion of a king. Is this why Isis is not visible in the Pre-dynastic Period?

Isis is not attested to before the 5th Dynasty but is an important deity in the *Pyramid Texts* which appeared during this dynasty. Described as "*the Great Isis*" she appears more than 80 times assisting the deceased king. Was Isis created to support the institution of monarchy? Even if she was it doesn't explain her continual rise in popularity amongst ordinary people. They were under no compulsion to worship a deity just because the rulers and elite did. A goddess manufactured for propaganda purposes wouldn't have taken such a hold over people's hearts.

The crown symbols of deities are often related to the original animal or object they were associated with. One suggestion is that Isis originally wore her fetish symbol as a crown and this was later adapted or merged with the hieroglyph for throne, but what the original symbol was is unknown. It is possible that she was merely the personification of the throne coming into being alongside the concept of the king. The word for throne is feminine and thus was personified as a goddess in the Egyptian way of thinking. Is it likely that the Great Goddess whom Isis became originated in a symbol of absolute monarchy? I do not think so.

There is no evidence for my theory but could the throne symbol originally have referred to the head of the family as the matriarch grandmother? Ancestors were important to the early tribes and the Great Mother Goddess was everyone's mother. Later periods saw depictions of Horus on his mother's knee as a reflection of the king on his throne. The throne hieroglyph can be seen as a much stylised seated woman. Was the original concept that of the daughter sat on her mother's knee reflecting the Great Mother Goddess, women and the continuation of the tribe?

The Birth of Isis

An Egyptian would have explained the origins of Isis by relating the myth of her birth. Plutarch records his version of the story, in which the Sky Goddess Nut and the Earth God Geb were lovers and embraced each other so closely that there was nothing between them. Ra (the Creator Sun God) was unhappy with this and told Shu (the God of Air) to separate them so life could have space to exist. Ra became furious when he found out that Nut was pregnant and cursed her so she couldn't give birth on any of the 360 days of the year. Thoth (the God of Wisdom and Magic) took pity on Nut and played a game of draughts with the moon. He won *"the seventieth of each of the lights"* and created five extra days from them *"and induced them into the three hundred and sixty days*.[6] These days were outside the time which Ra had created so Nut was able to give birth to her children during this period. In birth order they are Horus the Elder, Osiris, Seth, Isis and Nephthys. When Isis became the All-Goddess of the Greco-Roman Period this birth order was sometimes altered to emphasise her pre-eminence. In the hymns from Philae she becomes the eldest child of Nut.

The Names of Isis

Deities with many names are a feature of polytheist religions and a number of Egyptian deities have the epithet *"of many names"* but by the Greco-Roman Period Isis is Isis *Polyonymos*, the Many-Named, emphasising her unique position in the eyes of her devotees. A large number of names is a reflection of a diverse number of attributes.

Isidorus, a Greek who wrote a number of hymns to her, says that her true name is not Isis but *"the One"*.[7] In *The Golden Ass* Isis says that the Egyptians *"call me by my true name, Queen Isis"*.[8] Or should that be Aset? Diodorus says that *"Isis, in translation, signifies 'ancient' – a name bestowed for her ancient and immortal origin"*.[9] A reasonable theory but probably from an incorrect deduction. The word *"is"* does mean old in Egyptian but Isis was not her Egyptian name, she was called Aset.

Naming Isis

Names are an important part of a deity's character and help designate their essence or emphasise a particular feature. Wordplay was very important and the Egyptians appreciated puns. Many times Isis will do something *"in her name of"*. This name could be influenced by the verb describing the action or vice versa. Because names were powerful in their own right, owning a name, or being able to assume it, gave you the powers inherent in that name. These were often those

---

[6] *Plutarch: Concerning the Mysteries of Isis and Osiris*, Mead, 2002:194
[7] *The four Greek hymns of Isidorus and the cult of Isis*, Vanderlip, 1972:27
[8] *Apuleius: The Golden Ass*, Lindsay, 1962:179
[9] *The Antiquities of Egypt*, Diodorus Siculus & Murphy, 1990:15

with an etymological connection. The phrase *"in this your name of"* is equivalent to saying *"with this your special power"*.

In the *Coffin Texts* there is a reference to Isis standing before the Sun God *"as Maat"*. Here she takes on the role of Maat (the Goddess of Order and Justice) and upholds order in creation. When she is associated with the inundation then it is Isis *"who bringest the Nile...in thy name of Sothis"*.[10] (Sothis, Goddess of the star Sirius, was the herald of the inundation.)

She of Ten Thousand Names

In his lexicon of the titles of Egyptian deities Leitz lists all known titles and epithets of Isis; this covers 46 pages. What is more surprising is that those of Hathor cover 67 pages. Hathor is not referred to as Many-Named, probably because this was an epithet used in the Greco-Roman Period, but she obviously was. Hathor was an ancient Goddess worshiped for a long period over a wide area so will have accumulated plenty of names and epithets. The goddess with the third highest number is Neith (the Creator Goddess) with 8 pages illustrating just how many-named Isis and Hathor were.[11] One inscription from Philae refers to her as *"the goddess of the innumerable names"*.[12]

Many of the names are very similar and have the titles Lady of, Mistress of and Queen of as a prefix to the same phrase; such as *Mistress of Lower Egypt* and *Lady of Lower Egypt*. Other names just have a slight variation in the grammar such as *Mistress of the gods* and *Mistress of all the gods*. The same Egyptian name has also been translated slightly differently by the various translators as our understanding of the language changes and progresses.

Elusive and Endless

We will never know where Isis came from, her secret lies beyond her veil. Or maybe she always existed for she is the *"Lady of what*

---

[10] *Egyptian Religion*, Morenz, 1992:302
[11] *Isis in Roman Dakhleh: Goddess of the Village, the Province and the Country*, Kaper, 2010:149
[12] *Pagans and Christians in Late Antiquity*, Lee, 2000:27

exists".[13] Isis was the Beginning so there could be nothing or no one that came before. Her names appear endless, I have counted about 500 during my research for this book. A long way off her 10,000 but maybe one day such a number will have been brought together and listed.

---

[13] *An Ancient Egyptian Book of Hours*, Faulkner, 1958:12

CHAPTER 3

ICONOGRAPHY

"Their image is coming out of them, from their own body."[14]

Showing the Unseen

Isis of the Pharaonic Period is very different to the Greco-Roman Isis and nowhere is the contrast greater than in her iconography. An observer from the Old Kingdom would not recognise the Isis known to the Greeks and Romans. Over three thousand years changes in iconography are inevitable but there are two reasons why depictions of Isis have changed so much. Firstly, from the New Kingdom onwards she assimilated many other goddesses and with them their iconography. During the Ptolemaic Period Isis, as well as other deities, were portrayed in a more realistic less stylised manner. She was also identified with Greek goddesses, absorbing some of their attributes. Then, when she left Egypt, her form was changed to that of a Greek goddess.

Depictions of deities are not intended to show what they actually look like but to try and convey something about their nature. This does raise the question if you alter the image of a deity does it alter their identity? In a way it does because the image is a representation of the deity or some of their aspects. The Greeks certainly changed, or reinterpreted, Isis to align her with their own needs and perceptions.

---

14 *The Egyptian Amduat*, Abt & Hornung, 2007:170

Any other cultures which adopted her will have gone through a similar process.

Depictions of Isis Within Egypt

Like the other goddesses Isis is portrayed as a slender young woman in a long sheath dress. In the earliest depictions she wears the hieroglyph sign for "*throne*" as a crown. This is a stylised throne, or chair, standing upon a raised platform.

By the beginning of the 18th Dynasty Isis was increasingly identified with Hathor and began absorbing her attributes. She starts to wear Hathor's cow horn sun disc crown and in later periods to carry the Hathoric *sistrum* and *menat*. This means that the two Goddesses are often indistinguishable unless they are specifically named. Everything in Egyptian art has a purpose so when they chose to show Isis and Hathor looking exactly the same it was for a reason. Are they saying that Hathor no longer exists? This cannot be, because Hathor continued to be worshipped and referred to as an individual Goddess in her own right. Without the accompanying hieroglyphs the context can sometimes tell us whether it is Isis or Hathor, at other times we don't know for certain. Perhaps we should read it as "*here is the Goddess, call her what you will*".

In the Greco-Roman Period Isis continued to be portrayed in a traditional form in temples but in statues and *stelae* she can look very different because Hellenistic styles were incorporated. Instead of the traditional wig Isis can have tiers of curled hair. She keeps the cow horn sun disc crown but it is often surrounded by flowers, leaves and ears of wheat. These Hellenistic images of Isis were widespread in Egypt. They were mass produced using a mould and may have been adopted by the local population as well as the Greeks they were aimed at. A lone star, depicting Sirius, sometimes appears as Isiac emblems on figurines and frescos from the Greco-Roman Period.

A hoard of small bronzes and metal-working tools were found at Qalyub in the ruins of a house. They date to around 200 BCE. All the bodies and heads of the statues were designed as components so that any head could be attached to any one of the bodies. This meant that it was possible to get a statue of Isis customised to your own tastes. Although most are in the Greek style they do contain traditional

Egyptian motifs.[15] This is a clear indication of how the variations in the character and iconography of Isis were important to people.

Other Crowns and Headwear

Isis sometimes wears a vulture headdress beneath her cow horn sun disc. Both the Goddesses Mut (the pre-eminent Goddess of Thebes) and Nekhbet (the tutelary Goddess of Upper Egypt) have associations with the vulture and are shown wearing such a headdress (see chapter 10). It came to represent the female divine principle and as such a number of goddesses adopted it, especially Isis and Hathor.

In one of the depictions of Isis from the tomb of Sety I (19th Dynasty) she wears a red tie, or ribbon, in her hair. These ties were commonly worn to keep the hair in place and also for decoration. Red had both positive and negative symbolism for the Egyptians, as it does for all cultures. In this context it symbolised the life-giving and regenerative powers of Isis. This is alluded to in one of the funerary texts. *"Isis and Nephthys will rouse themselves with their head-covering, their bright red band and dark red cloth."*[16]

Depictions of Isis outside Egypt

The Greeks dressed Isis in a costume familiar to themselves, changed her crown and gave her new sacred objects. They also gave her a European face. Apuleius describes Isis as wearing a tunic of many colours with a black cloak. His description might be a blend of a number of different costumes. It was probably intended to evoke wealth, beauty and divine power rather than to give an accurate description of her statue's costume. Plutarch says that the sacred robes of Isis are *"variegated in their dyes, for her power is connected with matters producing all things and receiving all – light darkness, day night, fire water, life death, beginning end"*.[17]

Isis was particularly popular in Athens and about 100 gravestone reliefs have been found which show women in the dress of Isis. These

[15] *How Do You Want Your Goddess?* Naerebout, 2010:55-57
[16] *The Liturgy of Opening the Mouth for Breathing,* Smith, 1993:33
[17] *Plutarch: Concerning the Mysteries of Isis and Osiris,* Mead, 2002:251

range in date from the end of the 1st century BCE into the early 4th century CE. The costume consisted of two garments, a sleeved gown (*chiton*) and a fringed shawl (*mantle*) which is tightly draped around the body and tied into the Isis, or mystic, knot at the chest. This was the most common type of dress shown on statues of Isis at the time.

An inscription from Alexandria calls Isis "*fair-tressed*"[18] which probably means fair as in beautiful rather than blonde. In many Greek depictions her hair is long and has thick corkscrew curls which may be an echo of the ceremonial wigs of Egypt. Many Greek and Roman depictions show Isis with a crown of stars, a crescent moon, and a diadem of leaves and flowers or the more Egyptian *uraeus*. This is the protective fire-spitting Eye Goddess who sat on the forehead of royals and deities, covered in detail in chapter 4. "*The asp to which the Egyptians have given the name Thermuthis is sacred... and they bind it as though it was a royal headdress...about the statues of Isis.*"[19] If her headwear is topped by a lotus it symbolises purity, if topped by ears of corn it is a sign of abundance. One ritual *stele* from the 1st or 2nd century BCE shows Isis in the Greek style. The cow horn sun disc has been replaced with small horns on her forehead and a disc, representing the moon, resting upon her head.[20]

Depictions of Isis outside Egypt vary and the overall impression can often depend on which goddess she is being equated to and the artistic culture. Isis-Aphrodite is often shown nude or lifting her skirt in line with the sexual aspects of Aphrodite. Her body shape also varies as different cultures regarded different female shapes as the ideal. One such example is a 2nd century CE terracotta figurine of Isis-Aphrodite (now in the Louvre, Paris).[21] She stands with her hands by her sides and the very slender figure of the Egyptian goddesses has been replaced by a fuller European one. One Phoenician scarab depicts Isis nursing Horus and is in the distinctive Near Eastern style. She sits next to one of their traditional incense burners.[22] A gold pectoral from the Nabatean Period of Nubia depicts Isis as a winged Goddess but she

---

[18] *Apuleius of Madauros – The Isis Book*, Griffiths, 1975:124
[19] *On the Characteristics of Animals Volume II*, Aelian & Scholfield, 1957:329
[20] *The Complete Gods and Goddesses of Ancient Egypt*, Wilkinson, 2003:242
[21] *Gods and Men in Egypt: 3000 BCE to 395 CE*, Dunand & Zivie-Coche, 2004:273
[22] *Egyptian Scarabs*, Wilkinson, 2008:51

is portrayed in a more voluptuous African form than the slender Egyptian one.[23]

Animal and Other Forms of Isis

Unlike some of the other Egyptian deities Isis is very rarely shown with an animal head. She can however be portrayed in animal and tree form and this is covered in chapter 4.

Posture

Posture can be used to convey important information about the aspect of the deity being emphasised and Isis can be depicted in a number of poses. She is frequently shown standing with her arms outstretched in a gesture of protection. The hieroglyph meaning "embrace" (hepet) shows two arms reaching out and the position of arms in reliefs often mirror this position. Isis has her arms around Osiris, or the deceased, and is shown in this position on the corners of some sarcophaguses. In one depiction she is shown sheltering an image of herself further emphasising her protective nature. It is normal for any protective deity to stand behind the person or deity being protected. The arms are sometimes arranged with one angled upwards and the other downwards to give the impression of encircling the protected person.

The hieroglyph sign for *ka* is made up of two extended arms forming a U shape. The *ka* is an integral part of a person, or deity, and is usually translated as the soul or spirit which came into being at the same time they did. It is also used to signify the life-force. Figures of people and deities can be shown with their arms positioned to form the *ka* hieroglyph. On some statues Isis holds the Horus child in such a way that her arms form the sign of the *ka*. This alludes to the life-force that she imparts to him.

A number of stylised postures were associated with mourning. Tomb illustrations show mourners in the following positions: hands open by their sides, arms crossed above or on the waist, one hand

---

[23] *Jewels of Ancient Nubia*, Markowitz & Doxey, 2014:plate 8

grasping the other arm or one hand raised to cover the face. Isis and Nephthys are portrayed in such postures whilst mourning Osiris. A common pose is kneeling with one hand covering the face. Kneeling is usually associated with mourning. One Late Period statue of Isis depicts her in mourning. She kneels and holds her hands to her face. She wears her original crown rather than the adopted cow horn sun disc, probably to emphasise her role as the wife of Osiris over her later attributes.[24] In funerary contexts Isis can be shown kneeling with one hand resting on the *shen*, the hieroglyph sign for infinity. This is a circle of rope knotted at the base. During the New Kingdom Isis sometimes kneels on the hieroglyph sign for gold, *nebw*. This is a collar with hanging beads drawn to look like a stool. Gold was associated with Hathor, so much so that she was almost a personification of it. By depicting Isis in this way her Hathoric aspects, such as solar and rebirth, are emphasised. One such example can be found on the sarcophagus of Tutankhamun.[25]

Figure 1 - Isis Kneeling

---

[24] *The Great Goddesses of Egypt*, Lesko, 1999:157
[25] *The Royal Gold of Ancient Egypt*, Muller & Thiem, 1999:35

Nursing Isis

Statues and amulets of Isis nursing Horus became very popular from the 3rd Intermediate Period, although examples have been found dating back to the 19th Dynasty. This was a time of great upheaval and trauma and people wanted to emphasise security, home and family. A mother nursing her child was a comforting and familiar sight. Once it became popular the Nursing Isis remained widespread and was perpetuated in Christianity as the Virgin Mary and Christ child. Isis had become the archetypal symbol of the protective caring mother not just to Horus and the king but to everyone. Some of these amulets were for funerary purposes but they will also have been worn in life, probably by women and children, to bring them under the protection of Isis. They were also popular as votive offerings to Isis. Large volumes were deposited in her temples during the Late Period. One had the inscription *"Isis gives life"*.[26] The depiction of the Nursing Isis did change over the centuries. Isis usually sits on a throne and wears the cow horn sun disc. In one style that appeared in the 1st century BCE Isis holds the Horus child with her left hand and her breast with her right.[27]

Wing Symbolism

A number of goddesses are portrayed with wings; mostly Isis, Nephthys, Nut and Maat. Gods are rarely shown with wings unless they are in their bird form. Perhaps the protective aspects of wings suggested a feminine force. The solar disc and the *wedjat* eye (a depiction of the restored Eye of Horus which is covered in chapter 6) do have wings but then the Solar Eye is a goddess. Isis is associated with a number of birds (see chapter 4) but this was not the reason for portraying her as a winged goddess. The Egyptians were skilled naturalists and much of their symbolism comes from the natural world. Birds use their wings to shelter their young, providing essential shade and protection. When threatened a bird will sometimes hold its wings forward as a defensive posture. The hieroglyph *"to protect"* is a vulture

---

[26] *The Quest for Immortality: Treasures of Ancient Egypt*, Hornung & Bryan, 2002:178
[27] *The Royal Gold of Ancient Egypt*, Muller & Thiem, 1999:232

with its wings extended in such a way. Goddesses in both human and cobra form often have wings to emphasise their protective aspects.

A faience pectoral amulet in the form of a winged Isis was often sewn into the linen mummy bandages and positioned so that her wings would spread over the chest of the deceased to embrace and protect them in the afterlife. In Thebes in the 2nd Intermediate Period a form of coffin known as a *rishi* coffin was common. The word *rishi* is Arabic for feather and the coffin was so called as it was decorated with two large wings wrapped around the body. They are believed to represent the protective, enfolding arms of a winged goddess either Isis, Nephthys or Nut. Isis and Nephthys are often shown as winged cobras in funerary contexts to emphasise their protective aspects. The winged cobra is not a dragon in the Western or Oriental manner as this is absent from Egyptian beliefs for some reason, although the Chaos Serpent Apophis does take on a dragon-like role.

Hovering was also seen as a protective action. In some paintings depicting hunting in the marshes a bird can be seen hovering over her nest to protect the fledgelings. Wings and feathers were believed to create air allowing the deceased to breathe again. Isis is shown as a bird hovering over the mummy holding an *ankh* and a billowing sail, the hieroglyph for wind or the breath of life. Her beating wings create air for the deceased. Isis *"who makes shadow with her wings, who creates air for breathing with her wings...revives her brother"*.[28] In depictions of the conception of Horus, Isis hovers over the mummy of Osiris in the form of a kestrel or falcon. The wings on goddesses are symbolic rather than trying to mimic the wings of birds. They are shown hanging below the arms, as if attached to arm and wrist ornaments. However, when looked at from directly below the outstretched wings of a bird of prey can look similar to the outstretched wings of the Goddess.

Objects associated with Isis

Egyptian symbolism is very detailed and multi-layered. Much depends on wordplay and references to sacred stories. The same

---

[28] *Sheltering Wings: Birds as Symbols of Protection in Ancient Egypt*, Shonkwiler, 2012:53

symbol would have had different meanings in different contexts and we are unlikely to understand all the depths and subtleties. Flexible thinking is always useful when dealing with symbols. Unfortunately, in her earliest portrayals Isis has no defining objects. She carries only generic objects such as the *ankh* and the papyrus sceptre which are common to the other goddesses. Had she carried something unique to her it might have given us a clue to her origins.

– The Ankh

The *ankh* has been a sacred symbol since the early Old Kingdom and is a very familiar and popular symbol today. It has a wide range of symbolism all centred on concepts associated with life, such as the life-giving powers of air and water, the life force in plants and the divine power that births and rebirths. Despite being a generic sacred symbol the *ankh* was increasingly associated with Isis in the Greco-Roman Period. Although all Egyptian deities still carried the *ankh,* to many Greeks and Romans the symbol belonged to Isis. The *ankh* is the sign for divine life and Isis with the *ankh* was the source of all life.

The origins of the *ankh* symbol are unknown. Suggestions include a sandal strap, a mirror, a doll as either a fertility symbol or a portable symbol of a goddess and a variation on the *tyet* symbol (which is discussed below). Wilkinson suggests that it may have originally been a tie as early depictions show the leg of the *ankh* in two parts and in the earliest examples the ends of these legs are slightly separated.[29] This would give it a close connection to the *tyet.* The *ankh* was associated with air and the concept of the breath of life. Deities often hold an *ankh* to the nose of the deceased. Scent was associated with the life-giving air and floral bouquets were shaped into *ankhs* and given as offerings to both the deceased and the deities. The relief on a 20th Dynasty *stele* shows a man offering a huge *ankh* which has lotus flowers entwined around it.[30] The lotus was a symbol of the renewal of the sun and reinforces the life symbolism of the *ankh.*

The *ankh* was also associated with the life-giving properties of water. Deities are often depicted pouring *ankh* signs from a vessel over a person. This was a method of showing the life-giving power emanating from them. For this reason some ceremonial vessels, which

---

[29] *Reading Egyptian Art,* Wilkinson, 2011:177
[30] *Symbol & Magic in Egyptian Art,* Wilkinson, 1994:161

were used for liquid offerings, were in the form of an *ankh*. The power of the *ankh* would be transferred to the liquid making it more potent. Less common is the association of food offerings with the *ankh* but they do occur. A relief from an 18th Dynasty temple depicts altars piled with bread to imitate the form of an *ankh*. The bread is framed by a triangle, the hieroglyph sign for "*give*". This reads "*given life*" which forms a pun as food offerings give life to the deceased.

Functional objects, such as mirrors and spoons, were made in the form of the *ankh*. It is a very flexible sign and can easily be combined with other symbols to alter the emphasis of the symbolism. One such example occurs on an early Dynastic slate dish used for water offerings. A pair of arms form the shape of the *ka*, the spirit, and also embrace the *ankh*. Some 18th Dynasty *ankh* amulets are decorated with a small triangle at the top of the leg. These are often drawn like a lotus flower or papyrus umbel, both of which are associated with rebirth.[31]

Today the *ankh* is a popular amulet but in Egyptian times it was uncommon as an amulet and was mostly combined with other symbols such as the *djed* (a symbol associated with Osiris which has connotations of stability). It was constantly depicted on reliefs though. The earliest *ankh* amulets date to the late Old Kingdom and are of gold or electrum (gold mixed with a percentage of silver). In later periods green ones occur, the colour symbolising new life and regeneration. It has been suggested that the *ankh* was such a potent and recognisable symbol that it was taken by the Coptic Church as the *crux ansata*, the handled cross.

– The Tyet

The *tyet* (*tjet*) or "*knot of Isis*" is a very old sacred symbol, its earliest depiction is from the 3rd Dynasty. It is called a knot as it is similar to the knot used to tie the clothing of deities. Its shape is like an *ankh* with the transverse arms folded down. The *tyet's* original meaning is unknown and thus open to speculation. A number of authors have suggested a form of sanitary protection, but this seems unlikely to me, or a protective belt worn during pregnancy. Other suggestions include a form of *ankh*. When written the symbol has a

---

[31] *Symbol & Magic in Egyptian Art*, Wilkinson, 1994:160 & 169

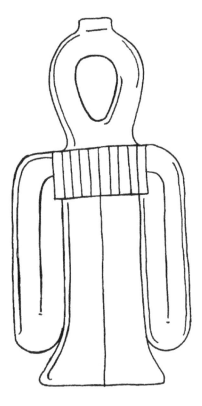

Figure 2 – Tyet

similar interpretation, that of "*life*" or "*welfare*". One 18th Dynasty bead necklace is strung with *tyet* and *ankh* amulets.[32] When the amulets are compared their similarity is striking. To me they suggest figures, the *ankh* being a figure with outstretched arms and the *tyet* one with arms by the side, which aligns with the doll theory of the *ankh*. Another suggestion is that the name is derived from *tayt*, meaning a shroud.

The earliest *tyet* comes from a woman's burial at Nag el-Deir dating to the 1st Dynasty. In the burial were three gold amulets; the beetle emblem of Neith, a bovine wearing the *bat* symbol of Hathor (a stylised cow head with horns) and an oryx with a *tyet* around its neck. The oryx occurs as one of the earliest amulets and has been found from the

---

[32] *Amulets of Ancient Egypt*, Andrews, 1994:87

Badarian Period. In later periods it was associated with Seth because it is a desert-dwelling animal. By the New Kingdom the *tyet* was closely associated with Isis but it was never solely her sacred object. Some *tyet* from the Old Kingdom portray the cow face of Hathor (or Bat, an ancient Cow Goddess) and are used as a cult badge. A 19th Dynasty statue shows a Hathor fetish necklace, in the form of a *tyet* with a Hathor head.[33] Even in the Late Period the sign can still be associated with Nut, Nephthys and Hathor in contexts of rebirth and eternal life.

Whatever its origin the *tyet* is an important magical symbol and was widely used as a protective amulet, particularly in funerary contexts. It was normally made of a red material (jasper, carnelian, red faience or red glass) reflecting its association with blood although green and blue ones have been found. Red is an ambiguous colour associated with death and hostile powers but also with birth and rebirth. Carnelian was a common crystal in Egypt, found in the Eastern Desert and Nubia, but was considered precious because of its orange-red colour and, in value terms, was ranked alongside silver, lapis lazuli and turquoise. It possessed both aspects of the colour red and could be linked to Seth as well as to beneficial deities. Its Late Period name was *herset* which can also mean "*sadness*". Red jasper was called *khenmet* which comes from the word "*to delight*" and is linked to the positive aspects of the colour red.

Spell 156 in the *Book of the Dead* states that the *tyet* should be made of red jasper. It is to be "*moistened with the juice of the 'life-is-in-it' fruit and embellished with sycamore-bast*"[34] (what these are is not known) and then placed on the neck of the deceased. Despite this instruction they are frequently found on the chest of mummies. "*The knot-of-Isis amulet has laid her hands on me.*"[35] The spell is often carved on the *tyet*. "*You have your blood, O Isis. You have your power, O Isis. You have your magic, O Isis.*"[36] As well as providing a protective function the *tyet* knot alluded to the restored body of Osiris and so to the integrity of the body of the deceased. "*Your head is knit to your*

---

[33] *An Unnamed Statue of a Late Middle Kingdom Vizier*, Thomas, 2011:10-14
[34] *Journey Through the Afterlife: Ancient Egyptian Book of the Dead*, Taylor, 2010:42
[35] *How to Read the Egyptian Book of the Dead*, Kemp, 2007:91
[36] *Journey Through the Afterlife: Ancient Egyptian Book of the Dead*, Taylor, 2010: 42

bones for you."[37] On a 25th Dynasty coffin the *tyet* is personified as a goddess.[38] Here she wears the *tyet* as a dress, her feet emerging from the ends and her arms and head from the hooped top. The *tyet* is often depicted with the *djed*. When shown together these two symbols could allude to Isis and Osiris and to the dual nature of life and death. They often occur in friezes on walls, columns and sarcophagus. The *tyet* might also have been carried as a protective amulet. Spell 156 from the *Book of the Dead* ends with the warning that no one should see the amulet being carried in their hands because *"there is nothing equal to it"*.[39] This suggests that it was worn as a protective amulet by the living but kept hidden. *Senet* was a very popular board game in Egypt and dates from the Pre-dynastic Period. It is shown in tomb decorations and even as a vignette (the illustrations accompanying the spells) in the *Book of the Dead* where it could be seen as a metaphor for the deceased's journey through the afterlife. The sides of the board are sometimes decorated with alternate *djed* and *tyet* symbols.[40]

Comparative symbols do not always help but Inanna of the Sumerians has a curved reed bundle as one of her symbols. In Crete the Minoans hung a knot made of cloth, corn or hair at the entrance to shrines to indicate the presence of the goddess.[41] Both these sacred knots look similar to the *tyet*. Were they all used as a symbol to represent a goddess either as a much stylised figure or through the association of cloth and its production to women or to their use of knot magic?

– The Sistrum

Originally the *sistrum* was the cult object of Hathor but by the Greco-Roman Period it had become strongly associated with Isis as a result of her assimilation of Hathor. The *sistrum* is a type of rattle, a musical instrument used in rituals. In Egypt it appears to have been used solely by priestesses and royals. The *sistrum* consists of a hoop mounted onto a handle. Metal rods are set into the loop and strung with small metal discs. Its shape is similar to that of the *ankh* and it

---

[37] *The Ancient Egyptian Pyramid Texts*, Faulkner, 2007:113 Utterance 355
[38] *Reading Egyptian Art*, Wilkinson, 2011:200
[39] *Journey Through the Afterlife: Ancient Egyptian Book of the Dead*, Taylor, 2010:42
[40] *Gifts of the Nile: Ancient Egyptian Faience*, Friedman, 1998:186
[41] *The Myth of the Goddess. Evolution of an Image*, Baring & Cashford, 1993:120

has a comparable significance. The sound made by the *sistrum* was considered pleasing to the deities and was also protective as it scared away demons and hostile forces.

Hathor's other cult object, the *menat* necklace, is not so strongly associated with Isis. It consists of a heavy bead necklace with a counterpoise and was used as a percussion instrument. During the 18th Dynasty Isis was increasingly associated with Hathor and began to be portrayed with the same attributes. In such depictions Isis carries the *menat* but it was never adopted by Isis cults outside Egypt, probably because they did not appreciate its significance.

– The Situla

The *situla* appears after the New Kingdom. It is a jug made in the form of a pendant breast, often mimicking the hieroglyph for breast, and was used to hold water or milk offerings. Water is associated with Isis through the Nile inundation and the rites of Osiris and milk with her maternal role as the mother of Horus. Breasts were associated with fecundity in general, as well as with the nursing Goddesses, and they suggest maternal and natural abundance. Although Isis is never shown with large breasts the goddess Taweret (the Hippopotamus Goddess associated with childbirth) and the God Hapy (who personified the inundation) are. The rise of the use of the *situla* appears to coincide with an increasing emphasis on Isis as a Mother Goddess.

The *sistrum* and *situla* are used in the cult of Isis throughout the Mediterranean and they were carried by priestesses, priests and participants. Depictions of Isis rituals in frescos at Herculaneum (Italy) show *situla* and *sistra* carried by women. The *situla* is usually held in the left hand. Grave reliefs from Athens (Greece) show women dressed as Isis. The *situla* is carried with the lowered left hand and the *sistrum* held up with the right hand.

– Boats

In a reflection of the importance of the Nile as a means of transport the Egyptian deities used boats. They were carried in procession in sacred barques and the Sun God was believed to travel across the sky in his Solar Barque. Originally Hathor rode in the Solar Barque but from the New Kingdom onwards Isis was increasingly portrayed in her place as she took over the role of protector of the Solar Barque and the Sun God. This is seen on a gold pectoral from Sheshonq II (22nd

Dynasty). Here a winged Isis and Nephthys stand either side of the sun disc on the Solar Barque.[42]

The Egyptians never had a deity associated with the sea but the Greeks and Romans did and so looked for one in the Egyptian pantheon. They may have seen depictions of Isis in the Solar Barque, or being carried in procession in her sacred barque, and assumed that it was a sea-going vessel. Many depictions of Isis in Greece and Italy allude to her maritime connection, she stands in boats and holds a billowing sail or a rudder.

Other Non-Egyptian Symbols

As the All-Goddess any symbol could be associated with Isis but there was still reasoning used when assigning the objects. Through her association with, and assimilation of, other goddesses there were plenty of objects to choose from. Whilst the Egyptians usually gave a deity one or two symbols the Greeks and Romans did not so restrict themselves. The cornucopia (a symbol of abundance in the shape of a horn overflowing with agricultural produce) belonged to the Fertility Goddesses, such as Demeter, who dispensed gifts from it. As Demeter was identified with Isis the cornucopia became one of the objects of Isis.

Isis the Healer was aligned with Hygeia, the Greek Goddess of Healing. Isis is portrayed as a Healing Goddess on a number of Alexandrian coins and also on an engraved carnelian gemstone. On her head she wears the *modius* (a cup used to measure corn) and holds an erect snake. In front of her is a globe and a flaming altar.[43] Through Hygeia's links to Asclepius comes the serpent and the altar, from Serapis the *modius,* and the globe alludes to Isis as Mistress of the World. (Serapis is her Greek consort, see chapter 9). A wall painting from Pompeii in Italy depicts Lunar Isis. She has large wings and wears a crescent moon with a lotus and stars on her head. She has a *sistrum*, a globe, a cornucopia and a rudder. The Roman Goddess Luna sits on a running hare holding a torch. Bearded and crested snakes sit at the

---

[42] *The Royal Gold of Ancient Egypt,* Muller & Thiem, 1999:225
[43] *A Collection of Gems from Egypt in Private Collections,* El-Khachab, 1963:147-156

altar.[44] The serpents represent the dynamic life force and the *sistrum* and lotus her Egyptian origins. The presence of Luna shows that Isis is the light in the darkness.

– Coins

Isis is depicted on coins from the last quarter of the 4th century BCE. Some coins from Alexandria during the reign of Alexander (356-323 BCE) have Isis on the reverse. She wears lotus flowers on her head, holds a *sistrum* and a spear and rides on a dog.[45] Isis coins in Greece occur over a wide geographic range but often over short periods. Corinth has the largest number and the most varied types, dating to 117-211 BCE. Isis is shown both on her own and with Serapis. She holds a *sistrum* and *situla*. Sometimes she is shown in front of the harbour of Kenchreai. When shown as Isis *Pelagia* she holds a billowing sail and part of her clothing blows in the wind.[46]

Isis is a common feature on many coins struck in Rome. The most frequent depictions are of Isis with a *sistrum* and *situla* or Isis standing on a ship. Many of these coins are anonymous, that is they do not carry the portrait of the emperor.[47] A 1st century BCE Roman coin shows Isis-Tyche-Panthea on one side and the Mother of the Gods on the obverse. A coin of Hadrian (117-138 CE) shows Serapis on a barge, Isis *Pharia* on his left and Demeter on his right.[48] On coins of Marcus Aurelius (161-180 CE) Isis is depicted with a peacock (the sacred bird of the goddess Hera) and a lion. She is also shown as Isis *Pelagia*. A veil flies from her head, behind her is a lighthouse and in front a mast and sail. Isis is shown on one coin welcoming Caracalla (198-217 CE) to Egypt.[49] She presents two ears of corn to the Emperor who is shown holding a spear and trampling on a crocodile. Coins of Antonius (138-161CE) show Isis seated on a dog holding a *sistrum*.

Many of the coins depict the Isis *Navigium* which was a very popular festival (see chapter 22). The issuing of coins depicting the Isis festival begins with Diocletian (248-305 CE) and the earliest one shows

---

[44] *Isis in the Ancient World*, Witt, 1997:83
[45] *Isis in the Ancient World*, Witt, 1997:236
[46] *Isis in Corinth: the Numismatic Evidence. City, Image and Religion*, Bricault & Veymiers, 2006:393-394
[47] *A Festival of Isis in Rome under the Christian Emperors of the IVth century*, Alfoldi, 1937:15-20
[48] *The four Greek hymns of Isidorus and the cult of Isis*, Vanderlip, 1972:21
[49] *Isis in the Ancient World*, Witt, 1997:236-238

Isis with Serapis-Neptune. Other depictions are of Isis and Nephthys as winged goddesses, Isis and Nephthys with a snake at their feet, the Horus child and Anubis either with a *sistrum* and caduceus or a palm-branch and caduceus.[50] Such coins depicting Isis were produced until the late 4th century BCE which was well after the Roman Empire had become officially Christian.

Portraying Isis

Depictions of deities will inevitably change over time and location but Isis shows the most diversity. This continues today, as can be seen in modern depictions where the artists do not feel constrained by anything wanting only to show how they feel about Isis and how she appears to them. In the end this is what iconography is all about. We can only portray the unseen and unknowable by how it comes across to us. If you can look at a depiction of a Goddess, or a sacred symbol, and immediately think of Isis then the artist has achieved what they set out to do.

---

[50] *A Festival of Isis in Rome under the Christian Emperors of the IVth century,* Alfoldi, 1937:20

CHAPTER 4

ANIMALS ASSOCIATED WITH ISIS

"I have flown like the swallow, I have soared like the falcon."[51]

Sacred Animals

Isis does not have a sacred animal and this absence is another reason why her origins remain a mystery. She was associated with certain animals and their number increased over time as her aspects grew and she assimilated other goddesses. Animals were not worshiped by the Egyptians but some deities were portrayed as animals because traits of the animal could illustrate a particular power or aspect of the deity; such as motherhood or protection. It was believed that the spirit of the deity could enter the body of their sacred animal and as a result the creature became a manifestation of the deity and a conduit for their power. Our concept of a sacred animal is one that is held in special regard by the deity and thus merits particular care and attention from us. The Egyptians viewed it differently and the sacrifice of sacred animals became very popular in later periods. They were considered a suitable offering which would act as an intermediary between the donor and the deity transmitting prayers and responses.

---

[51] *The Living Wisdom of Ancient Egypt*, Jacq, 1999:54

Birds

Birds feature a lot in Egyptian art and iconography. The distinct features of a particular bird alluded to both the deity and their specific aspects. A number of the bird illustrations are very accurate allowing the species to be clearly identified, others show a more generic form. Some artists will have been better at accurate representations than others or better naturalists. It is possible that portraying a particular species gave a slightly different meaning but it might just be a case of personal preference and ability. Birds have an obvious religious significance. As the deities were commonly perceived to reside in the sky contact could be established with them through flight. Birds flew between earth and sky and so were ideal messengers and symbols.

The *ba* was one of the components which made up a person, or deity. It was similar to our concept of personality and power. Because the *ba* was independent of the physical body it was portrayed as a human-headed bird. The *akh* was the form that the vindicated deceased took and was similar to our concept of the soul, being eternal and spiritual. It was depicted as a crested ibis.

– Falcon

Whilst the Egyptians didn't classify species as we do, it may make it clearer to know that a kestrel is a type of falcon and a kite is a type of hawk. The falcon is the most frequently depicted bird throughout Egyptian history. From the Late Pre-dynastic Period they appear on standards and palettes and were strongly allied to solar and sky deities. Their soaring was seen as the movement of the sun across the sky. As an aerial predator the falcon would swoop on its prey with the sun at its back, further emphasising its link to the sun. The falcon was particularly associated with the Sky God Horus and Ra-Harakhti (Ra-Horus of the Horizon). The kings, through association with Horus, also identified with the falcon. The bird was a solitary, dignified and fierce hunter and thus made an excellent representation for a god or king.

The kestrel in particular is associated with Isis and she is shown in this form in funerary settings. There was no need for her to have the same symbolism as her son Horus and she was not a Solar or Sky Goddess until much later. Does this point to some lost association with the falcon on her part? We can only speculate. In vignettes for spell 17 from the *Book of the Dead* Isis and Nephthys are depicted as kestrels standing next to the bier. As mentioned in chapter 3, hovering was viewed as protective and the kestrel is frequently observed hovering as it searches for prey. The kestrel was the most abundant species of falcon and so was the most frequently mummified raptor. It does not resemble the falcon used to depict Horus and might have been a popular offering because it was associated with Isis and Nephthys. However, an abundant species made a cheaper offering and so was more affordable to the majority of donors. The archive of Hor gives epithets to the mummified falcon offerings as the "*ba of Isis*" as well as the *ba* of other deities such as Nephthys, Osiris and Ptah.[52]

– Kite

The *Oxyrhynchus* papyrus calls Isis the Kite Goddess. When Isis and Nephthys are shown mourning for Osiris they are often referred to as kites (or screechers) and depicted as such. The kite has a shrill piercing cry and to the Egyptians this suggested the wailing of women in mourning. "*The screecher comes, the kite comes, namely Isis and Nephthys.*"[53] The kite is a scavenger and will have wandered the countryside and towns looking for carrion which will have suggested the wanderings of Isis as she searched for the body of Osiris. A 4th century BCE papyrus refers to "*stanzas of the Festival of the Two Kites*".[54]

Two species of hawk have been suggested from the depictions of Isis as a kite. One is the Black Kite (*Milvus migrans*)[55] while the other is the Chanting Goshawk (*Melierax musicus*)[56] based on the plumage and the shape. Chanting Goshawks are often seen in pairs, thus alluding to Isis and Nephthys. As their name suggests they have a melodic piping song which may have been similar to the sound of temple singers.

– Vulture

The word for vulture, *mwt*, sounds the same as that for mother and so it was associated with goddesses and maternity. Mut and Nekhbet were particularly associated with the vulture. Although it appears as a

---

[52] *Soulful Creatures. Animal Mummies in Ancient Egypt*, Bleiberg, Barbash & Bruno, 2013:53
[53] *The Ancient Egyptian Pyramid Texts*, Faulkner, 2007:203, Utterance 535
[54] *Between Heaven & Earth. Birds in Ancient Egypt*, Bailleul-LeSuer, 2012:134
[55] *The Animal World of the Pharaohs*, Houlihan, 1996:156
[56] *Pharaoh Was a Good Egg, but Whose Egg Was He?* Kozloff, 2012:59

Figure 3 - Isis as a Kestrel

scavenger to us the Egyptians liked its iconography. By the Late Period it was used to represent the female divine principle and was often paired with the scarab representing the male principle. The vulture was thus associated with a number of goddesses including Isis. Many goddesses wear a vulture cap beneath their crown. *"The Egyptians believe that the Vulture is sacred to Hera, and deck the head of Isis with Vulture's feathers."*[57] In spell 157 of the *Book of the Dead* an amulet in the form of a golden vulture is placed on the throat of the deceased to ensure their protection by Isis.

– Swallow

Plutarch says that Isis took the form of a swallow, rather than a kite, when she lamented the death of Osiris. It is possible that he misinterpreted especially if he heard the word 'screecher' used rather than 'kite'. Swallows do have a shrill, screaming call. There are illustrations of swallows in temples and tombs as this bird was often used to depict the *ba* of the deceased, usually in a human-headed form. This may have reinforced Plutarch's interpretation. However, it might simply have been a Greek bias against depicting Isis as a scavenger. Pliny refers to a folktale about swallows: *"Near to the town of Coptos there is an island sacred to Isis which they fortify with a structure to prevent it from being destroyed by the river."*[58]

– Ibis

The ibis is commonly portrayed in Isis cult scenes outside Egypt because it was considered a typical Egyptian bird. It is strongly associated with Thoth, with whom Isis has a close relationship (see chapter 9), and its presence may allude to him or his attributes rather than specifically to Isis.

– The Egg

A bird's egg could symbolise creation. In one creation theology either Geb (in the form of a goose) or Thoth (in his ibis form) laid an egg out of which the Sun God hatched. There is also a reference to the god Amun as the Great Cackler who laid the egg. The Egyptians were happy to overlook the biological problems of a male bird laying an egg. These myths may be the remnants of an earlier one in which the Pre-dynastic Bird Goddess laid the egg of creation. The goose is an emblem of Geb

---

[57] *On the Characteristics of Animals Volume II*, Aelian & Scholfield, 1958:315
[58] *Natural History Volume III*, Pliny & Rackham, 1940:353

and Isis as his daughter is sometimes called "*Egg of the Goose*".[59] There are references to a child being "*in the egg*" rather than "*in the womb*". The *Coffin Texts* allude to Horus in this way: "*I am Isis...a god's form has congealed in the egg*". It also refers to the egg as "*blue in aspect*".[60] Blue is the colour of the sky and the yellow yolk alludes to Horus as a solar god. Blue eggs are not particularly common but geese do lay them, one reason for the association of geese with Geb and Amun.

Mammals

– Dog

Isis was identified with Sothis, the Goddess who personified the star Sirius, in the constellation of Canis Major (see chapter 17). The Greeks and Romans knew Sirius as the Dog Star. During the Roman Period in particular, and in her cult outside Egypt, Isis was associated with the dog. Some Roman coins carry a depiction of Isis and in those she is often shown with a dog. Terracotta lamps show Isis seated on the back of a dog, these were probably used during the New Year's Eve vigil.

The temple of Isis in *Campus Martius* at Rome had a statue of Isis on a dog and there is a table, thought to be from the same temple, which shows a dog beneath her throne. The Egyptian Isis had no connection with dogs but to the Romans her companionship with the jackal-headed God Anubis will have suggested the connection. Processions for Isis outside Egypt were led by a priest wearing the jackal mask of Anubis. Less familiar with jackals, they called him dog-headed. Diodorus said that dogs led the processions during the Isis festivals in recognition of the fact that they guided and protected Isis during her search for the body of Osiris.

– Cow

"*In Egypt sculptors and painters represent Isis herself with the horns of a cow.*"[61] Isis has two connections with the cow. The first was through her assimilation of Hathor the Cow Goddess (see chapter 10), the second was that in later periods she became the Mother of the Apis Bull. The Apis Bull was considered a manifestation of the god Ptah of

---

[59] *Reading Egyptian Art*, Wilkinson, 2011:97
[60] *Pharaoh Was a Good Egg, But Whose Egg Was He?* Kozloff, 2012:59
[61] *On the Characteristics of Animals Volume II*, Aelian & Scholfield, 1958:323

Memphis. A male calf, who met the strict selection criteria, was chosen to be the Apis Bull replacing the previous incumbent on his death. In the 6th century BCE the cult of the Mother of the Apis Bull developed at Saqqara. Mummified cows were given a special burial, initially in a temple dedicated to Hathor. In this sacred animal necropolis a lot of bovine material has been found, offerings to the Apis Bull and to *"Isis, Mother of Apis"*. One inscription refers to Isis as *"the Great Goddess, who is in the House-of-Osiris-Apis"*.[62] There is a *stele* recording the burial of a cow in an area called the *"resting-places of Isis, mother of the Apis"*. The sacrificed cows were usually referred to as Isis but sometimes as *"she who belongs to Isis"*.[63]

25th Dynasty statues of cows portraying Isis as Mother of Apis look very similar to the Hathor Cow with a large collar, solar disc and *uraeus* and two plumes. Hathor was often depicted as a cow but seldom as cow-headed. A cow-headed bronze statue of Isis, the filial of a carrying pole from a shrine or bier, was found at Saqqara.[64] On this she wears the cow horn sun disc topped by two plumes. The Roman writer Tibullus refers to Isis as the Cow-Headed Goddess from Memphis.[65] However, many Romans found the idea of animal-headed deities repulsive so it may have been a derogatory comment.

– Cat

In Egypt the cat was sacred to Bastet but in the Isis cult outside Egypt it was considered a sacred animal of Isis. The *sistrum* was originally the cult instrument of Hathor and Bastet, both of whom have associations with cats and lions, so most *sistra* were decorated with these creatures. By the Greco-Roman Period the *sistrum* was strongly associated with Isis and the Greeks and Romans assumed that the cat symbolism belonged to Isis. They also associated the cat with the moon unlike the Egyptians who viewed it as a solar animal. As they saw Isis as a Moon Goddess this was a further link with the cat. Today the cat is considered lunar due to its nocturnal habits but its love of sunbathing betrays its solar origins.

---

[62] *Uncharted Saqqara: A Postscript*, Davis, 1998:45-56
[63] *Preliminary Report on the Excavations at North Saqqara, 1969-70*, Emery, 1971:3-13
[64] *Preliminary Report on Excavations in the Sacred Animal Necropolis, Season 1974-1975*, Smith, 1976:14-17
[65] *Isis in the Ancient World*, Witt, 1997:42

– Pig

The Egyptians had an ambivalent attitude towards pigs. To many they were associated with the Chaos God Seth and considered impure. Other groups valued them as a food source and in the Late Period the sow was associated with Isis and Nut as a symbol of fertility and motherhood. One epithet of Isis was the *"Great White Sow of Heliopolis"*.[66] Amulets and statuettes of a nursing sow were said to bring fertility and good luck.

– Gazelle

The gazelle was the sacred animal of Anuket, the Goddess of the Nile cataract region. She became associated with Hathor of Thebes which is probably how Isis became connected to the gazelle. *"People of Coptos worship and deify the female gazelle, though they sacrifice the male. They say females are the pets of Isis."*[67]

Other Animals

– Snake

In many cultures the snake is a creature of the Goddess because of its extensive symbolism. Egypt was no exception and any goddess could be portrayed as a snake. The determinative (a symbol used to clarify the meaning of the word) for the word goddess is a cobra. Why this was used rather than another snake is not known. Certainly a cobra with its hood extended is a very impressive and awe-inspiring sight. Cobras were said to be good mothers and perhaps their curved hood suggested the female body compared to the more phallic appearance of other snakes. Isis and Nephthys are frequently depicted as cobras in funerary scenes from the New Kingdom onwards. The ability of the snake to shed its skin symbolised rebirth and cyclical time. Their protective aspects were also useful in the dangerous afterworld.

Renenutet was a Snake Goddess from the Delta region. During the Late Period she was assimilated by Isis and passed on her snake attributes. The Greeks called her Thermouthis and as Isis-Thermouthis

---

[66] *The Routledge Dictionary of Egyptian Gods and Goddesses*, Hart, 2005:80
[67] *On the Characteristics of Animals Volume II*, Aelian & Scholfield, 1958:315

she was depicted as a snake. She has two main forms. One is with a woman's body which merges into a snake's body and her tail, often in a figure of eight, emerges from beneath her dress. The other depiction of Isis-Hermouthis is as a cobra with a woman's head.

Isis and Osiris (later Serapis) were also portrayed as snakes in the Greco-Roman Period. One jug used to hold Nile water shows a blend of Egyptian and Greek traditions. Here, Isis and Osiris are depicted as human-headed snakes. Isis wears the cow horn sun disc whilst Osiris has the hair and beard of Serapis.[68] In Ptolemaic Alexandria Isis was often paired with the Agathos Daimon, the Good Spirit of Alexandria. He was often shown as a snake with a beard and double crown and Isis is shown with a snake's body. Isis is also depicted as a snake in her role as Agatha Tyche, the protective Goddess of the city. The Greeks and Romans were aware of the strong association of the goddess with the cobra. On some Roman coins the benign Asclepion snake was used to depict the Agathos Daimon but the cobra was always used to show Isis as Agatha Tyche.[69]

– The *Uraeus* Serpent

The *uraeus*, depicted as a rearing cobra with its hood extended, is an Eye Goddess and a very potent symbol of life, protection, divinity and kingship. It occurs from the Pre-Dynastic Period and the myths describe its origin. The Eye of the Sun God, the visible disc of the sun, was considered a goddess as the word for eye is feminine. The word for eye also sounded like the word for "*doing*" and so became associated with an active, interventionist divine power. The Eye was considered the Daughter of Ra. The Eye became separated from Ra for various reasons and when she returned was furious because she had been replaced. To placate her Ra (or Thoth in some of the myths) transformed her into a cobra and placed her on his forehead.

Isis assumed the role of *uraeus* cobra through her assimilations, particularly of Hathor. Bastet, Sekhmet, Mut, Mafdet (an ancient Protective Goddess associated with a wildcat or mongoose) and Menhyt (a Lioness Goddess who was the consort of the Potter God Khnum) were also Eye Goddesses. Nephthys is often portrayed as a *uraeus* as

---

[68] *Egyptian Magic*, Raven, 2012:164
[69] *A Snake-Legged Dionysos from Egypt, and Other Divine Snakes*, Bailey, 2007:263-270

are Wadjyt (the Cobra Goddess of Lower Egypt) and Neith (the Creator Goddess of Sais).

– Crocodile

The crocodile was sacred to the Crocodile God Sobek and at his cult centre of Kom-Ombo Hathor was his consort. She was never associated with the crocodile so this is unlikely to be the reason for its association with Isis. In some of the myths a crocodile helps retrieve the body of Osiris from the Nile. The magic of Isis was said to protect those in papyrus boats in the Delta from being attacked by crocodiles, but many deities were invoked for protection against these dangerous creatures. To people living outside Egypt the crocodile was a typically Egyptian creature and as a result was frequently included in depictions of the fauna of Egypt. It was also large and fearsome and the fact that Isis had it under her control showed her power. Keeping crocodiles in temple precincts became popular at the end of the Late Period. A sacred crocodile lived in an Iseum in Libya and Juba of Mauretania gave a crocodile to the Iseum at Caesarea.[70]

– Scorpion

Isis has a strong link with scorpions through her relationship with the Scorpion Goddess Serket which is covered in detail in chapter 10. The scorpion was associated with the Isis cult at Coptos during the Greco-Roman Period. Part of the rites of the *Lamentations of Isis* involved women walking barefoot amongst scorpions, reflecting how Isis was protected by the seven scorpions of Serket as she walked in the Delta searching for shelter. "*Women in mourning at the temple of the goddess sleep on the floor, go about with bare feet, and all but tread on the aforesaid scorpions, yet they remain unharmed.*"[71]

Vegetation

Although they do not belong under the heading of animals, it is worth mentioning the few plants which were associated with Isis. Important trees were linked to deities and using the wood of these trees gave the object a stronger bond with the specific deity. The sycamore was originally considered a manifestation of Hathor or Nut who could

---

[70] *Isis in the Ancient World*, Witt, 1997:34 & 60
[71] *On the Characteristics of Animals Volume II*, Aelian & Scholfield, 1958:315

both be depicted as the Tree Goddess who provided the deceased with nourishment and shade. The sycamore became a manifestation of Isis in later periods when she assimilated these two goddesses. Thutmose III (18th Dynasty) is shown being suckled by a Tree Goddess on a relief in his tomb. The inscription says that the king is "nursed by his mother Isis".[72]

The persea tree has been identified as a *Mimusops* species, an evergreen which produces fruit. Because the persea fruit ripened at the time of the Inundation it was said to be sacred to Isis. Plutarch said "*the persea especially has been made sacred to the Goddess, because its fruit resembles a heart and its leaf a tongue*".[73] Reflecting this association with Isis, there is a tradition in Egypt that the persea bowed its head before Mary when the Holy Family were at Hermopolis.[74] In a 12th century BCE papyrus there is a reference to the "*plants of Isis*" which may refer to papyrus, another plant with a strong association with Hathor.[75]

Associations Outside Egypt

Most of the paintings and mosaics in temples that were outside Egypt included plants and animals from Egypt. They were originally included because they were considered Egyptian rather than because they were sacred to Isis but they soon became associated with her. In her role as the All-Goddess Isis was the life force present in all creatures and plants so the particular species was in effect irrelevant.

Isis the Animal Lover?

Although Isis was increasingly associated with different animals she does not seem to have had much of an emotional, or indeed any, connection to them and is never portrayed as a Goddess of Nature or of Animals. Despite her close association with Artemis she does not adopt Artemis' role as protector of animals. This may well be a reflection of

[72] *Reading Egyptian Art*, Wilkinson, 2011:47
[73] *Plutarch: Concerning the Mysteries of Isis and Osiris*, Mead, 2002:243
[74] *Isis in the Ancient World*, Witt, 1997:26
[75] *Isis in the Ancient World*, Witt, 1997:287 n.7

the Egyptian psyche. Wild animals may have been symbolic but they belonged to the untamed chaotic regions not the ordered world of their civilisation and so they didn't have a strong or romantic attachment to them. Even the revered cat and cow are only associated with Isis through her assimilation of Bastet and Hathor. The kite is probably the nearest we have to a sacred animal of Isis. Given her close association with the kite and the kestrel Bleeker debates whether Isis was descended from the prehistoric Bird Goddesses.[76] This is an intriguing idea but further research is needed into both these Bird Goddesses and the Pre-dynastic Goddess of Egypt before this can become a viable theory.

---

[76] *The Sacred Bridge*, Bleeker, 1963:193

CHAPTER 5

THE OSIRIS MYTHS

"I live, I die: I am Osiris... I live, I die, I am barley, I do not perish!"[77]

The Story of Osiris

There are many variations of the Osiris story and I will not be giving them in detail here. Comprehensive summaries are given in Tyldesley (2010), Watterson (2003), and Shaw (2014) amongst many others. Regardless of the changes over the millennia the fundamentals of the Osiris story remain constant. Isis and Osiris rule Egypt. Osiris is murdered by his brother Seth. Isis and Nephthys mourn and search for the body of Osiris and then resurrect him. Horus is then conceived to avenge his father's murder.

Osiris

The origins of Osiris are obscure. He is not considered a Pre-dynastic God as he doesn't appear on the tribal standards of the Pre-dynastic palettes. Given the vast timescales involved there is little trace of these early deities but there is no evidence of any god who could have been his predecessor. His earliest cult was Busiris in the Delta which suggests that he was a local God of this region. During the

---

[77] *Osiris. Death and Afterlife of a God*, Mojsov, 2005:8

Middle Kingdom his primary cult centred moved to Abydos. Osiris is usually depicted as a man with a mummified body whose hands emerge and hold the crook and flail, the symbols of kingship. He wears the *atef* crown, a tall conical crown with plumes at each side and rams' horns at the base. Osiris is associated with the *djed* symbol. This is a pillar with at least three cross-bars which originated in the Pre-dynastic Period. Its original meaning is unknown but it came to represent concepts of stability. In the *Book of the Dead* it is described as being the backbone of Osiris. Like Isis, Osiris has no sacred animals and he is not portrayed in animal form.

The Egyptians considered him the second-born son of Nut and Geb. They called him *Wsr* (or *Wsir*) and his name is written using the throne and eye hieroglyphs. The name of Isis is also written using the throne sign reinforcing the strong relationship between them and the concept of kingship. One suggestion is that Osiris' name originally meant *"that which has the power of the throne"*.[78] A number of studies have been carried out on his name in the hope of determining his origins but none are conclusive or widely accepted.

Troy has carried out research into the name of Osiris. She notes that both elements of his name, the throne and the eye, are feminine nouns which would normally associate them with goddesses. This does tie up with the feminine elements of his character, which are discussed below. Osiris has strong links to kingship but has no association with the Solar Eye. Troy suggests that the name of Osiris emphasises cosmic duality, resurrection and solar renewal and also that Isis and Osiris emerged as a consequence of the fragmentation of some of the aspects of the Great Mother Goddess.[79] Osiris is a very passive figure, a role normally associated with the feminine. He may play an important role in the afterlife but it is Isis who is the active partner. This fact was acknowledged by the Greeks and Romans, consequently it is Isis who takes the leading role in the cult's mysteries. Osiris has other feminine characteristics: an affinity with water and a connection to the underworld. In one variation of the myth Isis and Nephthys hurry to retrieve Osiris after he *"had drowned in his water"*.[80] The word 'his'

---

[78] *Patterns of Queenship in Ancient Egyptian Myth and History*, Troy, 1986:33
[79] *Patterns of Queenship in Ancient Egyptian Myth and History*, Troy, 1986:33-35
[80] *Ancient Egyptian Literature Volume I*, Lichtheim, 2006:53

suggests the association of Osiris and the Nile. It seems strange that a God of Water should drown in his own element. Was he merely reverting to type and unable to hold another form for long? Osiris was also associated with the sea. In one *Pyramid Text* spell he is referred to as *"great in your name of Sea"* and *"great and round in your name of Ocean"*.[81] Interestingly, given these epithets, Osiris is not portrayed as a Sea God but rather a God of Water in all its forms.

The remote creator deities are often beyond imagination but Osiris isn't. He is the innocent victim, the helpless one. Like humans he suffers but unlike Christ he does not suffer on their behalf. At the same time he is the power of revival and fertility, the power of the growth of vegetation. Through his death Osiris is the source of life.

Some Other Characters in the Myths

Seth is the villain of the story; the younger son who desires the throne and resorts to murder to obtain it. Seth may be the enemy of Osiris but there is no active conflict between them and Osiris is the passive victim. On one level the myth represents the helpless nature of the human element, such as the farmland, against the active chaotic forces of nature in the form of flood, storm or drought. Like Osiris, humans cannot control or act against such forces; they can only passively accept what happens and react or recover later.

Nephthys works closely with Isis, mourning with her and helping her retrieve the corpse of Osiris and resurrect him. Her role is discussed in more detail in the relevant chapters. Anubis is the Jackal God who oversees embalming and cemeteries. He plays an important role in the protection of the corpse and the resurrection of Osiris. Thoth appears in some versions of the story. He supports Isis, advises her and gives practical assistance. Chapter 9 covers this in more detail.

Isis the Excellent Wife

It was said that Isis and Osiris fell in love with each other in the womb, *"united even before they were born"*.[82] We have no record of any loving words spoken by Osiris to Isis. Perhaps he was the silent type,

---

[81] *The Ancient Egyptian Pyramid Texts*, Faulkner, 2007:120, Utterance 366
[82] *Plutarch: Concerning the Mysteries of Isis and Osiris*, Mead, 2002:195

which would be very much in keeping with his character. Isis, however, is forever proclaiming her love for Osiris. *"I love thee more than all the earth."*[83]

Isis and Osiris ruled Egypt and were well loved by their people. The early part of the myth emphasises her role as an ideal queen and wife; wise, supportive and faithful. Although she is the proactive partner after the murder of Osiris, during his life Isis did as good wives were meant to do. She remained in the background and didn't challenge or overshadow her husband. As the model housewife she taught the Egyptian women the arts of weaving, baking and brewing. Osiris also taught his people. These civilising gifts vary depending upon the source. By the time of the Greek *aretalogies* it was Isis who gave the people everything. One thing Isis isn't though is fertile. Sadly, producing sons is the primary duty of most wives. The fact that Isis conceives Horus posthumously and through magic tells us something important about both her and Osiris, which will be returned to later.

Osiris left Isis to rule on his behalf and he travelled the world to teach other people about wine and agriculture. Diodorus said that Osiris took his sons Anubis, Wepwawet (another Jackal God) and Min (a Fertility God) on his travels to Ethiopia and India leaving Isis in charge.[84] These three gods are all Pre-dynastic Gods. When Osiris came to power they must have been too important to ignore and so became allied with him. Osiris might have been naïve and trusting as far as Seth was concerned but, like any ruler, he would rather see his queen temporarily hold the throne for him rather than risk handing it to a brother who is desperate for power. During this time Seth *"attempted no revolution, owing to Isis keeping very careful guard, and having the power in her hands"*.[85]

The Murder of Osiris

The Pharaonic texts never mention directly that Osiris is dead. They use euphemisms such as *"Osiris was laid low by his brother Seth"*.[86] If his murder was stated directly, or even depicted, then his death would become a definite and fixed event, such was the power of

---

[83] *Isis in the Ancient World*, Witt, 1997:19
[84] *The Egyptian Myths*, Shaw, 2014:70
[85] *Plutarch: Concerning the Mysteries of Isis and Osiris*, Mead, 2002:195
[86] *The Ancient Egyptian Pyramid Texts*, Faulkner, 2007:231, Utterance 576

sacred words and images. Today we have no such beliefs but still prefer to use softer terms, such as 'passed away', especially when referring to loved ones. The *Pyramid Texts* allude to Isis and Nephthys as Kites searching for the body of Osiris after he had been *"thrown down upon his side"* by Seth.[87] Plutarch's version has Seth trick Osiris into trying out a coffin. Seth then sealed the coffin and threw it into the Nile. Isis was away at the time otherwise she would have cautioned Osiris against such a foolish act.

One fate the Egyptians feared was death by drowning because, in most cases, the corpse could not be found or else would be decomposed and partially eaten when it was. There is mention of Osiris drowning in the *Pyramid Texts*. The drowning theme continues into the later funerary literature. 26th Dynasty texts refer to Osiris being thrown into the river and his corpse floating to Imet in the Delta.[88] As Osiris is connected with the inundation his death by drowning in the Nile is not surprising.

Mourning Scenes

Isis and Nephthys are grief-stricken when they discover that Osiris has been murdered *"reducing the Two Sisters to widowhood"*.[89] They are often referred to as Kites or Wailing Women. *"You will hear the wailing sound of the Two Mourning Kites."*[90] For the Egyptians they are the archetypal image of mourning. *"My eyes are in tears. My heart is in sorrow. My body aches with burning flame."*[91] Isis and Nephthys are shown mourning at the bier of Osiris in many tomb decorations and vignettes during the New Kingdom. They are depicted in both human and kite form. The locks of hair Isis cut off in mourning were said to be preserved in the temple at Coptos. *"I pray for your health, continually making supplication for you before the hair of Isis at Coptos"* said one devotee.[92] Such a relic would have been treated with the same awe and reverence as the relics of saints were in the Middle Ages.

---

[87] *The Ancient Egyptian Pyramid Texts*, Faulkner, 2007:172, Utterance 485B
[88] *The Egyptian Myths*, Shaw, 2014:76
[89] *Traversing Eternity*, Smith, 2009:80
[90] *Traversing Eternity*, Smith, 2009:420
[91] *Traversing Eternity*, Smith, 2009:88
[92] *Cults and Creeds in Graeco-Roman Egypt*, Bell, 1957:67

Isis and Nephthys search for the body of Osiris as they mourn. It was essential that the body was found for without it there was no hope of resurrection. They are often helped in this task by Anubis. An 18th Dynasty hymn to Osiris tells of *"Beneficent Isis, who rescued her brother. Who searched for him and wouldn't surrender to weariness. Wandered this earth bent with anguish, restless until she found him."*[93] When they find the body of Osiris they bring it back and protect it as they continue to mourn over it.

The *Lamentations of Isis and Nephthys*, from the *Berlin* and *Bremner-Rhind* papyri, date to the Ptolemaic Period. They were designed to be recited by two priestesses taking the role of Isis and Nephthys. (The ceremony itself is covered in chapter 22.) *"I flood this land with tears today...we miss life though lack of thee."*[94] Her bemused grief is well known to all who have suffered the sudden loss of a loved one. *"Come to your house...you shall not part from me...long, long have I not seen you! My heart mourns you, my eyes seek you, I search for you to see you...I call to you, weeping to the height of heaven! But you do not hear my voice."*[95] Mourning was seen as an essential part of the process towards the resurrection of the deceased. *"You will be sated with the lamentations of her that weeps. Your ba will live by virtue of the songs of the mourners."*[96] The powerful emotion of grief and the energy put into mourning is transformed into *heka* which can then be used to revive the deceased.

The Corpse of Osiris

In some versions of the myth Isis finds the corpse of Osiris in Abydos. This was viewed as the burial place of Osiris from the 12th Dynasty. In another version Isis hides the corpse but not well enough. While Isis was away Seth *"taking his dogs out by night towards the moon, came upon it; and recognising the body, tore it into fourteen pieces, and scattered them abroad".*[97] The number varies, Plutarch says 14, texts on Greco-Roman temples say 42 (the number of *nomes* or administrative districts in Egypt). Diodorus says 26, others 12. According to Plutarch, Isis was not able to find his phallus because it

93 *Echoes of Egyptian Voices*, Foster, 1992:43-44
94 *Myths & Legends of Ancient Egypt*, Tyldesley, 2010:205
95 *Ancient Egyptian Literature Volume III*, Lichtheim, 2006:117
96 *Traversing Eternity*, Smith, 2009:420
97 *Plutarch: Concerning the Mysteries of Isis and Osiris*, Mead, 2002:200

had been eaten by a fish and had to make one. The loss of his phallus might have been in part an irreverent joke. The listeners would have known about the story of his infidelity with Nephthys. Dismemberment was a particularly dreaded fate for the Egyptians as a complete body was essential for rebirth and no-one wanted to live through eternity with part of their body missing or, even worse, in pieces. Isis buries the dismembered parts when she finds them. Some sources say that she just buried effigies so that Seth would be confused as to the location of the actual burial. Temples and cults grew up at these sites which led to rivalry between cities and several places claimed the same body part.

The 20th Dynasty *Salt* papyrus includes a *"ritual for the end of mummification"*.[98] Here the attack by Seth occurs in the Abydos *nome* and the details are specific. Osiris is attacked whilst under the *aru*-tree and this takes place on the 17th day of the 1st month of the inundation. Seth throws the corpse into the river and the Nile rises to cover Osiris and transport him away, providing another link with Osiris and the inundation.

The Late Period was a time of foreign influence and conquest. It is believed that this was the time when the concept of Isis going to Byblos (modern Jebail in Lebanon) in search of Osiris was introduced but the only source of this version of the myth we have is from Plutarch. The link with Byblos was not new though. Egypt had had important trade links with Byblos since the start of the Dynastic Period and Hathor had been identified with the local Goddess Baalat Gebal as Hathor of Byblos since the Old Kingdom.

The coffin containing Osiris is thrown into the Nile and eventually floats to Byblos. After much wandering Isis travels to Byblos and discovers that the coffin had been washed ashore and concealed by an *erica* tree (a tree heather) which grew protectively around it. Unfortunately the king had the tree felled and turned into a pillar for his palace. For some reason Isis does not go to the king and explain who she is. Perhaps she is wary of the news of her discovery of the corpse of Osiris reaching Seth. Instead she sits by a spring and mourns and is found by servants of the queen. Isis talks to them, dresses their

---

98 *The Egyptian Myths*, Shaw, 2014:76

Figure 4 - Isis and Nephthys

hair and gives them perfumes to wear. Perfume has a strong association with Hathor as does hairstyling. Isis is not normally associated with this and this action has probably come via Hathor of Byblos. When the queen smells their perfume she asks for Isis to be brought to her. Isis then becomes a nurse for the queen's baby. When Isis finally retrieves the coffin she treats it like a corpse wrapping it *"in fine linen, and pouring the juices of sweet herbs over it"* before taking it back to Egypt. Once found the corpse must be preserved to stop it from decaying as the physical body was considered an essential component of a person in the afterlife. Anubis and Thoth create and then carry out the embalming rites for Osiris. He becomes the archetypal mummy.

Adonis was the dying and resurrected lover-son of Aphrodite and his rites were celebrated in Byblos. The *erica* tree is sacred to Adonis who was originally a Phoenician Vegetation God. The link between him and Osiris is strong. *"Unto this day the people of Byblos venerate the wood lying in the holy place of Isis."*[99]

Resurrection

There are no details as to exactly how Isis and Nephthys resurrect Osiris but part of the magic is in the restorative power of her wings. *"She shaded him with her feathers and gave him air with her wings."*[100] Many of the spells command Osiris to *"live"*. The correct and powerful utterance of this word by Isis carries with it the magic powers which breathe life into the inanimate. The *Lamentations of Isis and Nephthys* express grief but also act as a spell. *"Isis provides thee with life...raise thyself, thou art risen, thou shalt not die, thine soul will live."*[101] The resurrection of Osiris is also covered in chapter 14.

The Conception of Horus

Once Osiris has been resurrected Isis conceives a child with him, but Osiris is the passive partner. In fact he is not in a state which we would consider as being alive, perhaps this is because he now belongs

---

[99] *Plutarch: Concerning the Mysteries of Isis and Osiris,* Mead, 2002:199
[100] *Myth and Symbol in Ancient Egypt,* Clark, 1978:106
[101] *Isis as Saviour,* Bleeker, 1963:8

to the afterworld and so cannot maintain a full presence in this world. What is still vigorous within him is his regenerative power. In the *Pyramid Texts* the conception of Horus is described in basic biological terms. "*Your sister Isis comes to you rejoicing for love of you. You have placed her on your phallus and your seed issues into her.*"[102] Tomb illustrations show Isis as a kestrel hovering over the mummy of Osiris and his erect phallus.

The *Coffin Texts* tell of a more mystical process where the conception is from a flash of lightning or, in this translation, a meteorite. Could it have been an actual impact with the accompanying sound of the shock wave that inspired the change in the story? "*After the blast of a meteorite such that even the gods fear, Isis awoke pregnant by the seed of her brother Osiris.*" Isis announces to the deities that "*I have conceived the form of a god...as my son*". Atum is a Creator and Sun God, he is often coalesced with the Ra as Ra-Atum. He questions what Isis says, perhaps he does not believe that Isis is capable of creating life through her own magic. It is he who is the Creator and she has just usurped his territory. Isis replies "*there is indeed a god within this womb of mine! It is the seed of Osiris*". She states the destiny of Horus and asks the deities for assistance in protecting her unborn child.[103] Atum gives his support and advises Isis to conceal her pregnancy from Seth. This support will only extend as far as the birth; after that Isis has to rely on other protection.

This protection doesn't appear to have been very effective as Seth manages to imprison Isis in his spinning-house. Isis is "*more rebellious than an infinite number of men, smarter than an infinite number of gods*"[104] so why was Seth not only able to imprison her in the spinning-house but stall her attempts to escape? What had happened to Atum's promise of protection of Isis and her unborn child? Isis appears to have been reluctant to escape and it is Thoth who urges her to do so, reminding her that she needs to listen to his advice. Why does Thoth have to persuade Isis to escape? Perhaps she was imprisoned psychologically not physically. Are we looking at the fear and despair that keeps a woman in an abusive relationship, having lost so much of

---

[102] *The Ancient Egyptian Pyramid Texts*, Faulkner, 2007:120 Utterance 366
[103] *The Emergence of Horus. An Analysis of Coffin Text Spell 148*, O'Connell, 1983:66-87
[104] *The Egyptian Myths*, Shaw, 2014:44

her power that she cannot flee? The stories that we live by are of great importance in our lives. Children will have grown up with these stories as their religious and cultural heritage. Tales that portrayed even the mighty Isis as a victim will have had a grave psychological impact on them. The fact that a goddess can be imprisoned and intimidated will have told girls that they could never be safe and gave the men an excuse for this behaviour.

The Mythic Levels of the Osiris Story

The Osiris story can be read on many levels and is continually being reinterpreted, as any good myth should be capable of. The Osiris myth went through a number of transformations from the 5th Dynasty when it is first attested to. We have no narrative of the myth, just allusions to parts of it, until Plutarch gives his version. There are at least three levels of understanding with myths. They explain cosmic order, the natural environment and its relationship with humans and they try to give an understanding of the afterlife. At any level they can relate to the psyche or soul and its development.

– Osiris the Vegetation God

At one level the myth of Osiris can be understood as an explanation of the cycles of nature. He is buried as the inundation recedes and ploughing and sowing commence. Isis breathes life into him and by harvest time has borne his son. This is hinted at in this speech of Isis. *"Thy divine seed, which was in my body, I put it on the back of the earth so that it should partake in thy nature."*[105] As Isis resurrects Osiris so he, in the form of the inundation, brings the rebirth of vegetation to Egypt. Osiris appears wherever and whenever there is a flow of water; that is, plant growth occurs when water is added to dry earth and his soul is reflected in the sprouting vegetation. The murdered Osiris is seen in the dry land and dead vegetation. His rescue by Isis is the rising waters of the inundation. This would have been more profound in a desert climate than it is for those of us who live in a wet one.

---

[105] *Isis as Saviour*, Bleeker, 1963:9

Osiris has a strong connection with trees. He could be the "*unique one in the acacia tree*".[106] The tree enclosing the corpse of Osiris can also be the mulberry, most frequently called the sycamore fig. This is the sacred tree of Hathor. In the *Pyramid Texts* there is an address to a sacred tree referencing the "*tree which encloses the god*".[107] Towns where Osiris was said to be buried such as Memphis, Heliopolis and Herakleopolis had sacred willow groves. It is thought that the species of willow referred to (*tcheret*) is the tamarisk. There was an annual festival of the *Raising of the Willow* which ensured the fertility of the ground. In one version of the myth the corpse of Osiris is enclosed by a tree so raising the tree is symbolic of raising his body enabling him to live again. Once the mummification was complete the mummy was lifted into an upright position and the *Opening of the Mouth* ceremony carried out to allow the deceased to breathe again. The willow tree was sacred to Osiris because it was believed to have sheltered his body while his *ba*, in the form of a bird, sat in its branches.[108] At Philae an inscription tells how a milk offering was poured at the foot of trees at the sacred tomb of Osiris in order to revive him.

– Kingship

The myth legitimised the new king after the death of the old one by transforming the old king into Osiris and the new king into his son Horus. This strong link to kingship is unusual compared to the dying and reborn Vegetation Gods of the Near East. Was the kingship role appended to Osiris' original role as a Vegetation God?

– The Afterlife

Osiris, despite his resurrection, is the only deity who actually dies when he is murdered and has to remain in the afterworld. Seth is often killed but, like Apophis, his killing doesn't seem to have any impact on him. Isis has her head chopped off by her son Horus in a brutal tantrum but again it doesn't cause her any harm. This does suggest that Osiris was originally a Vegetation God as no other deity needs to die. In the Old Kingdom only the king was believed to be resurrected but after the 1st Intermediate Period every person became an Osiris on their death and could benefit from the magic of Isis and be resurrected.

---

[106] *Traversing Eternity*, Smith, 2009:420
[107] *The Ancient Egyptian Pyramid Texts*, Faulkner, 2007:229, Utterance 574
[108] *Ancient Egypt*, Oakes & Gahlin, 2004:333

– Lunar Cycles

Pinch suggests that the mutilations described in myths are linked to the lunar calendar to explain or intermesh with eclipses and the lunar cycles. For example Osiris is cut into 14 pieces, the duration in days of the waxing and waning moon.[109]

– Plutarch's Theory

Plutarch interpreted the myth as a reflection of duality with two opposing powers, one benevolent and one destructive, in a perennial struggle for dominance. This was very similar to the Persian concept which Plutarch would have been familiar with. *"The soul of Osiris is eternal and indestructible but his body is frequently dismembered and destroyed...whereupon Isis...put it together again. For what is spiritually intelligible and is good prevails over destructive change."*[110]

Isis Without Osiris

In the Late and Greco-Roman Periods Isis and Osiris usually had temples in close proximity to each other. His most important cult centre was at Busiris in the Delta and about 10 miles away at Behbeit el-Hagar was the cult centre of Isis. Her temple was built in the 4th century BCE and dedicated to Isis as the Mother of the God.[111] Osiris had a temple at Philae where he was closely connected to the inundation.

Isis and Osiris were together from the earliest periods but when Isis left Egypt she often left Osiris behind. Osiris was never as popular with the Greeks and Romans although he played an important role in the Mysteries of Isis (see chapter 21). Perhaps he was too passive for their liking, they preferred a more active heroic god and Serapis often replaced Osiris as the husband of Isis (see chapter 9). There was a very close relationship between Osiris and kingship and although this was critical to the Egyptians it was irrelevant to other nationalities.

---

[109] *Egyptian Mythology*, Pinch, 2002:91
[110] *Plutarch: Concerning the Mysteries of Isis and Osiris*, Mead, 2002:232
[111] *Isis in the Ancient World*, Witt, 1997:18

Who is Osiris?

Witt argues that the basis of the Osiris myth was not rebirth and eternal life, nor the cycles of nature but the importance of hereditary kingship. Both Isis and Osiris have the hieroglyph for throne in their names and the kings can justify their claim to the throne and absolute rule by claiming descent from Horus.[112] Certainly Horus is referenced many more times than Osiris is in the *Pyramid* and *Coffin Texts* and the *Book of the Dead*. Kingship may be important in the Osiris myth but it is far too detailed and significant a myth to be solely about this.

If Osiris is a Vegetation God then he dies and is reborn every year. He does not need a son to inherit his power, he is the son reborn back into the womb of the Earth Goddess each year. Was Horus as the justifier of hereditary kingship grafted onto a pre-existing agricultural myth? Is this why Isis can't conceive until Osiris is dead? He is in effect his own son. Osiris is the spirit of becoming, the personification of the "*coming into being*". It is he who fulfils the promise of new life at all levels but he cannot function alone. Isis provides the spark to ignite life, without her magic and power it would exist only as potential - a seed forever dormant in the earth.

---

[112] *Isis in the Ancient World*, Witt, 1997:37

CHAPTER 6

THE HORUS MYTHS

"Isis the Great, the god's mother...nurse of the falcon of gold." [113]

Mother of Horus

Isis was known as *Mut-Netcher* "*mother of god*"[114] where the god in question was her son Horus. Her maternal aspect expands and by the New Kingdom she was often referred to as "*mother of all gods*".[115] Motherhood becomes an important part of the cult of Isis from the Late Period and she is frequently depicted nursing Horus. This could be a consequence of her transformation from the mother of Horus and the king to a universal Mother Goddess. One of the hymns from the temple of Isis at Philae puts specific emphasis on Isis as the divine mother of Horus.

A Confusion of Horus

There are a number of different Horus gods referred to in the various myths and it is not always clear exactly which one is being referred to. Horus is a Falcon God whose name, Hr or Hrw, has its root

---

[113] *The Triumph of Horus*, Fairman, 1974:80
[114] *Reading Egyptian Art*, Wilkinson, 2011:33
[115] *Conceptions of God in Ancient Egypt*, Hornung, 1996:147

in a word meaning "high" or "far off". He is the Sky God soaring in the heavens and in this aspect is a very ancient God appearing on late Pre-dynastic palettes. It is likely that there were many local Falcon and Hawk Gods who were absorbed into the Horus cult and so are known to us only as Horus. They will have differed considerably over the country resulting in the two major Horus Gods and endless confusion between them.

– Horus the Elder

The situation is not helped by the fact that Nut gave birth to Horus the Elder as her first born but he plays no part in the ensuing myths. Was this Horus the original son of the Sky Goddess (Nut or Hathor) and they didn't want to lose him so merely gave him four siblings? The myth of their birth gives the explanation for the additional five days of the calendar so five deities were needed. This was essential to realign the calendar to bring it in line with the actual year (excluding leap years). Alternatively, Horus the son of Isis and Osiris could be an incarnation of Horus firstborn son of Nut. In the *Coffin Texts* there is a reference to him being born *"before Isis came into being"*.[116]

– Horus as the Sun God

In this context Horus is the Celestial Falcon whose wings form the sky, his right eye the sun and his left eye the moon. Horus as a solar deity is often merged with Ra to become Ra-Harakhti. Hathor was considered to be the mother of the Celestial Falcon and she is also the wife of Horus of Edfu (Behdet).

– Horus Son of Isis and Osiris

Throughout this book when Horus is mentioned it is as the son of Isis and Osiris, unless stated otherwise. Nothing is simple in this mythology though, the temple calendar of Edfu says that Horus was conceived on the 4th day of the 3rd month of *Shomu*. It refers to Horus as the son of Isis and Osiris but in the next sentence refers to him in the womb of Hathor. [117]

---

[116] *Conceptions of God in Ancient Egypt*, Hornung, 1996:151
[117] *Temple Festival Calendars of Ancient Egypt*, el-Sabban, 2000:177

The Horus Child

The swamps of the Delta were the traditional birthplace of Horus and he was brought up hidden in the papyrus thickets. *"The son of Isis, conceived in Pe and born in Chemmis"*. Khemmis was said to be near Buto in the Delta. The exact location is unknown and it was probably a mythical place. In a New Kingdom hymn to Osiris, Isis tells how she *"nurtured the child in solitude and unknown was the place where he was"*.[118] His destiny was to inherit the throne of his father Osiris and to avenge his death by killing Seth. The birth of Horus is told in spell 148 of the *Coffin Texts*. Here Isis addresses Horus as *Bik*, which is the ornithological name for falcon. *"O Falcon, my son Horus, dwell in this land of your father."*[119]

Judging by his many mishaps and misadventures, the magical protection granted by Atum seems only to have lasted until Horus was born. Like all Egyptian children Horus was very vulnerable. Many healing spells refer to the times that Isis had to leave her young child alone in the marshes whilst she searched for food. Given that the other Goddesses, as well as the people of Khemmis, were meant to be looking after the Horus child this seems strange. Here Isis is portrayed as a very vulnerable and friendless single mother. This dreaded situation will have been familiar to many so perhaps it is a way of aligning Isis with the ordinary woman. A way of showing that she understands their plight as she has experienced it for herself. It is the healing of Horus that forms the basis of many of the healing spells and rituals, which are covered in chapter 15.

Some Other Mothers of Horus

In the funerary texts Hathor can be the mother of Horus. Mut, Serket, Neith, Nephthys, Wadjyt and Nekhbet were also said to have cared for the Horus child and are sometimes cited as his mother either in their own right or conflated with Isis. From texts at Dendera there is

---

[118] *Horus the Behdetite*, Gardiner, 1944:23-60
[119] *An Egyptian Etymology of the Name of Horus*, Gilula, 1982:259-265

Figure 5 - Isis Nursing Horus

reference to Wadjyt "*making shelter for her infant amid the marsh-plants, bringing up her son Horus in the papyrus marshes*". At Edfu Wadjyt is called "*the protection of Horus in Chemis*".[120] One myth says that it was the Ihet Cow who gave birth to Horus and nursed him in the marshes. She was usually identified with Hathor or Isis.

The Adult Horus

The adult Horus is closely aligned to the reigning king and much of the mythology surrounding him is a justification and celebration of the divine right of kings and hereditary kingship. Isis "*introduced him, with his arm grown sturdy, into the court of Geb*".[121] The *Turin* papyrus says that Seth took the throne and ruled for many years. This seems plausible as Horus wouldn't have been able to claim the throne until he was perceived as being of an appropriate age. Now that "*my son Horus has grown up in his strength and was from the first ordained to avenge his father*"[122] the trouble begins. Isis wishes to see Horus take the throne, for as the son of Osiris he is the legitimate heir. She also wishes to see Seth punished for the murder of Osiris. This is what guides and motivates her throughout the cycle of stories.

The *Contendings* of Horus and Seth

The *Contendings* stories are longwinded and convoluted. It is possible that they were largely told to audiences by storytellers who would have embellished them to incorporate local mythology, topography and current events. The key plot is as follows. Isis takes Horus to the council of the deities to begin the legal fight for the throne. Isis is ejected from the meeting and then tricks her way back in and also tricks Seth into condemning himself. Seth tries to seduce, or rape, Horus and Isis advises Horus on the best course of action. The action moves away from the law court and Horus and Seth begin fighting. Isis helps both Horus and Seth during their battle in the form of hippos and is decapitated by Horus who is angry at this perceived betrayal. After 80 years of conflict the tribunal finally award Horus the throne.

---

[120] *Horus the Behdetite*, Gardiner, 1944:23-60
[121] *Hymns, Prayers and Songs*, Foster, 1995:51
[122] *The Triumph of Horus*, Fairman, 1974:92

As with the Osiris stories I will not attempt to retell them in detail. Versions are given in many books such as Shaw (2014), Simpson (2003) and Tyldesley (2010).

The battles of Horus and Seth provided an endless source of stories which could be adapted to the socio-political climate of the time and the locality. The theme of conflict is unfortunately timeless and Horus and Seth give us sibling rivalry, claims to the throne and power struggles between countries as well as between good and evil. Horus continually fights Seth. The *Cairo* calendar marks the 22nd day of the 1st month of *Akhet* (Inundation) as unlucky, the day on which they both fought as hippos. Horus does not have the strength of his uncle but he is more cunning and patient and he has the help and advice of Isis. Sometimes Isis tries to act as the peacemaker. "*Make peace...life will be pleasant for you.*"[123] Not that they paid her much attention. As Horus was conceived with the purpose of avenging his father such counsel is slightly contradictory. It is reasonable to ask why Isis couldn't have avenged the death of Osiris herself as she has much more power and skill than Horus. The main reason is that the myth justifies kingship and the inheritance of the throne by the eldest son. The queens might have got unacceptable ideas if Isis had claimed the throne and acted without the need of a son.

Some Details from the Conflict

– The Eye of Horus

The sun was considered to be the right eye of Horus the Elder or Ra, and the moon his left eye. In later periods Horus, son of Isis, was associated with the Lunar Eye. The Eye of Horus was symbolic of many important things; soundness and perfection, the strength of the monarchy and the moon. It was also very vulnerable and in the battles between the two gods Seth tears out the Eye of Horus. In some versions the Eye escapes or is thrown away. The Eye is retrieved and restored by Thoth which results in the *wedjat* eye a symbol of divine life, the power to overcome death and the moon restored to wholeness. It is depicted as a combination of a human eye and eyebrow with the facial markings

---

[123] *Ancient Egyptian Literature Volume I*, Lichtheim, 2006:53

of a cheetah. A widespread symbol, it is often shown being offered to deities especially Horus, Ra and Osiris.

Isis performs a lot of healing on Horus when he is a child but she does not heal the wounded Eye. Why was this? On one level Isis was not the All-Goddess when the myth first originated so would not have been expected to do everything. The myth was not a monologue but an interplay of various deities with differing interests and abilities. Thoth is best suited to heal the Eye due to his knowledge and skill in magic and healing. He was a Lunar God and the Eye can be considered the moon which was under his jurisdiction and care. The restoration of the Eye restores cosmic order, *maat*, which was another major preoccupation of Thoth. When Seth tears out the eyes of Horus in retaliation for his decapitation of Isis, it is Hathor who takes pity on Horus and heals him. Although it is understandable why Isis would not be rushing to his aid over this incident.

The Eye of Horus was also associated with wine and wine offerings. The king offers wine to Osiris with the words *"take to yourself the Eye of Horus which has been freed from Seth"*.[124] Wine has a long association with blood in many cultures especially when it is red. The damaged Eye would have bled so offering it wine helped restore it to completeness. Wine was offered to both deities and the deceased. Wine and vines are surrounded by symbolism. The vine appears dead in winter and revives in the spring and its products, wine and dried fruit, survive for long periods of time after the apparent death of the vine. Wine's intoxicating properties reflect good and evil, in small volumes it is a social lubricant and makes people happy but over-indulgence results in chaos and illness. Intoxication can be a portal into other worlds and ease communication with the deities. In the Greco-Roman Period wine used in offerings was often referred to as the *"Green-Horus Eye"*.[125] Green has connotations of freshness and prosperity, the land after the inundation. Although Isis is strongly connected with the inundation she never took over the wine association from Hathor, another reason perhaps for her lack of involvement in the healing of the Eye.

---

[124] *Wine and Wine Offering in the Religion of Ancient Egypt*, Poo, 1995:78
[125] *Wine and Wine Offering in the Religion of Ancient Egypt*, Poo, 1995:24

– Sexual Assault

In one bizarre turn of the story Seth tries to seduce then assault Horus one night after they'd been drinking together. Horus catches Seth's semen in his hands and runs to seek the advice of Isis. She is horrified and chops off his *"corrupted"* hands and throws them in the Nile, using her magic to replace them. Isis takes semen from Horus and smears it on lettuce in Seth's garden which Seth then eats. At the tribunal Seth boasts that he has had intercourse with Horus who denies the allegations saying *"call forth our semen, and see whence it answers"*.[126] Seth's semen answers from the river and Horus's from within Seth. The deep meaning to this escapes me. Was it just a bawdy interlude? When Horus goes to Isis she suspects trickery rather than lust on the part of Seth and she is correct. She is well equipped to deal with the situation having a clever, slightly trickster side to her character. Knowing trickery and deceit she is well equipped to recognise it in others. Her wisdom allows her to see beyond the first emotive issue, sexual assault, to the true objective behind the act.

– Horus Turns Against Isis

"Beneficial is Isis to Horus her god"[127] but Horus doesn't always reciprocate. The New Kingdom *Sallier* papyrus contains the story of Horus decapitating Isis. He was angry that she had not killed Seth for him when she had the chance. Thoth gave Isis a cow's head in replacement. Plutarch gives an alternative explanation. *"Laying hands on his mother, he drew off the crown from her head. Whereupon Hermes crowned her with a head-dress of cow horns."*[128] Both descriptions seem to be a way of explaining why Isis began to wear Hathor's cow horn crown. Later myths have Horus rape Isis. Some authors have excused this saying that Horus as king needs to possess the throne, namely Isis. I disagree. The rape of goddesses is a way of disempowering them. It is a way of showing power over them and, through them, over women. *"Her tears falling into the water. See, Horus has had intercourse with his mother Isis."*[129]

---

[126] *Myths & Legends of Ancient Egypt,* Tyldesley, 2010:140
[127] *The Ancient Egyptian Coffin Texts Volume I,* Faulkner, 2007:205 Spell 269
[128] *Plutarch: Concerning the Mysteries of Isis and Osiris,* Mead, 2002:202
[129] *Ancient Egyptian Magical Texts,* Borghouts, 1978:89

– Mutilations

There is a lot of graphic violence in the stories and all the key players involved are victims at some stage. Osiris is murdered and dismembered. Horus tears off the testicles of Seth and sometimes Horus, Isis and Anubis castrate and dismember Seth. Seth damages the Eye of Horus. Isis cuts off the hands of Horus. Horus beheads Isis. Mutilating the body would put the deceased at great risk and so was greatly feared. Is this the only reason why there is so much mutilation going on in the Horus myths? Despite mutilation the deities are always restored which provided confirmation and reassurance that this could also happen to the deceased. At one level the mutilations appear as transformations, albeit very violent ones. The healed Eye becomes a powerful healer and Horus and Osiris gain new powers. When Isis is beheaded she gains the power of Hathor as Thoth gives her the cow-head or crown of Hathor.

Eyes are very vulnerable. On a mundane level blindness and other eye problems were endemic and very much feared in Egypt and this is reflected in the myths. As mentioned above eyes have very important symbolism and the Eyes of Horus are the sun and moon. Attacks on these bodies were attacks on the order and stability of the universe. In the *Contendings* Seth tears out both eyes of Horus to punish him for beheading Isis. Hathor heals Horus using gazelle milk. She plants his mutilated eyes and they grow into lotus flowers. The sun was born from the first lotus so the damaged solar and lunar eyes regenerate as the lotus which first bore them. The *Jumilhac* papyrus gives an alternate story. Here Anubis places each eye in a box and buries them on the mountainside. Isis waters them and they grow into the first grape vine. This reinforces the identification of the Eye of Horus with the wine offering.

The Triumph of Horus

A separate saga, the *Triumph of Horus*, describes one battle between Horus and Seth. It can also be read as the king battling and triumphing against invaders. *"Horus the Behedite...sallied forth into battle with his mother Isis protecting him."*[130] Isis is present throughout

---

[130] *The Triumph of Horus*, Fairman, 1974:80

the battle and advises and encourages Horus. *"Be of good courage, Horus my son. Be not wearied because of him."*[131] Horus battles Seth, in his hippo form, and eventually dismembers him. *"I fortify thy heart, my son Horus, pierce thou the hippopotamus, thy father's foe."*[132] The war-galley is described in a similar way to the boat used by the deceased, where the components are assigned to various deities. The boat has two masts *"one is Isis, the other Nephthys"*.[133] At the end of the battle *"Isis the divine said to her father Re 'Let the winged disc be given as a protection to my son Horus as he has cut off the heads of the enemy and his confederates"*.[134] This is presumably to protect Horus from the repercussions of this act as Seth never dies. Kingship and the right to rule is a strong element throughout these myths. The kings aligned themselves with Horus as the legitimate heir who will be supported and protected by Isis. *"Your son Horus is established upon your throne...whilst his mother Isis safeguards him by creating his magical protection upon earth."*[135] The Egyptian name of Khemmis was *Ahk-bity* which translates as *"papyrus thicket of the king of Lower Egypt"* emphasising the king's divine birth.[136]

The Reconciliation of Horus and Seth

The Egyptians knew that chaos and conflict were an integral part of creation, a part which could not be destroyed because the very act of destruction was a chaotic act. They were keen to reconcile and control opposing forces and the reconciliation of Horus and Seth was stressed in many sources, it is only in the later periods that this was ignored in the rush for revenge. Horus and Seth are often depicted tying together the heraldic plants of Upper and Lower Egypt, the reed and the papyrus, to symbolise the union of the Two Lands.

---

[131] *The Myth of Horus at Edfu: II. C. The Triumph of Horus over His Enemies a Sacred Drama (Continued)*, Blackman & Fairman, 1943:2-36
[132] *The Triumph of Horus*, Fairman, 1974:81
[133] *The Myth of Horus at Edfu: II. C. The Triumph of Horus over His Enemies a Sacred Drama (Concluded)*, Blackman & Fairman, 1944:5-22
[134] *The Myth of Horus at Edfu: I*, Fairman, 1935:26-36
[135] *The Tomb of Maya and Meryt I: The Reliefs Inscriptions, and Commentary*, Martin, 2012:48
[136] *The Routledge Dictionary of Egyptian Gods and Goddesses*, Hart, 2005:81

Horus and the Greeks and Romans

Much of the mythology about the adult Horus refers to kingship which the Greeks weren't particularly interested in and so he had little to offer the Isis cult outside Egypt once it had been separated from the cult of the king. In the Greco-Roman Period we have two distinct forms of Horus; Harsiese who is the adult son of Isis and Osiris and Harpocrates who is the Horus Child. Harpocrates was more important because of his healing aspect and as a reflection of the maternal aspect of Isis. When the cult of Isis spread outside Egypt Horus wasn't always included. For example, in the Isis *Navigium* procession Isis is accompanied by Anubis as her companion and herald. In Alexandria, and in a number of Greek cities, Anubis was invoked with Isis and Serapis as the son of Isis. Harpocrates was either left out or only ranked fourth.

Horus wasn't totally ignored outside Egypt. He was sometimes allied with Apollo, the Greek Sun God, and came to symbolise the triumph of good over evil. December was the month for the birth of solar deities. According to the *Philocalus* calendar of the 4th century CE the festival of *Sol Invictus* was held on 25th December.[137] Horus was also the "*saviour child of light*" born at the winter solstice.[138] Plutarch gives the birthday of Horus in the latter half of December. Another date quoted is 23rd December. All these are near the important winter solstice date of the birth of a Sun God.

The Mother of Us All

Isis certainly is a very proactive and determined mother, some would say domineering and interfering, as she drives Horus to his destiny. But could Horus have achieved this on his own? It seems unlikely given what we can glean about his abilities. Only through the active intervention of Isis can *maat* (peace and prosperity) return with the triumph of Horus over Seth and his chaos. Was this what the myth was originally about and it gradually got hijacked by kings in their search for victory and divinity? The maternal aspect of Isis as the caring, protective mother comes from her role in the Horus myths and

---

[137] *Isis in the Ancient World*, Witt, 1997:213
[138] *Osiris. Death and Afterlife of a God*, Mojsov, 2005:xii

through this she becomes the caring Mother of all. She eventually comes to symbolise and idealise all that is good and powerful about motherhood. Statues of her nursing Horus are a powerful evocation of this aspect which survived into Christianity as the Virgin Mother nursing the Christ Child.

CHAPTER 7

NEPHTHYS

"Hidden are the ways for those who pass by; light is perished and darkness comes into being' - so says Nephthys."[139]

The Quiet Goddess

Nephthys, the youngest daughter of Nut and Geb, is often overlooked as a Goddess in her own right purely because she is so closely identified with Isis. She is either perceived as one of the Two Kites and Two Sisters or seen as the shadow side of Isis. Both Goddesses can appear identical apart from their crowns, a closer look is often needed to see the individual Nephthys.

Name and Origins

To the Egyptians Nephthys was *Nbt-Ht*, Lady of the Mansion or House. She wears the hieroglyph sign for this as a crown; a basket upon a rectangle, which is the sign for a house. The house she was associated with could be the palace or the temple, which was the home of the deities. This is an important title but nevertheless still a fairly bland one and, together with the lack of specific sacred objects and animals associated with her, gives little clues as to her origins or

---

[139] *The Ancient Egyptian Coffin Texts Volume II*, Faulkner, 2007:9 Spell 373

character. Like Isis she is usually portrayed as a woman but can take the form of a cobra or kite. Nothing is known of her origins. Nephthys appears to have been a Pre-dynastic Goddess and there are hints that she was once more important. Her husband Seth and her son Anubis are both ancient gods as is Min whom she was associated with in some areas. Like many important ancient deities she may have been incorporated into the rites of Osiris and the Solar theology when these became dominant.

Aspects

The Greco-Roman *Book of Hours* calls Nephthys by the following epithets; *"kindly of heart...mistress of women...valiant...potent of deeds...the wise"*.[140] Like a number of other goddesses Nephthys can be one of the divine mothers and protectors of the king. In one scene at Philae the king is shown offering myrrh to Nephthys whom he addresses as his mother. The kings were happy to align themselves with as many goddesses as possible.

Her main role is as Mistress of the West, the protective afterlife Goddess, and here she plays an important role. *"I have placed Nephthys for you under your feet, that she may beweep you and mourn you."*[141] Alongside Isis she mourns the deceased, assists in their rebirth and protects them on their journey through the afterlife. She was a popular protective Goddess in funerary art but she never achieved the high status of Isis. An inscription from the tomb of Thutmose III (18th Dynasty) refers to her as *"Nephthys of the bed of life"*[142] and she is depicted as a kite guarding the funerary bed. Along with Isis she works the magic of resurrection and shares the epithet *"Lady of Eternity"*.[143] Nephthys does decline in importance and appears fewer times in the later funerary texts compared with the *Pyramid Texts*. However, she is present with Isis in the funerary text *the Amduat* (see chapter 14). In this text Nephthys can be viewed as the restorative waters of the *nun*, or the uterine waters of the womb, where Osiris and the Sun God are

---

[140] *An Ancient Egyptian Book of Hours*, Faulkner, 1958:13
[141] *Cracking Codes: The Rosetta Stone and Decipherment*, Parkinson, 1999:75
[142] *The Routledge Dictionary of Egyptian Gods and Goddesses*, Hart, 2005:103
[143] *The Tomb of Maya and Meryt I: The Reliefs Inscriptions, and Commentary*, Martin, 2012:48

regenerated and new life is formed. She plays a decisive role and symbolises the *"ultimately anonymous feminine power"* that is powerful because it is anonymous.[144]

Nephthys can be seen as a Goddess of edges, boundaries and transitions; between light and dark and life and death. *"They call the extremities of the land, both on the borders and where touching the sea, Nephthys; for which cause they give Nephthys the name of End."*[145] Although Isis is an important funerary Goddess Nephthys is often associated with the western horizon, death and the afterlife while Isis is associated with the eastern horizon and life. *"Ascend and descend; descend with Nephthys, sink into darkness with the Night-bark. Ascend and descend; ascend with Isis, rise with the Day-bark."*[146] Plutarch says that she was called *"Aphrodite while some call her also Victory"*.[147] She is also a Goddess of hidden and sacred knowledge. *"I hide the hidden thing."*[148]

Relationships

– Osiris

Nephthys, the youngest sister of Osiris, is often referred to as the *"Sister of the God"*.[149] According to Plutarch, Nephthys and Osiris had an adulterous relationship. *"Osiris in ignorance had fallen in love and united himself with her sister."* His explanation was that they looked similar, which is a somewhat feeble attempt as excuses go. The resulting child was Anubis and Nephthys *"exposed it immediately she bore it, through fear of Typhon"*. The exposure of unwanted babies was a Greek habit not an Egyptian one and it has been suggested that this was an addition by Plutarch. When Isis found out she searched for the abandoned baby and with *"dogs guiding Isis to it – it was reared and became her guard and follower"*.[150]

---

[144] *The Sungod's Journey Through the Netherworld*, Schweizer, 2010:106
[145] *Plutarch: Concerning the Mysteries of Isis and Osiris*, Mead, 2002:219
[146] *The Ancient Egyptian Pyramid Texts*, Faulkner, 2007:50 Utterance 222
[147] *Plutarch: Concerning the Mysteries of Isis and Osiris*, Mead, 2002:195
[148] *The Gods of the Egyptians Volume I*, Budge, 1969:456
[149] *The Tomb of Maya and Meryt I: The Reliefs Inscriptions, and Commentary*, Martin, 2012:45
[150] *Plutarch: Concerning the Mysteries of Isis and Osiris*, Mead, 2002:197-198

This adultery doesn't seem to be mentioned in the Egyptian texts. Many goddesses were said to have had sons by a number of gods but this isn't seen as adultery in the same way as it would be between married humans. Perhaps the Greeks didn't understand the Egyptian concept and, having serial adulterers in their pantheon, applied their own concepts to the Egyptian mythology.

– Seth

Seth was the husband of Nephthys. Plutarch tells of her as an unwilling wife but this may not have been the situation in the earlier periods. Certainly in the *Pyramid Texts* they sometimes work together. "*O Seth and Nephthys, go and proclaim to the gods of Upper Egypt.*"[151] Nephthys was never condemned as a result of her relationship with Seth and she is always supportive of Isis and never takes his side.

– Isis

Nephthys is a constant support and companion to Isis. The alleged adultery with Osiris doesn't seem to have affected their relationship at all. Egyptian kings were polygamous and Nephthys may just have been viewed as the second wife of Osiris. There are many references to them both as widows.

Nephthys works alongside Isis supporting her and reinforcing the magic, particularly in the funerary texts. In many of the myths Nephthys is with Isis but takes no action, often just watching or joining in her lamentations. When Horus is dying Nephthys cries alongside Isis and it is another Goddess who gives advice. In the story of *Queen Ruddedet* Ra sends Isis, Nephthys, Heket and Meskhent to help the queen give birth. Nephthys stands silently by whilst the others act. Why is Nephthys present if she is not contributing to the story or the outcome? Is she merely a shadow of Isis or is she included because she was once a more important Goddess and they didn't want to leave her out? Perhaps she is contributing in her secret fashion with a silent power or protection which is essential but unobserved.

Nephthys may not be the active one in the partnership but she performs a vital role in supporting Isis through her troubles. In one spell Isis comes out of the spinning house and says to Nephthys "*my deafness has overtaken me. My thread has entangled me. Show me my*

---

[151] *The Ancient Egyptian Pyramid Texts*, Faulkner, 2007:44 Utterance 217

way that I may do what I know to do.[152] As Horus is now a child she
shouldn't have still been imprisoned in the spinning house, was she
merely working there? Why had she forgotten how to heal? That is a
very worrying condition for such a Great Magician. Was she still
psychologically trapped by her past trauma and unable to function
properly in the present? More likely it was the patriarchal Greek
influence on the myths. Isis is being portrayed as a helpless mother
who cannot cope rather than an all-powerful dignified Goddess.

Associations

– Seshat

Seshat is the Goddess of writing, numeracy and all forms of
notation as well as the patron Goddess of architecture, mathematics,
astronomy and secret learning. She is often considered to be the wife of
Thoth. Seshat is identified more with Nephthys than she is with Isis.
One *Pyramid Text* spell states that *"Nephthys has collected all your
members for you in this her name of Seshat"*.[153] At first Seshat, with her
logical and academic character, seems the very opposite of Nephthys
but Seshat does have an afterlife role and a very strong involvement
with the secret teachings of the House of Life. Seshat is also a Pre-
dynastic Goddess.

– Anuket

During the Late Period Nephthys was associated with Anuket, the
Goddess of the Cataracts of the Lower Nile. There is a reference to
Nephthys as a gazelle which was the sacred animal of Anuket. At Komir
(south of Esna) is a Greco-Roman temple dedicated to Nephthys and
Anuket. Nephthys was worshiped here in the form of a kite. There are
hymns to both Goddesses on the temple walls.[154]

---

[152] *Ancient Egyptian Magical Texts*, Borghouts, 1978:25
[153] *The Ancient Egyptian Pyramid Texts*, Faulkner, 2007:119 Utterance 364
[154] *Egypt from Alexander to the Copts*, Bagnall & Rathbone, 2004:224

A Life Apart or a Life Conjoined?

Does Nephthys have a distinct role without Isis? Certainly a number of spells from the *Pyramid Texts* and the *Coffin Texts* refer to Nephthys alone. It is Nephthys who will *"gather you together...for such is this great lady, possessor of life in the night bark"* and *"Nephthys has favoured you, you being renewed daily in the night"*.[155] One *Pyramid Text* spell refers to the king as a star who fades at dawn. *"I have come to you, O Nephthys. I have come to you, Sun Bark of night."*[156] This is not conclusive proof though as many deities are cited in this way. If Nephthys originally had a separate role it is long lost. There is no evidence that she had a cult of her own but she is still portrayed as an individual Goddess as well. She is the *"god's sister, lady of heaven, mistress of the Two Lands"*.[157]

Some authors refer to Nephthys as the dark sister of Isis, her shadow, but that implies that Isis has no negative aspects and Nephthys no positive ones. Even a quick review of these Goddesses will show that this is not so. Another suggestion is that Isis and Nephthys are opposites. The Egyptians were fascinated by dualities and the pair do have contrasting representations such as Isis representing day and Nephthys night. Often Isis and Nephthys are referred to as the Two Sisters and at times they appear inseparable. The Egyptians believed that each person, and deity, was made up of a number of essential components; such as the body, the soul and the name. The *ka*, the life force, came into being at the same time and was viewed as the person's double. All these elements needed to be recombined to ensure survival in the afterlife. *"Mine are Isis and Nephthys, the two fair sisters; may your doubles be joined in peace."*[158]

Nephthys Abandoned

By the time we get to the Greco-Roman period Nephthys is fading away and she plays no part in the mystery cults, which is surprising given her mysterious but helpful nature. Why didn't the Greeks take to

---

[155] *Patterns of Queenship in Ancient Egyptian Myth and History*, Troy, 1986:39
[156] *Hymns, Prayers and Songs*, Foster, 1995:30
[157] *The Tomb of Maya and Meryt I: The Reliefs Inscriptions, and Commentary*, Martin, 2012:47
[158] *The Ancient Egyptian Coffin Texts Volume I*, Faulkner, 2007:275 Spell 341

Nephthys? It is possible that they, viewing Isis as the All-Goddess, saw no need for her to have a female companion? Or was it because she was less important at the end of the Pharaonic Period? My suggestion is that they didn't understand the importance of duality which is embodied in her role. They also wouldn't have liked the idea of women sharing power as it strengthens them, they preferred to weaken their powers by presenting them as rivals.

The Loyal Sister

Because Nephthys works so very closely with Isis it has been suggested that she is merely an aspect of Isis. I do not support this position but certainly their dual role is critical and is discussed in detail in the following chapter. Nephthys is not the shadow of Isis. She is not the dark, dangerous aspect which is hidden away. Isis does far more smiting than Nephthys. The roles which they play suggest that they have a strong internal relationship and a complementary nature. Nephthys embodies beneficent and selfless care for others, she is a true sister to the other deities. She is "*Nephthys, the benefactress of the gods*".[159] Nephthys is a Goddess in her own right but she does work closely with Isis and this fact is critical in the understanding of both of them.

---

[159] *A Pious Soldier: Stele Aswan 1057*, Ray, 1967:169-180

CHAPTER 8

THE POWER OF TWO

"The Two Weeping and mourning women, the Two Sisters, protect him; they are the Two Kites." [160]

The Two Sisters

Isis and Nephthys are the Two Sisters who work closely together. Nephthys has been discussed as a Goddess in her own right in the previous chapter, but one of her most important aspects is her ability to work closely and effectively with Isis. The Two Sisters work together to protect and resurrect Osiris and to protect and re-energise the Sun God. However, Isis works by herself to raise Horus and support him in his endless battles with Seth. Why should this be? Despite being Seth's wife Nephthys works with Isis against Seth, surely she would be just as loyal as regards the Horus child? Perhaps her energy is incompatible with that of Horus. He often represents anger and aggression albeit harnessed for what is arguably a good cause. Horus is the masculine solar energy compared to the mysterious dark energy of Nephthys but there is nothing to suggest that they could ever be opposites united. Could it be that Nephthys is just not maternal? She did abandon her son Anubis and let Isis bring him up. She is the guide and supporter of the adult phase of life rather than the nurturer of the young.

---

[160] *The Temple of Edfu*, Kurth, 2004:58

The Egyptian Concept of Duality

Two can be considered a number of both duality and unity. The Egyptians didn't always emphasise the differences between the two extremes of a pair, often they used these differences to stress their complementary nature and as a way of hinting at unity. This is similar to our use of phrases such as 'young and old' or 'great and small' to mean everyone or everything.

Duality was deeply ingrained in the Egyptian world-view. Virtually everything consisted of paired opposites. People have their *ka*, their spiritual double. There is a dual mode in creation with the concept of "*as above so below*". Some of the Egyptian pairings are common to all cultures; heaven and earth, life and death, day and night, north and south. The geography of Egypt further emphasised duality in nature with the desert and the fertile land (the red land and the black land), the predominantly north-south Nile and the split between the Delta and the Nile Valley. Furthermore the country was split into Upper and Lower Egypt and although the unity was stressed it was always referred to as the Two Lands. Duality fascinated the Egyptians. They wanted to work out how two opposing forces could work together and how they might eventually be reconciled. This fascination goes back a long way. Prehistoric rock art from the Eastern Desert contains many depictions of figures in boats. It is believed that the larger figures represent deities and a number of these are in pairs.[161]

The different characters of Isis and Nephthys can reflect the duality in nature. Isis and Nephthys are associated with the two horizons (the place of sunrise and sunset), the east and west banks of the Nile and through that with the east-west life cycle of the sun. The horizon marks the border between two states of being; day and night, life and death or pre-birth and life. Solar Barques have been depicted since the 1st Dynasty but in the New Kingdom it was common to show two placed prow to prow. Thomas suggests that this represents perceived solar movement, east to west during the day and west to east during the night. Isis and Nephthys are shown in many of the solar barques. In one depiction they stand next to the barques and Nephthys passes the solar disc to Isis. As Isis is associated with the east and Nephthys with the west, Isis could be seen as the diurnal cycle of the sun and

---

[161] *Genesis of the Pharaohs*, Wilkinson, 2003:190

Nephthys as the nocturnal cycle.[162] *"His bow rope is taken by Isis, his stern rope is coiled by Nephthys."*[163]

Working as a Team

Regardless of any symbolic aspects, two people are just more effective than one in many circumstances. They can achieve more, give alternate opinions, are more likely to identify errors and provide a mutual support mechanism. Nephthys provides an essential supporting role to Isis. *"O Isis and Nephthys, come together, come together! Unite! Unite!"*[164] Particularly in funerary literature Isis and Nephthys are paired and referred to as the *Two Great Ladies*, the *Two Kites*, the *Two Mourning Kites* or the *Two Hawks*. In funeral processions for the wealthy of the New Kingdom two professional mourners, the *"two mourning birds"*, were hired to take the role of Isis and Nephthys.[165]

"We unite your flesh, we put your limbs in order. Live! You will not die."[166] In the darkness of the underworld the Sun God is renewed by the Two Sisters. In the funerary text the *Amduat* this is depicted as a scarab emerging from a mound flanked by Isis and Nephthys. Paralleling this, in the darkness of the tomb the deceased is resurrected by the Two Sisters. A hymn to Re in the *Book of the Dead* describes this. *"Isis and Nephthys honour you, they cause you to appear in glory in the two divine barks their arms protecting you."*[167]

The Echo Function

Having the two Goddesses work together reinforces the power of what they are doing. It also can give an echo or nuance to the power, providing two differing energies when slightly different words are used. For example, *"I ascend upon the lap of Isis; I climb upon the lap of*

---

[162] *Solar Barks Prow to Prow*, Thomas, 1956:65-79
[163] *Patterns of Queenship in Ancient Egyptian Myth and History*, Troy, 1986:39
[164] *The Ancient Egyptian Pyramid Texts*, Faulkner, 2007:46 Utterance 218
[165] *Religion and Ritual in Ancient Egypt*, Teeter, 2011:138
[166] *New Light on the Recarved Sarcophagus of Hatshepsut and Thutmose in the Museum of Fine Arts, Boston*, Manuelian & Loeben, 1993:121-155
[167] *Hymns, Prayers and Songs*, Foster, 1995:89

Nephthys"[168] and "*Isis speaks to you, Nephthys calls to you*".[169] This echoing function is common in the *Pyramid* and *Coffin Texts* but less so in the *Book of the Dead.* By the later funerary texts Nephthys plays a lesser role even though she appears in the vignettes. This practice was not abandoned completely, the Late Period and Greco-Roman Period *Books of Breathing* have many examples. "*She speaks, namely Isis, saying one thing. She speaks, namely Nephthys, saying another.*"[170] It is also used in spells. A spell against Apophis, or a snake, states that Isis has chained him whilst Nephthys has bound him.

Power Gradient and Polarity

Polarity is a state of having poles or opposites compared to duality which is a state of having two parts. A gradient is needed for power to flow, whether it is electricity created by the positive and negative terminals on a battery or the higher and lower levels of land turning standing water into a stream. Isis and Nephthys are different as well as complementary. It is this polarity that enables them to create a differential allowing the life-giving power to flow through Osiris and reanimate him. They invariably stand on either side of Osiris to revive him. The echo function discussed above may also have the same effect where similar but distinct actions are carried out by the pair. "*Rise up Osiris on your side in Gehesty; Isis has your arm and Nephthys has your hand. Go between them.*"[171] Isis and Nephthys were depicted at the foot and the head of the coffin for the same reason. "*Isis at your head and Nephthys at your feet.*"[172] Their power gradient creates *heka* which can be used in all magic and healing. In one spell for a scorpion sting it states that Isis sits down and Nephthys stands upright.

The earth is Geb and the life force is Osiris but the circle of life has to be driven by the feminine divine power in the form of Isis and Nephthys. This is very different to the passive female role in other mythological cycles. The relationship between Isis and Nephthys is the

---

[168] *Hymns, Prayers and Songs*, Foster, 1995:32
[169] *The Ancient Egyptian Pyramid Texts*, Faulkner, 2007:139 Utterance 422
[170] *Traversing Eternity*, Smith, 2009:300
[171] *Patterns of Queenship in Ancient Egyptian Myth and History*, Troy, 1986:37
[172] *Traversing Eternity*, Smith, 2009:364

feminine polarity which resurrects Osiris and is reflected in the phases of cosmic cycles.

Becoming the Continuum

Many things viewed as opposites are merely different ends of a spectrum, such as hot and cold which are just positions on a scale of temperature. As the original unity of pre-creation was split into two so two can merge to become one. This idea of re-joining was used in the *Coffin Texts*. There are a number of spells in the *Coffin Texts* to join the river-banks. One spell states that *"the hair of Isis is knotted to the hair of Nephthys"*[173] associating the two Goddesses with the east and west banks of the Nile. The idea behind the spells is that the deceased joins the river banks in the afterworld so that they can walk across. *"The western bank is joined with the eastern, and they are closed together...while I have passed by...I have come that I may be joined to the two Sisters and merged in the two Sisters, for they will never die."*[174] The spell is also about uniting what has become separated. The banks were once the same land but were separated by the river. The joining of the Two Sisters merges the Two into the One. Similar versions of this spell refer to the east and west banks kissing and of the king (Horus) being reconciled with his brother (Seth).

The Double Goddess

Research carried out by Noble into the early Goddesses suggests that the Double Goddess is a very old concept given the many depictions of twins in the ancient world especially of goddesses with their associated sacred creatures; bird, snake and lion. She says that this represents the *"yin-yang female biological cycle and its shamanic relationship to life"*.[175] The Great Mother has a dual nature encompassing all that is perceived as good and all that is perceived as bad. A healthier approach than denying the dark side of the divine and ending up with an irreconcilable personification of evil. Noble proposes that the healed whole isn't male-female but is the two components of

---

[173] *The Ancient Egyptian Coffin Texts Volume I*, Faulkner, 2007:145 Spell 168
[174] *The Ancient Egyptian Coffin Texts Volume II*, Faulkner, 2007:169 Spell 562
[175] *The Double Goddess*, Noble, 2003:1

the female archetype or energy. There is an oscillation between two phases in every natural cycle and the Double Goddess illustrates this perpetual motion.

Female Dualities in Egypt

The Egyptians used symbolic forms to express their world view. Dualism was central to this and it is not always male-female polarity. They may not have shared the concept of a Double Goddess or sole Mother Goddess but they expressed the totality of creation in dualistic terms using female-female symbolism as well as male-female symbolism. The duality of the feminine was a common theme in Egyptian symbolism and concept which may well be an echo of the Double Goddess or the splitting of the Great Mother. The duplication or pairing of goddesses is common as it is for inanimate symbolic objects whose names are feminine nouns and so are related to pairs of goddesses.

There are a number of references in the literature to two goddesses or two females. In some instances it can be read simply as more than one such as *"the two female guardians of the threshold"* from the *Pyramid Texts.*[176] Others have a deeper meaning. *"Two women have given birth to Horus on the waters of the w'rt."*[177] Troy suggests that this is a statement about the double role of the feminine in conception and birth or it may just refer to the confusion over Horus as discussed in chapter 6. There is a similar concept in an inscription from Elephantine where Thutmose refers to *"his mothers Satis and Anukis"*.[178] Or are we reading something too deep into this? Does it simply refer to the king's birth mother and his wet-nurse?

The gazelle can also be paired. The gazelle is the sacred animal of Anuket who was later associated with Nephthys. It is also sacred to Hathor. Two gazelles appear on diadems of royal women in the Delta area during the late Middle Kingdom and 2nd Intermediate Period. In the *Pyramid Texts* and the *Coffin Texts* Osiris dies at a place called Geheset whose name means the place of two gazelles. Troy suggests

---

[176] *Patterns of Queenship in Ancient Egyptian Myth and History*, Troy, 1986:47
[177] *Patterns of Queenship in Ancient Egyptian Myth and History*, Troy, 1986:69
[178] *Temple Festival Calendars of Ancient Egypt*, el-Sabban, 2000:36

that the place where Osiris is killed and enters the afterworld is a feminine duality and a reflection of the Mother Goddess as creator-destroyer.[179] Feminine duality guards the entry into the next world, hence the two female guardians mentioned above, and it has a generative role. Conception and birth occur along this duality and are complementary functions. This may be one reason for the concept of two mothers mentioned above.

The *uraeus* is often paired and referred to as the Two Ladies of Egypt, the same title as given to the Goddesses Wadjyt and Nekhbet. The double *uraeus* represents the duality of the Eye which is overlaid onto the Two Ladies and then the Two Lands. In the *Coffin Texts* there is a reference to the "*two mrwty*". Grammatically the word is feminine and plural. They appear to be a combination of the double *uraeus* and Isis and Nephthys. They are described as "*companions of Re*". There is also mention of a pair of *mrty*-snakes in the *Book of the Dead* who accompany the sun disc. In some versions of the *Book of the Dead* the *mrty*-snakes are replaced by the Two Sisters.[180]

A pair of feathers was a symbol of kingship from the 4th Dynasty. They also appear in the crowns of gods such as Min. A solar hymn treats them as the eyes of the sun and moon. "*Your two feathers go out to the sky...your east is your left eye and your west is your right eye. These two eyes of yours...are set in your head like the two feathers.*"[181] There are two crowns of Egypt and crown is a feminine noun. The country was unified at the start of the Dynastic Period but the Red Crown of Lower Egypt and the White Crown of Upper Egypt remain distinct as does the Upper and Lower Egypt split. For a country so focused on the unity of the Two Lands it is surprising that they retained these separate distinctions. It must have been more important to emphasise the duality than to combine the symbols to show unity or power over.

The *Book of the Dead* refers to the "*Two Sycamores of the Horizon*". These are two trees of turquoise which stand at the point of sunrise and protect the newborn sun. The sycamore tree was equated to Hathor in her Tree Goddess aspect. Isis and Nephthys also protect the

---

[179] *Patterns of Queenship in Ancient Egyptian Myth and History*, Troy, 1986:47
[180] *Remarks on Beings Called mrwty or mrwryt in the Coffin Texts*, Bianchi, 1987:206-207
[181] *Patterns of Queenship in Ancient Egyptian Myth and History*, Troy, 1986:128

newborn sun and in later periods Isis was associated with the sycamore tree. At the temple of Edfu the flagpoles that stood on the entrance are *"the Two Sisters Isis and Nephthys, who protect the Prince of the White Crown (Osiris) and watch over the Ruler of the Temples of Egypt (Horus)"*.[182]

Other Paired Goddesses

Apart from Isis and Nephthys the most important pair of goddesses is Wadjyt and Nekhbet the Two Great Ladies. The duality of Wadjyt and Nekhbet as cobra and vulture is integrated into the symbolism of the female duality. It is possible that they are descendants of the prehistoric Bird and Snake Goddesses but there is no direct proof of this. Their relationship parallels that of Isis and Nephthys. They also represent the night sky, the Solar Eye and Upper and Lower Egypt. In effect they express the dual nature of the feminine. Is this why Upper and Lower Egypt retained their separate identity whilst the unity of Egypt was continually being stressed? At Medinet Habu, Rameses III is called *"he of the Two Goddesses"* namely Wadjyt and Nekhbet.[183] There is also reference to him at the *Festival of the Two Goddesses*. By the 18th Dynasty the Two Ladies increasingly appear as two cobras wearing the crowns of Upper and Lower Egypt. Royal women started to wear two *uraei* at this time.

A number of other goddesses can be paired together without losing their individuality. Mut and Sekhmet, Bastet and Sekhmet and Hathor and Sekhmet. The common denominator in this example is Sekhmet, probably because they are all Eye Goddesses and Sekhmet has the aspect of the Angry Eye. Together they become the Whole Eye symbolic of the totality of creation. It is no surprise that the Eye is a dual symbol. All vertebrates have two eyes and eyes are the most distinct aspect of a face. The sun and moon were viewed as the Eyes of Heaven.

Another goddess pairing is Anuket and Satet. Anuket is an ancient Goddess with a cult based around Elephantine. She is another one of the daughters of Ra. In the New Kingdom she was considered the daughter of Satet, the Goddess who guarded the frontier with Nubia

---

[182] *The Temple of Edfu*, Kurth, 2004:67
[183] *Temple Festival Calendars of Ancient Egypt*, el-Sabban, 2000:63

and was associated with the inundation. In the New Kingdom they formed a triad with the ram-headed God Khnum from Elephantine, who was believed to control the inundation. The Two Goddesses of the Cataracts could be thought of as either side of the river banks, upstream and downstream from the cataracts or the cataracts and the normal river flow. Maat, the Goddess of truth, order and justice can be doubled. In the *Pyramid Texts* she is referred to as the "*Two Maats*" and in the *Book of the Dead* the deceased are judged in the "*Hall of the Two Maats*".[184]

Isis assimilated many goddesses but with Renenutet (Hermouthis) and Sothis they are frequently referred to as Isis-Hermouthis and Isis-Sothis. This was probably to emphasise the particular quality and function of their combined powers – combined without being totally merged and subsumed by Isis. Despite absorbing many aspects of Hathor, Isis rarely has the appellation Isis-Hathor. As she took Hathor's crown the two Goddesses can appear identical from the New Kingdom. In this situation it is their combined and merged powers that is the most important rather than their working together.

When Isis and Hathor merged in the New Kingdom why did Isis assimilate Hathor rather than the other way round? Hathor was a very popular and ancient Goddess with wide-ranging aspects. She could easily have absorbed Isis. I have debated this question in chapter 10 but was the duality of Isis a major factor? Hathor does have a Sekhmet persona but it is restricted. Hathor did not represent duality to the extent that Isis did, who was immersed in it, and duality was important to the society at the time.

Male Duality

There are very few examples of male pairings unless it is the various aspects of the Sun God, such as Ra-Harakhti the Hawk-headed Sun God or Osiris as Osiris-Sokar (Sokar is the Hawk-headed God of the necropolis at Memphis). The two gods Horus and Seth continually battle for dominance. This is in contrast to the many female pairs who complement each other and work together. The duality of the Gods wreaks havoc whilst that of the Goddesses brings eternal renewal.

---

[184] *Journey Through the Afterlife: Ancient Egyptian Book of the Dead*, Taylor, 2010:205

The Greek and Roman Point of View

This is one of the few chapters where the focus is on Isis in the Pharaonic Period rather than in the Greco-Roman Period. The Greeks and Romans did not have the same fascination with, and understanding of, duality that the Egyptians did. To them Isis was the All-Goddess and she had absorbed dualities alongside everything else. This is probably why they did not see the need to have Nephthys in their Isis cult. The emphasis is on Isis and her helper Anubis and sometimes her son Horus. The prominence of the battles of Horus and Seth disappears as well. Isis and Nephthys are a good example of what women can achieve when they work together. This might have set a dangerous example, the Greek and Roman patriarchs didn't want to see women cooperating as it was a risk to social order. The lack of women working together in productive harmony is another disempowering aspect of the Greek and Roman input into the mythology.

However, the one thing which Greek myth has is the strong mother-daughter bond in the form of Demeter and Persephone. The goddesses of Egypt rarely have daughters. Nut may be the mother of Isis and Nephthys but there is no relationship between them. The gods do have daughters and the father-daughter bond is strong; Maat and Hathor (and the other Eye Goddesses) are the daughters of Ra and are much loved and needed by him. Atum displays a similar attitude in the *Coffin Texts* explaining that he lives by his two daughters. The lack of a bond between Nut and her daughters could be seen as a way of breaking the relationship between mothers and daughters and weakening matriarchy but I am not entirely convinced. A more likely explanation is that Nut was a very remote Goddess who had very little direct involvement in people's lives. Egyptian society was probably structured so that it was other female relationships which were power sharing; such as between sisters or mother-in-law and daughter-in-law. The latter was certainly important in royal circles with the wife and mother of the king.

Figure 6 - The Greco-Roman Isis

Two As One

For the Egyptians duality appears to have been an important aspect of the feminine divine. Pregnancy and childbirth may have had an influence in this way of thinking. One becomes two when a woman is pregnant and one pregnant woman becomes two separate individuals when she gives birth. Every fertile female of every species has the potential to become two (or more). In the beginning there was only the Great Mother Goddess but as her power was eroded by increasingly patriarchal religions she became fragmented into an array of deities. Is the strong feminine duality present in Egyptian philosophy and religion an echo of this? The duality of the Great Mother first split into the Double Goddess then into Goddesses who work together, such as Isis and Nephthys. These will always create a complementary pair as they are really part of the same whole. The Double Goddess is collaborative female power integrating all components of female energy and this collaboration is seen perfectly in the work of Isis and Nephthys. As Isis evolved into the All-Goddess did she become increasingly whole so lost the need to have her paired sister as they were now one?

At Dendera, the birth of Isis was celebrated and she was said to have been born *"in the shape of a black and red woman"*.[185] Could red refer to her solar aspect and black to the night sky and underworld or as Isis and Nephthys as one? The Egyptians liked well balanced and harmonious opposites and pairs and in Isis and Nephthys they found it. Female unity in Egypt was not about conflict but cooperation. This is in direct contrast to the attitude of patriarchal societies and religions which used the 'divide and rule' philosophy and worked hard to turn women against each other rather than risk allowing them to unite and turn against the oppressing males. The inherent female duality was sadly transformed into conflict.

---

[185] *Hathor and Thoth: Two Key Figures of the Ancient Egyptian Religion,* Bleeker, 1973:64

CHAPTER 9

RELATIONSHIPS WITH OTHER GODS

"All the gods of the South and the North come to you, and you love them." [186]

Working Together

Isis forms very close relationships with many deities outside her immediate family. Relationships and the support and power that they bring are important to Isis. Despite being the All-Goddess she still needs and values her strong bonds with the other deities.

Thoth – the Friend and Teacher

Thoth, the Ibis and Baboon God of wisdom and magic, is an important friend of Isis throughout her story. It was his compassion and wisdom that allowed him to break the curse Ra had placed on Nut enabling Isis to be born (see chapter 2). Thoth *"catches the suffering of Isis as though in a net"*.[187] He helps her in both practical and emotional ways advising, comforting, counselling and offering magical assistance.

---

[186] *The Hellenistic Face of Isis: Cosmic and Saviour Goddess*, Gasparro, 2006:69
[187] *Hathor and Thoth: Two Key Figures of the Ancient Egyptian Religion*, Bleeker, 1973:118

As the Master Magician and Healer, Thoth helps Isis and Nephthys to revive Osiris and acts as a guide and protector of Osiris in the afterlife. The 4th century BCE *Metternich stele* tells how Isis was imprisoned by Seth in a spinning house at Sais. She was pregnant with Horus at the time but Seth appears not to have noticed, otherwise why didn't he try to harm them both? Thoth realises that they are both in peril and encourages her to escape and go into hiding. Isis appears to have been paralysed by her grief at the death of Osiris and has lost the ability to act decisively due to her abusive relationship with Seth. Thoth is able to cure Horus when he has been poisoned by Seth (see chapter 15) and Isis is unable to save him. He acts as advocate for Osiris and Horus during the legal proceedings in the afterlife and when Horus appears before the Tribunal of the Gods to claim his father's throne. He aids Horus in his battles with Seth and tries wherever possible to defuse the situation. He also protects and supports Isis during this time.

Originally there was no family relationship between Isis and Thoth. In the Greco-Roman Period Thoth was aligned with his Greek counterpart Hermes and Thoth-Hermes was referred to both as her father and as her son. "*Many have set down that she is Hermes' daughter.*"[188] A spell for obtaining a divine dream involved drawing the ibis of Thoth on a band of linen. His name was written in myrrh along with an incantation which referred to his father Osiris and his mother Isis.[189] By the 6th century BCE there was a cult of Isis as the Mother of the Apis Bull at Saqqara alongside the cult of Thoth and here Thoth was considered the father of Isis. These seem to be fictitious relationships for no apparent reason other than the desire to force the deities into family groups. What is really important is their teamwork and Thoth's support.

In the time of Domitian (81-96 CE) Middle Egypt was an area of interest to philosophers and Hermopolis, the cult city of Thoth, was viewed as an important source of wisdom. Isis is increasingly associated with Thoth particularly in relation to her intellectual aspects. Thoth-Hermes became Hermes Trismegistus who was the Mage who taught Isis. In this role he acts as the Logos, the divine word of God which creates all things, and Isis is his pupil. This may be

---

[188] *Plutarch: Concerning the Mysteries of Isis and Osiris*, Mead, 2002:184
[189] *The Greek Magical Papyri in Translation. Volume One: Texts*, Betz, 1996:159

where the idea of Isis as his daughter first came from, describing not a family relationship but a tutor-pupil one.

Originally Thoth was the principal judge and lawgiver. In the Greco-Roman Period Isis takes over this role. The *aretalogies* tell how she devised contracts, upheld justice and oaths and put an end to tyranny and murder. Thoth was seen as the keeper of the ancient wisdom and the inventor of writing but in the *aretalogies* we see Isis in these roles. "*With Hermes I have invented the signs for writing, sacred ones and those of the vernacular.*"[190] She also takes over his role of allocating separate languages to the different peoples of the world and becomes the Lady of Secret Wisdom.

Given the link between Isis and Thoth it may seem surprising that she does not feature in the *Book of Thoth*. The surviving parts of this book date to the 1st and 2nd centuries CE but it is believed to date to the Ptolemaic Period and to incorporate earlier elements. It is written in the form of a dialogue between Thoth and his pupil. The *Book of Thoth* aims to instruct the initiate in all forms of learning and uses scribal training as a metaphor for the journey through life and the afterlife. There are only a few references to Isis in the *Book of Thoth* and Seshat is the dominant goddess in this work. Isis is rarely associated with Seshat, but in a text from Edfu it does say that "*Isis is beside him as Seshat*".[191] In addition, Isis does not have any links with scribes so her absence in this work is understandable. Isis does differ from goddesses such as Seshat. She may be very wise but she doesn't appear to appreciate learning for its own sake. She likes knowledge to be acquired for a specific purpose and then put to good use.

A relief at Ariccia (Italy) depicts Isis seated on a throne holding a scroll on her knee. In niches on either side are four baboons. The *Book of Thoth* allowed the priests and priestesses to access the divine realms and here Isis is Lady of the Sacred Word.[192] In Isis temples outside Egypt baboons and ibis were often used in decorations, for example at Herculaneum and Benevento (Italy). This is not just to show Egyptian fauna but to emphasise the intellectual link between Isis and Thoth.

---

[190] *Egyptian Religion*, Morenz, 1992:336
[191] *Egyptian Religion*, Morenz, 1992:336
[192] *The Flavians: Pharonic Kingship Between Egypt and Rome*, Vittozzi, 2014:254

Thoth has little part in the Isis cult outside Egypt. Anubis assumed the relevant attributes of Hermes-Thoth and even became Hermanubis. Plutarch refers to Hermes as the Dog confusing, or identifying, him with Anubis. Thoth-Hermes does play a role in some forms of the Isis cult and this role parallels that of Anubis who physically guides the initiate. Here Thoth-Hermes guides the mind of the initiate. This turned him into a God more appealing to philosophers and theologians than to the ordinary worshipers.

Anubis – the Nephew and Guide

Anubis is the Jackal God of cemeteries, embalming and the afterlife. He is depicted either as a jackal-headed man or as a crouching jackal with long ears and tail. As a jackal he wears a large collar and is shown with the flail of Osiris. Diodorus said that he accompanied Osiris on his travels as a soldier. The Romans also viewed Anubis as a soldier, and often depicted him as a legionary. A later Greco-Roman role for Anubis was that of the carrier of the keys to the afterworld. A number of portraits of Anubis outside Egypt show him as a jackal with a bunch of keys around his collar. The Egyptians did not have the concept of the keys to the afterworld but Greeks did. Hekate was also a well-known key-bearer and she has a strong link to dogs.

Anubis is a very old God from Abydos who is attested to in the 1st Dynasty. He is associated with the other Jackal Gods Wepwawet and Khentimentiu. They were all afterlife gods, a role taken over by Osiris as his cult expanded. Because he was important Anubis was assimilated into the Osiris cult at an early stage. According to Plutarch, Anubis is the nephew of Isis and the illegitimate son of Osiris and Nephthys (see chapter 7). Anubis belongs to the heavens, the earth and the underworld and so can easily move between them. He can be seen as the guardian of the boundaries between the worlds. Plutarch says that "*Nephthys is that which is below the earth and non-manifest, while Isis is that which is above the earth and manifest*". Anubis reconciles the opposing characteristics of Isis and Nephthys and thus forms the curving horizon connecting the two. The horizon "*as being common to both of them, has been called Anubis*". He also says that Anubis has the same power as Hekate "*being at one and the same time chthonian and*

Olympian.[193] In *The Golden Ass* Anubis is referred to as a traveller, a messenger between the deities of heaven and the underworld.

Anubis accompanies Isis and Nephthys in their search for Osiris and guards the corpse. He then works closely with Thoth in embalming the body of Osiris and through this act becomes the patron God of the embalmers. Like Thoth he is a *psychopomp*, guiding and protecting the deceased as they journey through the afterworld. Vignettes of judgement scenes in the *Book of the Dead* show Anubis leading the deceased by the hand into the Judgement Hall.

In terms of sky symbolism Isis is associated with the star Sirius, which was known as the Dog Star to the Greeks, providing an immediate link between Anubis and Isis. In the temple of Isis in Rome, as in many others, Isis is depicted riding on a dog. This alludes both to her identification with Sothis and the Dog Star and her reliance upon Anubis.

The Greeks and Romans took a liking to Anubis and he became one of the fashionable deities. He had his own cult as well as a prominent role in that of Isis. A shrine was dedicated to Isis and Anubis at Canopus in 276 BCE by Callicrates of Samos, the king's admiral.[194] A hymn from Kios (Greece) calls him King of the Gods.[195] Plutarch said *"there is, then, for the worshipers of Anubis some mystery or other that may not be spoken of"*.[196] Anubis connects this world to the afterworld as the gatekeeper or ferryman. Thoth plays a similar role and because of this Anubis was identified with Hermes, even though they had little in common, to become Hermanubis. Although Thoth was a much better match the Greeks were happy to ignore the incompatible elements and accept that Hermes was sometimes Thoth and sometimes Anubis. Both versions of Hermes retain their individual characters and although Thoth was respected by the Greeks he never became one of the fellow temple gods of the Isis cult.

Anubis plays a major role in the cult of Isis outside Egypt. He is a very close companion to Isis and often displaces her son Horus. Anubis was always at the head of processions. The priests who took this role wore the dog-headed mask of Anubis and carried the herald's wand of

---

[193] *Plutarch: Concerning the Mysteries of Isis and Osiris*, Mead, 2002:224
[194] *Ptolemaic Alexandria*, Fraser, 1972:271
[195] *Isis in the Ancient World*, Witt, 1997:199
[196] *Plutarch: Concerning the Mysteries of Isis and Osiris*, Mead, 2002:224

Hermes and a palm branch. Specimen masks have survived, one being in the Hildesheim Museum (Germany). In the Greek cults Anubis is the regular attendant and bodyguard of Isis. He is the eternally present herald in the rituals and provides endless support for Isis. He shares her sorrows and mourning and the search for Osiris. Some later myths have him search for Horus when the child wandered off into the marshes.

Why was Anubis so important to the cult of Isis outside Egypt, especially given the fact that the Greeks and Romans found animal-headed deities repulsive and objects of derision? Detractors of the cult made much of this, Virgil calls him *"the barker"*. Another writer asks how a member of the Senate can stoop so low as to attend a parade wearing a dog's head. Many Greeks considered the dog to be unclean and viewed the merging of Hermes with a dog as insulting. Why didn't Anubis give up his jackal head? He could have performed his duty as herald and supporter of Isis just as well with a human head. Though why should he alter his personality and appearance to suit his detractors? *"Take me as I am or not at all"* is obviously his motto. The dog has a strong afterlife connection in Greek mythology so being dog or jackal-headed will have further emphasised his role. Anubis survives in the Eastern Orthodox Church as St Christopher depicted with a dog's head. There he acts as the ferryman for the deceased.[197]

Seth – the Adversary

Seth is the troublesome brother of Isis and Osiris. He is a Chaos God full of aggression, demonic energy and destructive, impulsive urges. He is strong but not clever, often the personification of 'brute force and ignorance'. In other words he is the shadow, the uncontrollable emotions. He causes confusion whenever he finds the opportunity and acts as a catalyst to force changes however unwelcome they are. The Egyptians had a profound understanding of and appreciation for duality and opposites. The shadow, in the form of death and destruction, is a reality which cannot be ignored. It is the opposite which can never be resolved.

---

[197] *Isis in the Ancient World*, Witt, 1997:201

Isis has a complex relationship with her brother Seth. She intervenes in a battle between Horus and Seth, who have changed into hippos, and spears Seth. He reminds Isis that he is her brother and she relents, much to the fury of Horus. In the *Contendings of Horus and Seth* Isis usually tracks down and punishes Seth and his followers. In some versions though they are handed over to her but she is unable to hurt Seth. "*When Isis received Typhon in bonds, she did not make away with him...she unbound him and let him go.*"[198] Isis does not have the uncontrollable anger of Sekhmet, in her heart she is a peacemaker and healer who wants reconciliation as well as justice. She is also wise, she knows that Seth cannot be defeated only contained and that his powers are an essential part of creation. The battles with Seth can be seen as the tension between the desert and the cultivated land and between individual desires and the imposed regulations of the collective.

Isis is increasingly the enemy of Seth and it has been suggested that this is a result of non-Egyptian influences. The Greeks did not have the Egyptian understanding of the roles of opposites believing the enemy, however defined, exists only to be annihilated. In the myth of *Horus at Edfu* Thoth advises "*let the company of Seth be given to Isis and her son Horus that they may do whatever their hearts desire with them*".[199] She and Horus behead the followers but Seth transforms himself into a snake and disappears into the ground. Isis is not the only shape-shifter. Seth cannot die despite being killed in various ways. Chaos is ever present in creation and also pre-dates creation.

In the Ptolemaic *Jumilhac* papyrus Isis chases after Seth and his followers taking a number of forms until she finally poisons them in her snake form at Geheset, probably Komir near Esna in Upper Egypt. Their blood turns into juniper berries where it falls upon the mountain. Illustrating the many additions to and deviations from the myth, the same papyrus gives an alternate version of the story. Here Isis and Nephthys transform into *uraeus* serpents who attack Seth and his party and throw lances at them.[200] A strange method of attack for a *uraeus* serpent.

---

[198] *Plutarch: Concerning the Mysteries of Isis and Osiris*, Mead, 2002:202
[199] *The Myth of Horus at Edfu: I*, Fairman, 1935:26-36
[200] *The Egyptian Myths*, Shaw, 2014:134

Seth imprisons Isis when she is pregnant with Horus. In one spell Isis refers to being imprisoned by Seth in his spinning house.[201] The Greco-Roman myths have Isis suffer increasingly at the hand of Seth. He robs and rapes her and in one instance a child is born as a result of this assault. Interestingly the child, who is born premature, is a hybrid of baboon and ibis which are the sacred animals of Thoth.[202] Is this trying to suggest that rape could have a beneficial end result? That the offspring is wisdom? An insulting and patriarchal conceit. Seth is unlikely to father offspring comparable to Thoth. I believe that this increasing emphasis on the rape of Isis comes from the Greeks. They have plenty of rapists amongst their gods, it stops the goddesses becoming too powerful and secure. Rape is less about lust and more about power over the female, something close to the Greek male's heart.

The Egyptians never viewed Seth as totally evil. As the Eldest Magician he is a crucial partner in the fight against Apophis. It is Seth who has the ability and power to fight off Apophis and Isis fights alongside him. "*The magic of Isis and the Eldest Magician is enacted to ward off Apophis*".[203] Unlike Seth, Isis is in direct opposition to everything that Apophis represents. Her opposing feminine energy works with that of Seth to defeat the ultimate evil. Without Seth by her side neither Isis nor any of the other deities could defeat Apophis. If Seth had really been destroyed the annihilating energy of Apophis could not have been contained and the universe would have been destroyed. In psychological terms he is the chaotic rebel and murderer who can defeat Apophis because he is like fighting like with like. We unfortunately have need of Seth's dark side for survival and Isis is aware of this which is why she doesn't slay Seth when she has the chance.

Ra – the Father Figure

The Sun God doesn't always appear as a kindly god in the myths. He is a remote authority figure and has to be persuaded by the other deities to help in times of need. It was only when Isis forced the Solar

---

[201] *Ancient Egyptian Magical Texts*, Borghouts, 1978:59
[202] *The Egyptian Myths*, Shaw, 2014:91
[203] *The Egyptian Amduat*, Abt & Hornung, 2007:229

Barque to a standstill that he dispatched Thoth to save the Horus child. In the *Contendings of Horus and Seth* he wants to give the throne to Seth because he is the strongest, regardless of the legitimacy of Horus' claim. Given that she tricked him into telling her his true name it could be expected that Ra would view Isis as an adversary, but this is not so. Perhaps he admired her cunning or understood why she had to take that action.

When the Solar and Osiris theologies are merged in the New Kingdom Isis becomes an increasingly important aide to Ra. As Isis assimilates Hathor her relationship with Ra changes. Hathor is a daughter of the Sun God and has a strong bond with him and Isis adopts this relationship with Ra. He now comes across as less of a patriarch and more of a father who needs and appreciates support. Isis becomes his loyal daughter and protector. One of the hymns to Isis in her temple at Philae describes her as the Daughter of Ra. The pylons at the entrance to temples in the New Kingdom mirrored the hieroglyph for "*horizon*" where the sun rose. An inscription at the entrance to the Greco-Roman temple at Edfu states that the pylons are called "*Isis and Nephthys who raise up the sun god who shines on the horizon*".[204]

Other Partners

Although eternally married to Osiris Isis is sometimes partnered with other gods.

– Mandulis of Nubia

Mandulis is a Nubian Sun God and usually wears an elaborate crown consisting of ram's horns with cobras and plumes on a sun disc. He can be depicted as a hawk with a human head. At Philae he is called the companion of Isis and has a chapel in the temple of Isis.

– Min

Min is an ancient God responsible for the fertility of humans and crops. Isis is often linked to him either as wife or mother. He is also a protector, scaring away evil spirits. Spell 15 of the *Book of the Dead*

---

[204] *Symbol & Magic in Egyptian Art*, Wilkinson, 1994:29

explains the crown of Min. "*He has two plumes on his head*" which are "*Isis and Nephthys...they put themselves on his head as two hawks*".[205] Min's cult plant was the lettuce because its juice resembled semen. In the *Contendings* Seth becomes pregnant after eating the "*seed of Horus*" which Isis had smeared on lettuce leaves (see chapter 6) which illustrates the powerful regenerative powers of Min. He was sometimes combined as Min-Horus and was said to unite with his mother to beget himself. Was it this myth which was the source of Horus raping Isis? From the Middle Kingdom Min was often identified with Horus as the son of Isis. He had a cult centre at Coptos and also at Akhmim and by the Middle Kingdom there was a cult of Isis attested to in these cities. Here Min was said to have been "*born of divine Isis*".[206]

– Ptah

Ptah is an ancient God with a cult at Memphis where he was viewed as the Creator. Ptah is depicted as a man wearing a tight skull-cap and he holds a *was*-sceptre topped by a composite *ankh* and *djed*. He only has a tenuous link to Isis and his consort was Sekhmet, or sometimes Hathor. In the funerary texts he can be merged with Osiris and Sokar to give a triple god symbolising rebirth. The Apis Bull was considered a living embodiment of Ptah and Isis is linked to him in her role as Mother of the Apis Bull.

– Serapis - her Greek Consort

Ptolemy I (323-283 BCE) embarked on a religious policy which he hoped would bring the Greeks and Egyptians closer together and an Egyptian priest, Manetho, was believed to have had a major input. They wanted a pair of deities who would be popular with all people at all levels of society. At the *Serapeum* in Memphis there was a temple to Osiris-Apis who was worshiped alongside Isis as Mother of the Apis Bull. Greek settlers worshiped Amun (the ram-headed Creator God) in the same area, viewing him as a form of Zeus. Where the Egyptians saw Osiris and Apis the Greeks saw Dionysus and the chthonic Zeus-Hades. The two were easily merged to form the artificially constructed Serapis. Isis was the obvious consort to Serapis as she was already the partner of Osiris and a very popular Goddess in her own right. Alexander (356-323 BCE) had already dedicated a temple to her in his

---

[205] *The Rainbow*, Bleeker, 1975:99
[206] *The Great Goddesses of Egypt*, Lesko, 1999:169

city and Ptolemy I built the first *Serapeum* in Alexandria. Isis and Serapis were thus set to become the official deities of the Ptolemies.

Serapis is depicted in the form of a Greek god but he occasionally wears the *atef*-crown. In the Roman Period he was associated with Jupiter, as Ruler of the Gods. Serapis has connections with the underworld and seafaring. He has a strong healing aspect, which is absent in Osiris but strong in Isis. Official patronage helped but the pair were genuinely popular because both the Greeks and Egyptians could see their own deities in them. By the end of the 4th century BCE their cult had spread quickly throughout the eastern Mediterranean. "*Reverence Isis and Serapis, the greatest of the gods, saviours, good, kindly, benefactors.*"[207]

The Value of Friendship

In a pantheon, relationships, friendly or otherwise, between the deities are always going to be important but they are a major part of Isis' personality. She might be all powerful but she is not independent or aloof. Even as the All-Goddess of the Greco-Roman Period she still valued friendship. When two deities, or people, interact energy flows between them creating a temporary or permanent connection and these connections are an important part of their character.

---

[207] *Cults and Creeds in Graeco-Roman Egypt,* Bell, 1957:68

CHAPTER 10

ASSIMILATING EGYPTIAN GODDESSES

"Isis in all her Manifestations...Isis in all her aspects." [208]

Growth by Assimilation

The Pre-dynastic tribes of the area which would one day become the kingdom of Egypt all worshiped different deities. Over time these merged, allowing one deity to absorb the aspects and characteristics of another. As tribal areas were replaced by kingdoms local deities transformed into national ones. Some local deities disappeared completely; others would have retained traces of individuality as a particular aspect of the national deity. The Egyptians were totally accepting of this approach as they perceived the deities to be fluid and above definition. They saw value in multiple approaches rather than the restricting dogma of one cult's point of view. Contradictions were to be expected, so competing cults were often embraced and assimilated. Important deities could find a home anywhere.

During the Late Period, Isis was universally worshiped. How much of this was due to her assimilation of the other popular goddesses? Isis absorbed Hathor in the New Kingdom and from then on was merged and associated with many other goddesses. Through her absorption of these other goddesses, some of whom may be completely unknown to

---

[208] *The Great Goddesses of Egypt*, Lesko, 1999:181

us, Isis becomes the Queen of Heaven and the pre-eminent Goddess of Egypt. The power of Isis grows with each assimilation and the power of the assimilated goddess must therefore diminish. Was this intentional? Some changes probably were deliberate being politically and financially motivated. Each of the goddesses that Isis assimilated had some shared attribute but they also brought new ones. By assimilating multifunctional goddesses and assuming their various qualities Isis becomes *"the unique one"*,[209] the All-Embracing Goddess. Her two most important assimilations were those of Hathor and Renenutet.

Hathor

Hathor was an ancient, well-loved and widely worshiped Goddess. She was a Cow Goddess, originating in the anonymous Cow Goddesses of the Pre-dynastic Period. As the Celestial Cow she rose from the *nun*. She was also a Solar Goddess, a daughter of Ra and his protector. Hathor has important funerary and afterlife aspects as the Lady of the West and the Sycamore Goddess and was the divine mother and protector of the king. She has a strong sensual aspect as Goddess of love, wine, music and dance. All foreign lands were considered to be under her domain. Hathor had previously assimilated many other local goddesses making her a Universal Goddess before she was in turn absorbed by Isis. She was frequently regarded as a form of the indigenous goddess in areas where she didn't have a cult of her own.

Isis' most important syncretism was with Hathor. It allied her with the solar tradition and combined the powers of the two most powerful goddesses in the country. From the New Kingdom onwards Isis wears Hathor's cow horn sun disc crown. Hathor was the only goddess so completely assimilated that she was identical to Isis in depictions, and they could only be differentiated if their names were added. Isis took much of her iconography from Hathor; such as the *sistrum, menat,* and cow horn sun disc crown. The *sistrum* often has a stylised face of Hathor with cow ears, and Plutarch refers to a *sistrum* having *"the face sometimes of Isis"*.[210] A bronze and electrum *menat* counterpoise was excavated at Amarna. Isis is shown in profile holding a *was*-sceptre

---

[209] *Hymns to Isis in Her Temple at Philae*, Zabkar, 1988:132
[210] *Plutarch: Concerning the Mysteries of Isis and Osiris*, Mead, 2002:239

and a cow in a boat, another symbol of Hathor. It is inscribed to *"Isis, Mother of the God, Mistress of Heaven"*.[211]

Isis' dramatic rise in importance in the New Kingdom is reflected by the fact that she was incorporated into the dominant state cult of the Heliopolitan Ennead (Ra and his entourage). The Egyptians did not like to neglect important deities and they were always found a place in the major cults. This philosophy may have been partly through a fear of offending them but also through a desire to increase the power of the receiving cult. Hathor has a very strong solar aspect for she is the daughter of Ra and one of the Eye Goddesses. This is emphasised by her crown, the sun disc draped by the *uraeus* cobra. As the Eye Goddess Hathor is a force of illumination, renewal and creativity. During the New Kingdom Isis took Hathor's place in the Solar Barque and it is she who protects the Sun God during his travels through the underworld. Isis' solar aspect was particularly emphasised at Philae. Here she is the Mother Goddess who gives birth to the sun but she has also taken on the active aspect of Hathor and can be viewed as the sun herself. One hymn to Isis from Philae addresses her as the *uraeus* which Ra has placed on his forehead. It describes her role traveling in the underworld in the Solar Barque: *"You are the one who rises and dispels darkness, shining when traversing the primeval ocean, the Brilliant One in the celestial water."*[212]

The other major role which Isis took over was that of Afterlife Goddess. By the end of the 18th Dynasty Isis is *"Lady of the Beautiful West"*[213] and takes over the role of the Sycamore Goddess who provides food and shelter for the deceased. In the tomb of Thutmose III (18th Dynasty) she is depicted nursing the king. As an aside, his birth mother was called Isis.

Hathor has a very distinct personality, and it is easy to see the Hathoric element in a number of the attributes and epithets of Isis in the later periods. Lady of Imu was an early epithet of Hathor, used at Philae for Isis. One hymn describes Isis as one who *"fills the palace with her beauty, fragrance of the palace, mistress of joy"*.[214] Although it is normal to praise the beauty of goddesses the address is very

---

[211] *Private Religion at Amarna: the Material Evidence*, Stevens, 2007:36
[212] *Hymns to Isis in Her Temple at Philae*, Zabkar, 1988:80
[213] *The Great Goddesses of Egypt*, Lesko, 1999:175
[214] *Hymns to Isis in Her Temple at Philae*, Zabkar, 1988:42

Hathoric as is the image from Plutarch where Isis searches for the dismembered Osiris *"in a papyrus skiff sailing away through the marshes"*.[215] Memphis was a major cult centre of Isis and here she was identified with the Cow Goddess aspect of Hathor. Ovid calls her the Sacred Cow of Memphis. By the 30th Dynasty Isis was the pre-eminent Goddess but Hathor still retained her high prestige. By the Ptolemaic Period all Hathor's epithets were associated with Isis. Some still continued their devotion to Hathor. There is a small temple of Hathor at Philae and inscriptions dedicated to her continue until the end of the pagan period.

Whilst taking many of Hathor's important aspects, Isis appears to have rejected the fun side of Hathor. Take love for example. Hathor's love represents the joy of physical love and sex as well as the romantic love of couples. Isis does not take on this aspect and retains her love as maternal and social. Bastet has a similar sensual side. Perfume was strongly associated with Hathor and Bastet yet there is no link to Isis. Music, dance and alcohol were very important to Hathor. She took a healthy enjoyment in all sensual pleasures but Isis appears to have rejected them. Isis does display a more puritan streak. Is this because of the sorrow in her life? Does she have a more sombre approach to life having experienced its trials?

It was probably inevitable that the two greatest Goddesses of Egypt would become increasing close then merge. Hathor is a much older Goddess than Isis and had a wider range of aspects. Why didn't Hathor absorb Isis instead of the other way round? I suspect that it was largely because the character of Isis was a better fit to the cultural and religious environment of the times. She was a devoted wife and mother compared with the independent, fun-loving Hathor. The other reason is that Isis was intimately connected with Osiris and the Osiris cult was very popular.

Renenutet

Renenutet was a Cobra Goddess, the Goddess of Harvests and Green Fields. In a 12th Dynasty temple at Medinet Madi, Renenutet is depicted with Sobek giving the king life, happiness, eternity and health.

---

[215] *Plutarch: Concerning the Mysteries of Isis and Osiris*, Mead, 2002:201

She is frequently shown with an offering table piled with food. Her name is derived from the verb *rnn* meaning "*to bring up*" or "*nurse*". She was originally a protector of the king but in later periods became the protector of all families. *Rnn* is also the stem of the word for fortune, *rnnt*, and she was one of the deities responsible for assigning a persons' fate and apportioning their lifespan. Renenutet was the mother of the god Neper who personified corn. This links him to Osiris as a Grain God making it easy for Isis to be associated with Renenutet.

Renenutet's main centres of worship were in the fertile, agricultural areas. In the Delta she had a shrine at Tebtunis and possibly one at Terenuthis. In the Fayum, a large fertile oasis in the Libyan Desert, her principal temple was at Medinat Madi. In the Fayum she was part of a triad with Sobek and Horus. The Greeks called her Thermouthis or Hermouthis. In the Late Period Renenutet was assimilated with Isis and referred to as Isis-Hermouthis or Isermuthis. Vanderlip suggests that hers was also a mystery religion. There was a synod of Thermouthis on 13th July 24 or 25 CE.[216]

Although the only aspects which Isis absorbed from Renenutet were that of Grain and Harvest Goddess and the allocation of fate they were key aspects and important additions to her character. They were particularly significant for the Greeks as it gave Isis an immediate link to one of their major Goddesses, Demeter. The Egyptians credited Osiris with teaching them agriculture and viticulture but by the Greco-Roman Period it was Isis who had invented agriculture. Diodorus says that "*Isis had discovered the value of the wheat and barley which happened to be growing among the other grasses...unappreciated by men*". This association was strengthened when he saw "*during the festival of Isis, stalks of wheat and barley are borne in procession among the other cult objects*"[217] not realising that they were a reference to Osiris.

Other Assimilations

It would serve no purpose to list every goddess assimilated by or associated with Isis but a few of them are discussed below. In some

---

[216] *The four Greek hymns of Isidorus and the cult of Isis*, Vanderlip, 1972:20
[217] *The Antiquities of Egypt*, Diodorus Siculus & Murphy, 1990:19

cases Isis appears to have just taken their epithets rather than any specific characteristics.

– Anuket

Anuket was the Goddess of the First Cataract region and was closely connected with Hathor at Thebes. Isis takes the epithet Mistress of Biggeh, which Anuket shared with Satet.

– Bastet

The Feline Goddess Bastet is a daughter of Ra. She is best known as the Cat-headed Goddess but was originally portrayed as a lioness. In the *Pyramid Texts* she is closely linked to the king as his mother and nurse. Bastet was associated with childbirth and motherhood. Like all Eye Goddesses she has an aggressive side. Texts from the temple of Edfu explain that the soul of Isis is present as Bastet. Isis is invoked as Bastet in her temple at Aswan. In the *Kyme aretalogy* it states that Isis built the city of Bubastis, which was sacred to Bastet. She is called the Goddess of Bubastis, an epithet of Bastet, and there is reference to her carrying the *sistrum,* an instrument originally associated with Hathor and Bastet.[218] At Ostia in Italy a priestess of Bastet dedicated an altar to Isis Bubastis.[219] The Greeks identified Bastet with Artemis.

– Maat

Maat is the Goddess who personifies cosmic harmony, truth, justice and morality. The word *maat* was used to encompass the whole concept from the balance of the cosmos to the truth spoken by an individual. She is an integral part of the universe coming into being at the instant of creation and is a daughter and guide of Ra. Her crown and symbol is the ostrich feather. In the Judgement Hall the heart of the deceased is weighed against this feather. The concept of the judgement of each individual was introduced in the New Kingdom. In the *Book of the Dead* the judgement scene is prominent and is presided over by a variety of deities. Osiris sits in judgment and Isis and Nephthys stand beside him. Spell 17 in the *Book of the Dead* says that Isis and Nephthys are in charge of those who are to be "*examined*",

---

[218] *Isis in the Ancient World*, Witt, 1997:30
[219] *Isis in the Ancient World*, Witt, 1997:81

namely judged, in the Solar Barque. *"May you reckon up every good thing for...Semminus"*[220] in the judgment hall.

In the Pharaonic Period Isis at times assumes the role of Maat without really assimilating her. In the Greco-Roman Period Isis takes on more of an Olympian judgement role, like Zeus, watching over people and judging them. The moral lives of her worshipers were important to her. *"Looking down on the manifold deeds of the wicked and gazing down on those of the just...you witness men's individual virtue."*[221] To the Egyptians the concept of *maat* has cosmological, political and ethical meanings. The Greeks interpreted it more narrowly as legislation and the civilising aspect of law and order.

– Mehet-Weret

The name Mehet-Weret originally meant Great Flood, later Great Swimmer, and she is the female counterpart of *nun* who is portrayed as the Celestial Cow. Mehet-Weret existed before creation as a fertile current within the *nun* and rose from it to create the universe. She gave birth to the sun and placed it between her horns. Mehet-Weret was commonly represented but never had her own cult. She was closely associated with Neith and then with Hathor before being linked to Isis. Her name is used as an epithet for the other Creator Goddesses such as Hathor, Neith and Isis. The starry patterned cows on the sides of the golden bed of Tutankhamun are called Isis-Mehet. The deceased king ascends into the afterworld supported by the Celestial Cows.

– Neith

Neith is an ancient Goddess. Her symbol of the shield and crossed arrows occurs in the Pre-dynastic Period. She was a Creator Goddess and Isis may have acquired her cosmic aspects from Neith. Her cult centre was in Sais. Neith was originally the Goddess who couldn't be unveiled; that is understood. *"I am all that has been, and is, and shall be, and my robe has never yet been uncovered by mortal man."*[222] Isis' epithet *"exalted in Sais"*[223] originally belonged to Neith. From the 3rd Intermediate Period Busiris was an important cult centre for Isis and Osiris, as it had been for Neith. She was associated with the *Festival of*

---

[220] *Traversing Eternity*, Smith, 2009:488
[221] *The four Greek hymns of Isidorus and the cult of Isis*, Vanderlip, 1972:51
[222] *Isis in the Ancient World*, Witt, 1997:67
[223] *Hymns to Isis in Her Temple at Philae*, Zabkar, 1988:107

Lamps which became an important festival of Isis (see chapter 22). The Greeks honoured Neith as Athena, the warrior and weaver.

– Nekhbet

Isis merges with Nekhbet, the Vulture Mother Goddess who was the tutelary Goddess of Upper Egypt. From Nekhbet came her epithet Lady of el-Kab.

– Satet (Satis)

Satet was the original Lady of Elephantine and Mistress of Biggeh. She guarded the border with Nubia and her cult was centred around the First Cataract region. By the Greco-Roman Period Satet was called "*Mistress of the water of life*"[224] and identified with Isis-Sopdet.

– Sekhmet

The Lioness Goddess Sekhmet was originally the aggressive aspect of Hathor, when she wasn't being a Goddess in her own right. At a later period she was considered the aggressive aspect of Mut then finally of Isis. A hymn to Isis at Philae calls her "*Sakhmet, the fiery one, who destroys the enemies of her brother*". Through Sekhmet Isis became the "*Mistress of battle*"[225] and is depicted holding a curved sword in the company of Tiberius (14-37 CE).

– Serket (Selkis)

Isis is closely connected with the Scorpion Goddess Serket who appears in spells as her helper. Isis does not appear to have assimilated Serket the same way that she has the other goddesses; the relationship appears to be that of two goddesses working together in the same way as Isis and Nephthys. Serket is an ancient Goddess and is depicted as a woman with a scorpion on her head. She protects the king and has a funerary role. As a Scorpion Goddess she is able to heal poisonous bites and stings.

When Isis was pregnant with Horus she wandered the marshes in search of shelter so that she could hide from Seth. Seven scorpions accompanied her, believed to be the seven manifestations of Serket. A rich woman refused to help, but a poor woman invited Isis into her home. The scorpions became angry at the injustice, shared their

---

[224] *Egyptian Mythology*, Pinch, 2002:187
[225] *Hymns to Isis in Her Temple at Philae*, Zabkar, 1988:69

venom, and one went back to the rich woman's house and stung her baby. Isis took pity on the woman and her dying infant and drove out the poison with a spell in which she recited the true names of all seven scorpions. The fact that Isis knew their true names suggests that Serket may be an aspect of Isis. There is nothing in the literature to support this so it may just be a reflection of Isis' wisdom and *heka*.

There were other Scorpion Goddesses who were associated with Isis as they had power over poisonous bites and stings. Hededet, who was very similar to Serket, and Ta-Bitjet who was sometimes considered to be the wife of Horus.

– Shentayet

Shentayet is a Cow Goddess who is regarded as a form of Isis. Her origins are uncertain. She is depicted as a cow or a cow-headed woman. Her name means "*widow*" an obvious connection to Isis. She is called Isis-Shentayet where she is associated with the resurrection of Osiris and is often identified with his sarcophagus.

– Sothis

This is covered in chapter 17.

– Tayet (Tait)

Tayet is the Goddess of weaving and spinning cloth, particularly in a funerary context. She usually holds the hieroglyph for cloth, which is a folded length of cloth. New Kingdom texts refer to Isis-Tayet and texts at Dendera frequently show Tayet in relation to Isis. She is shown with the king offering cloth to Isis and Horus. It is thought that her presence signifies the funerary rebirth which was associated with the New Year. Tayet can also be identified with Nephthys. She is shown with Isis as one of the *drty*, the kites who carry the deceased to heaven.

– Wadjyt

Wadjyt was the Cobra Goddess of the Delta region and the tutelary Goddess of Lower Egypt. She can take on the role of the Eye Goddess. Wadjyt was a nurse to Horus son of Hathor and so was associated with Isis and her son Horus. Her epithets taken by Isis are Lady of Pe and Dep and Lady of Buto.

Isis the All-encompassing

Plutarch commented on some of the names of Isis. "*Isis is sometimes called Muth, and again Athyri and Methyer. And by the first of the names they mean 'mother'; by the second 'cosmic house of Horus.*"[226] Even in the Greco-Roman Period the goddesses behind the multi-named Isis were still acknowledged, in this instance Mut and Hathor. All assimilations can be seen as a trend towards monotheism. It certainly simplifies a complex pantheon if all goddesses are mere aspects of the One Goddess. But is this what was happening? Isis seems to think so at times. In one *aretalogy* she says she is the "*single embodiment of all gods and goddesses*".[227]

---

[226] *Plutarch: Concerning the Mysteries of Isis and Osiris*, Mead, 2002:234
[227] *The Golden Ass*, Apuleius & Walsh, 1994:220

CHAPTER 11

INTERACTION WITH NON-EGYPTIAN GODDESSES

"You alone are the goddesses that the peoples call by other names." [228]

Did Isis Assimilate All Before Her?

In his hymns Isidorus tells Isis that all her worshipers *"pronounce your beautiful name, with all honour, each in his language, each in his country"*.[229] He then goes on to list the names that different people call Isis; the Syrians address her as Astarte, the Greeks as Aphrodite and so on. As Lucius says, the whole world worships *"this single godhead under a variety of shapes and liturgies and titles"*.[230] Does this mean that Isis has assimilated each of these goddesses as she did with the Egyptian ones? I would argue that she did not. The goddesses outside Egypt were different and they had many attributes and aspects that could not fit with Isis. Nothing in religion is easy and many of the Greek (and other) goddesses are equated with each other. There could never be a complete fit and there is a limit to how much change can be made before one goddess loses her personality. If Isis had not had

---

[228] *Gods and Men in Egypt: 3000 BCE to 395 CE*, Dunand & Zivie-Coche, 2004:275

[229] *Gods and Men in Egypt: 3000 BCE to 395 CE*, Dunand & Zivie-Coche, 2004:275

[230] *The Golden Ass*, Apuleius & Walsh, 1994:220

such a strong personality she would have been swamped by all the new additions.

Herodotus, and other Greek writers, regarded the Greek deities as universal and so saw them everywhere. Today we would use the term archetypes. He does admit that they have different names as well as varying cult practices. The Greeks would take an aspect of Isis and look for one of their goddesses who possessed a similar attribute and equate the two. If they wanted to stress the purity of Isis she was Isis-Artemis but if beauty and sexual allure was important she was Isis-Aphrodite. At times it seems as if some of the Greeks took their favourite goddess and just appended some of Isis' Egyptian attributes. Conversely, the devotees of Isis saw nothing wrong in seeing an admirable aspect in another goddess and assigning it to Isis. Sometimes the important aspects of both goddesses were merged to give a composite goddess such as Isis-Demeter. Some of the attributes Isis took on did have a basis in her Egyptian form, as the Greeks and Romans understood it. Others were simply additions to her already complex character. It can appear as though Isis is incarnating herself in another goddess but it must be remembered that the majority of people in these countries continued to worship the same goddess as they had always done.

There are references to many other goddesses who were identified with Isis. Some names were to emphasise her importance and the extent of her cult without having much basis in fact. In the *Oxyrhynchus* hymn Isis is identified with many goddesses. This may be poetic licence - did the author really know what the Persians called their goddess and whether she had any relationship to Isis? The aim of the liturgy was to emphasise her universal powers rather than give an accurate geographical list.

– Aphrodite (Venus)

Aphrodite was the Goddess of Love and Beauty and the embodiment of sexuality. She rose fully formed from the foaming ocean where the genitals of her castrated father, Uranus, had been thrown. She originated in Cyprus and had close links to the Near Eastern Goddesses Inanna and Ishtar. She had been identified with Hathor and Bastet through their love and sexual aspects. Aphrodite had no obvious link with Isis and wasn't even a very good match to Hathor and Bastet but their sexual aspects distracted attention away from their other attributes. For one thing they were Solar Goddesses whilst Aphrodite was from the ocean. Because of this she was a protector of sailors and harbours - an attribute Isis needed when she was amongst the seafaring Mediterranean peoples. Lucius addresses Isis as *"heavenly Venus...you united the opposing sexes and multiplied the human race"*.[231] A priest of Isis-Aphrodite is attested to in the 4th century BCE.[232] The sexual aspect of Aphrodite is much reduced in Isis-Aphrodite.

– Artemis (Diana)

Artemis was the one *"whom all Asia and the world worshiped"*.[233] She was born on the island of Delos, the daughter of Zeus and twin sister of Apollo. Artemis was a Virgin Goddess, but the emphasis was more in the sense of not being subject to any man or the whims of love and lust. She is freedom, belonging to no-one and defined by no-one. Artemis had a number of manifestations such as the many-breasted Artemis of Ephesus. The Greeks originally equated Bastet with Artemis, although they had little in common, and as Isis had assimilated Bastet it was easy to equate her to Artemis. Witt considers Artemis the most important association or assimilation of Isis.[234] The link between Isis and Artemis appears to have been particularly strong in Macedonia.[235]

Artemis was a Moon Goddess and through the moon was ruler of all waters; including the tides, the menstrual cycle and human emotions. She was associated with seafaring and harbours and had similar waterside processions to Isis. By the Greco-Roman Period Isis had a strong water aspect which tended to overpower her Hathoric solar attributes. Isis the wife and mother was not an obvious fit to the virgin Artemis. In one hymn to Osiris Isis is referred to as the Great Virgin,[236] an odd epithet for a Goddess who is almost the personification of motherhood and a model wife. Unlike Artemis, Isis is very much defined by her relationships both with her husband and son and also with Nephthys and Anubis amongst others. Despite being a virgin Artemis has strong connections with childbirth and was considered a protector of young children, especially girls. In this aspect she is much like Hathor.

---

[231] *The Golden Ass*, Apuleius & Walsh, 1994:218
[232] *Apuleius of Madauros – The Isis Book*, Griffiths, 1975:149
[233] *Isis in the Ancient World*, Witt, 1997:149
[234] *Isis in the Ancient World*, Witt, 1997:151
[235] *Isis in the Ancient World*, Witt, 1997:145
[236] *Isis in the Ancient World*, Witt, 1997:15

Artemis was associated with the natural world and was the protector of wild creatures. There was no such deity in Egypt although many had sacred animals and trees. The *Oxyrhynchus* papyrus calls Isis "*Artemis of the three-fold nature*" an epithet usually associated with Hekate.[237] There are aspects which Isis and Artemis shared but the major factor in their association was probably the fact that Artemis, like Isis, was a very popular and strong Goddess.

– Astarte

The Great Goddess was known as Inanna by the Sumerians. To the Assyrians and Babylonians she was Ishtar, later the Phoenicians called her Astarte. All were associated with a dying-resurrected consort who was a Vegetation or Fertility God. Amongst other aspects, they are associated with the underworld, water, the moon and love and fertility. The Phoenicians had trading links with Egypt and there was a cult of Astarte at Memphis in 2nd century BCE. Astarte was linked to Aphrodite by the Greeks. Herodotus mentions a temple to the "*foreign Aphrodite*" at Memphis who was worshiped by the Phoenicians living there.[238]

Isis shares a number of aspects with Astarte, in particular the annual death and resurrection of her husband Osiris. The love and sexual aspects are absent, with Hathor assuming that particular role. An inscription on Delos refers to Isis-Astarte and an inscription to Isis in Rome equates her to Astarte.[239]

– Athena (Minerva)

Pallas Athena sprung fully armed from the head of Zeus to become a Warrior Goddess yet one who was ruled by her head. She was a Goddess of Wisdom and patron of the city of Athens. Like Artemis she was a Virgin Goddess. There was a large Greek settlement in the town of Sais and Plato said that the local people were especially friendly towards the Greeks. The statue of Neith in her temple at Sais was regarded by them as a representation of Athena. When Isis became identified with Neith she was equated to Athena. Plutarch said "*they often call Isis by the name of Athena, which expresses some such*

---

[237] *Apuleius of Madauros – The Isis Book*, Griffiths, 1975:152
[238] *The Histories*, Herodotus & Selincourt, 2003:137
[239] *Isis in the Ancient World*, Witt, 1997:131

meaning as 'I have come from myself'.[240] Both are Wisdom Goddesses but here the similarity ends. Isis didn't really have a warlike aspect despite being invoked as such and she is a loving wife and mother unlike the celibate Athena. Isis is linked to Minerva Chalcidica at the *Iseum Campense* in Rome.[241]

– Cybele

Cybele is a Mother Goddess from Asia Minor. She was brought to Rome at the end of the 3rd century BCE and as Isis became more important she was identified with her as the All-Mother. From about 55 BCE there is reference to Isis equated to Cybele.[242]

– Demeter

Demeter is the Earth Goddess, a bringer of fertility. Her daughter is Persephone and their myth is one of the richest in Classical mythology. Persephone is abducted by Hades, the god of the underworld. Demeter wanders the earth grieving and searching for her daughter. Finally Hermes descends to the underworld to retrieve her, but as she has eaten in his realm Persephone has to return to Hades each winter. The myth became the basis of the Eleusinian Mysteries. Demeter's was one of the most popular Greek cults. By the reign of Ptolemy I (305-283 BCE) there were temples to Demeter in Alexandria.

Herodotus identifies Isis with Demeter, saying she is *"the Egyptian equivalent of Demeter".*[243] Both Goddesses are benevolent and compassionate having a strong saviour aspect but what really equates them is their mourning aspect. Demeter loses her daughter Persephone to the underworld and Isis loses Osiris. As well as mourning they both wander the earth searching for their missing loved ones. Isis is assisted by Thoth, who was equated to Hermes. Through the myth of this loss comes the mysteries of both Goddesses. Diodorus claimed that the Eleusinian rituals had come from Egypt.[244] In the Homeric Hymn to Demeter it tells how Demeter was received at Eleusis. This is very similar to Isis and the palace at Byblos. Demeter becomes nursemaid to the Queen's baby. Each night *"she buried him in the fire's might...she*

---

[240] *Plutarch: Concerning the Mysteries of Isis and Osiris*, Mead, 2002:238

[241] *The Flavians: Pharonic Kingship Between Egypt and Rome*, Vittozzi, 2014:257

[242] *The four Greek hymns of Isidorus and the cult of Isis*, Vanderlip, 1972:29

[243] *Isis Among the Greeks and Romans*, Solmsen, 1979:8

[244] *The Antiquities of Egypt*, Diodorus Siculus & Murphy, 1990:36

would have made him unaging and immortal.[245] When the queen discovered the ritual Demeter revealed herself and her mysteries. It is thought that these hymns were written in 7th century BCE so they may have been influenced by the myth of Isis in Byblos.

By the Greco-Roman Period Isis was viewed as a Grain and Harvest Goddess through her assimilation of Renenutet. With this aspect the Greeks found another logical connection with Demeter, particularly as the part of Egypt they were most familiar with was the extremely fertile Delta region. To them, Isis was the Lady of Bread and the Harvest. In the temple of Kellis was a life-size bust dedicated to "*Isis-Demeter, the greatest goddess*". It was dedicated by the cult leader and his family "*on account of gratitude, for the best*".[246] Like Demeter, Isis is depicted with the cornucopia and ears of corn. The Romans identified Isis with Ceres the "*bountiful and primeval bearer of crops*".[247] As Egypt was in effect their breadbasket this was an understandable and important connection. Ceres was a Roman Vegetation Goddess who, with her daughter Proserpina, was assimilated by Demeter and Persephone. Isis takes a number of Demeter's epithets. In one *aretalogy* Isis says that she is called Lawgiver, *Thesmorphoros*, which was a classical epithet of Demeter. Isis and Demeter tended to retain their separate characters even though they had a common cult. This is probably because they both had strong characters and well-established cults.

– Hekate

Hekate is an ancient Goddess, predating the Olympian pantheon. She is associated with magic, the underworld, the moon and the night and is a protector of sailors and witches. The triple aspect is very strong with Hekate and her three-fold aspect was placed at crossroads. In her triple form she is associated with Artemis and Persephone. In Greece, Artemis was often closely associated with Hekate and could even be Artemis-Hekate. It was a simple step to associate Isis with Hekate as well and they do have a number of shared aspects. Both are strongly associated with the underworld and this world. To the Greeks they were both Lunar Goddesses who bestow wisdom, grant victory and are known for helping those at sea.

---

[245] *The Homeric Hymns*, Raynor, 2004:25
[246] *Isis in Roman Dakhleh: Goddess of the Village, the Province and the Country*, Kaper, 2010:170
[247] *The Golden Ass*, Apuleius & Walsh, 1994:218

Magic is a major aspect linking Isis to Hekate. There is a bronze statue in Rome that depicts Hekate wearing the lunar crown of Isis, topped by lotus blossoms, and carrying a lighted torch in each hand. The statue is dedicated to Hekate and Serapis from someone who was saved by them from an unnamed danger.[248] Both Isis and Artemis are shown carrying a torch as is Torch-bearing Hekate who illuminates the secrets of the underworld.

Lead tokens found in Memphis depict Isis-Hekate so the conflation of Isis and Hekate may have been common in some areas.[249] One hymn says that Isis is called Hekate in Caria (Turkey). But was she actually worshiped as such? Solmsen says there is no evidence for an alliance or relationship between Isis and Hekate in Caria, said to be the homeland of Hekate.[250] Hekate refused to give up her identity as easily as some other goddesses, being too strong a personality to lose much to Isis.

– Hygeia

Hygeia, the Goddess of Health, was the daughter of Asclepius. Isis is linked to her through her healing aspect. In Epidaurus a temple was dedicated to Hygeia under the name of Isis.[251]

– Io

Io was originally a priestess who was pursued by Zeus and turned into a cow. Hera chased Io out of Greece and the Greeks could easily find her presence in the cow horn crown of Isis. "*The statues of Isis show a female figure with cow's horns, like the Greek representation of Io.*"[252] A wall painting shows Isis welcoming Io to Egypt. She is depicted as a Roman lady in white wearing a garland of ivy. She holds a cobra wrapped around her left hand. Io is shown as dishevelled, with small horns protruding from her forehead. Two assistants stand behind Io holding *sistra*, wands and an offering vessel.[253]

---

[248] *Isis, or the Moon*, Delia, 1998:549
[249] *Apuleius of Madauros – The Isis Book*, Griffiths, 1975:153
[250] *Isis Among the Greeks and Romans*, Solmsen, 1979:59
[251] *Isis in the Ancient World*, Witt, 1997:192
[252] *The Histories*, Herodotus & Selincourt, 2003:111
[253] *Egypt at Pompeii*, Phillips, 2013:33-47

– Nana

Nana (or Nania) is an ancient Goddess from the Near East; Anat is another of her forms. She was known at Alexandria and is often equated to Artemis. There is a 3rd century CE reference to Isis-Nania.[254]

– Nemesis

Nemesis is a Goddess of divine anger and retribution, also known as Adrastia. She brings retribution to wrongdoers. Nemesis is sometimes equated to Maat but is more focused on punishment and revenge than cosmic harmony and justice. Both goddesses were identified with Isis. A magical papyrus gives a protection charm addressing Isis, Nemesis and Adrastia.[255] In Alexandria there was a dedication to Isis-Adrastia by a priest of Serapis.[256]

– Sophia

Sophia, the Goddess and personification of wisdom and philosophy, was a popular concept in the Greco-Roman world in both pagan and Jewish-Christian theologies. *Hagia Sophia*, Holy Wisdom, was considered to be the mother of the divine Logos. When identified with Isis we get Isis-Sophia who gives birth to Harpocrates as the Logos. The Wisdom of Solomon was written in Roman times. Its author was unknown but he knew Greek and had studied various philosophies including Egyptian rites so was probably based in Alexandria. Sophia was described as *"more beautiful than the sun and all the orders of stars: being compared with light, she is found beyond it"*.[257] She was important in Gnosticism. The similarity to Isis is noticeable as is the fact that the Christian Virgin Mary took over the role of Sophia.

– Tyche (Fortuna)

Tyche was the Goddess of Fortune and the personification of luck. Isis-Tyche as Mistress of Destiny is covered in chapter 16. Isis is linked with Tyche at Rhodes, Rome and Lyon.

---

[254] *Cults and Creeds in Graeco-Roman Egypt*, Bell, 1957:15
[255] *Apuleius of Madauros – The Isis Book*, Griffiths, 1975:153
[256] *Isis in the Ancient World*, Witt, 1997:293
[257] *Osiris. Death and Afterlife of a God*, Mojsov, 2005:113

The Degree of Assimilation

The assimilated Egyptian goddesses lost some of their power and independence. Did the same happen with the other goddesses? Was it calculated manipulation? It didn't seem to upset the worshipers of the period but we have so little written evidence that we can't say for sure. No doubt some would have seen Isis in every goddess whilst others carried on worshiping Artemis or Hekate as they had always done. It must be remembered that the cult of Isis was always a minority religion outside Egypt. Why would anyone readily accept that their beloved Goddess was actually Isis? Even if they knew someone who had recently returned from Egypt with stories about her, their first impression was more likely to be that it was their Goddess who was worshiped in Egypt under the name of Isis. The goddesses of Greece and Rome were instantly understandable to someone who had grown up in that culture whereas it took extra effort to understand the Egyptian deities. Did she appeal to those disaffected with their own religion or was her call too strong to ignore?

Is this the same Isis we had before the assimilation of foreign goddesses? I don't think so for she has changed, but this made her more versatile and thus acceptable to the people outside Egypt. Despite her power, prestige and gifts to her followers it probably wouldn't have been possible for Isis to enter the Greek world before she had become Hellenised. Her early Greek devotees in Egypt altered some of her attributes and reemphasised others so that she would be approachable to Greeks without an understanding of the Egyptian religion. In the end Isis was portrayed more as a Greek Goddess with interesting foreign connections than an Egyptian Goddess in Greece. It was the Hellenised Isis not the Egyptian Isis who went on to conquer the Mediterranean world and compete with Christianity.

CHAPTER 12

KINGSHIP AND ISIS

"The king stands upon his throne according to her word."[258]

Isis the Throne

Isis was an essential part of royal cosmography as she birthed, nursed and protected kings. The king gets his authority and dignity from the throne, in effect the throne making the king just as Isis the Throne Goddess makes the king. A statue of the king on his throne is paralleled with the concept of the Horus child sat in the lap of his mother. Isis is the living throne.

Isis as Mother of the King

Isis was the symbolic mother of the king and the king imbibed divinity and the right to rule through her divine milk. Isis was not the only mother of the king as Hathor, as well as some other goddesses, also took on this role. Kings describe themselves as the *"son of Isis"*, or one of the other goddesses. Some took no chances listing all of them as their mothers. In his Luxor temple Amenhotep III (18th Dynasty) is shown between Isis and Hathor. As with everything there was a fashion, some dynasties favouring Isis over the other goddesses and others not. Kings in the New Kingdom in particular aligned themselves with Isis.

---

[258] *Egyptian Religion*, Morenz, 1992:302

Legitimising the King

The king took on the identity of Horus, the son of Isis, who was the rightful heir to the throne of Egypt. Isis says *"I give thee the strength of my son Horus, so that thou occupyest his throne in triumph"*.[259] One hymn to the Red Crown says *"Let your kas rejoice over this king...as Isis rejoiced over her son Horus when he was a child in Chemmis"*.[260] Not only did this legitimise the king's position it 'proved' his divine descent showing that he ruled with the approval of the deities. Rameses III (20th Dynasty), in an inscription at Medinet Habu, is portrayed as Horus on the throne and called *"Horus...great in kingship"*.[261] Many kings are shown worshiping and offering to their mother Isis. An inscription on the back of a statue of Horemheb (18th Dynasty) refers to his queen as *"beloved of Isis"* and himself as *"son of Isis"*.[262] Thutmose I (18th Dynasty) describes himself as *"Born of Isis"*[263] and Rameses II (19th Dynasty) calls himself *"beloved of Isis the great"*.[264]

Osiris was the rightful ruler of Egypt and his son, Horus, succeeded him. It was this that set the precedent for the inheritance of the throne. The deceased king became Osiris and the new king became Horus son of Osiris when he ascended the throne. A king who claimed the throne by conquest rather than inheritance did not have a legitimate claim. This was only a temporary inconvenience: the incoming king could still claim his accession was legitimate because he had become Horus the legitimate king and the king only ascended the throne on the wish of Isis. Kings who ruled by conquest often married (forcibly or otherwise) the queen of the late king or one of the princesses as this helped to legitimise their rule. Is this echoed in the concept of the Goddess having sovereignty of the land whom the king had to symbolically marry and also that of Isis as the Throne Goddess? Although she is speaking to the unborn Horus, these words of Isis were important to the new king: *"Come and go forth on the earth so that I*

---

[259] *The Significance of the Ceremony Hwt Bhsw in the Temple of Horus at Edfu,* Blackman & Fairman, 1949:98-112

[260] *Ancient Egyptian Literature Volume I,* Lichtheim, 2006:201

[261] *Temple Festival Calendars of Ancient Egypt,* el-Sabban, 2000:63.

[262] *The Coronation of King Haremhab,* Gardiner, 1953:13-31

[263] *New Light on the Recarved Sarcophagus of Hatshepsut and Thutmose in the Museum of Fine Arts, Boston,* Manuelian & Loeben, 1993:121-155

[264] *Temple Festival Calendars of Ancient Egypt,* el-Sabban, 2000:38

may give you honour such that the retainers of your father may serve you...go forth in power from within my flesh."[265]

Worship by Kings and Emperors

The kings worshiped all the state deities as part of their duty as rulers of Egypt. Who they were privately devoted to was irrelevant. They were there to act as intermediaries between the deities and the state and people of Egypt. The king was the highest-ranking priest and the queen was the highest-ranking priestess. They performed the critical rituals which maintained order and preserved the state and creation and ensured that the deities were satisfied. Daily ceremonies in each temple were similar and in each the priests carried out the rituals on behalf of the king, who obviously could only perform them in one of the temples. Kings and queens are depicted in the temples carrying out various rituals such as purifying the sanctuary, playing *sistra* and making offerings of wine, food and flowers.

Royals had their preferred deities and although many kings were depicted with Isis it is not until the Greco-Roman Period that she became the special favourite of some of the rulers. The Ptolemies and the Roman Emperors were as keen to show their devotion to Isis as their predecessors had been. Regardless of personal belief, keeping in with the Egyptians deities when in Egypt was seen as a sensible move and it emphasised their divine right to rule Egypt. At Philae Ptolemy II (285-246 BCE) is shown playing the *sistra* in front of Isis, to pacify her as well as worship her.[266] Ptolemy III (246-221 BCE) promoted the cult of Isis and Serapis. He decreed that only the names of Isis and Serapis could stand with those of deified royals in royal oaths.[267] Ptolemy XII (80-51 BCE) is shown smiting his enemies before Isis and Hathor. Isis holds a curved sword and tells Ptolemy that she has given him control of the lands and backed his conquests of foreign territories.[268]

The Roman Emperors varied in their attitude towards Oriental religions in general and Isis in particular. Tiberius (14-37 CE) hated

---

[265] *The Emergence of Horus. An Analysis of Coffin Text Spell 148*, O'Connell. 1983:66-87
[266] *Hymns to Isis in Her Temple at Philae*, Zabkar, 1988:107
[267] *The four Greek hymns of Isidorus and the cult of Isis*, Vanderlip, 1972:77
[268] *Hymns to Isis in Her Temple at Philae*, Zabkar, 1988:63

them whilst Caligula (37-41 CE) adopted Egyptian deities and their cults and dedicated a large temple to Isis. At Dendera, Augustus (27 BCE – 14 CE) is depicted with the Red Crown of Egypt offering to Isis and the Horus child although he opposed the cult of Isis in Rome. Domitian (81-96 CE) was a well-known devotee of Isis as was Hadrian (117-138 CE). Hadrian had sculptures of Isis in his garden at Tivoli. One has two faces; the face of Isis with a cow's head at the back – a nice depiction of the syncretism between Isis and Hathor.

Isis and the Queens

In the New Kingdom there was a deliberate association of queens with goddesses and the queens of this period were a lot more visible than in previous dynasties. During the 17th and 18th Dynasties there was a close association between queens and Hathor. As Isis began to assimilate Hathor both could be aligned with the queen. Isis and Hathor began to be depicted wearing the traditional queen's crown consisting of *uraeus*, double feathers and vulture cap. The mortuary temple of Rameses II in Abydos had a life-size sculpture of Sety I (19th Dynasty) as Osiris next to Isis wearing a contemporary queen's crown. It has been suggested that it was the increased power of royal women, and queens in particular, during the 18th Dynasty which helped elevate the cult of Isis in the New Kingdom.

The Ptolemaic Queens

– Arsinoe II

Arsinoe II (about 316-270 BCE) identified with Isis and did a lot to popularise her cult. At the temple at Philae Ptolemy II is depicted offering to Isis and Arsinoe II. She used Isis as one of her names calling herself Isis-Arsinoe. One mortuary inscription says *"Arsinoe, image of Isis and Hathor...costumed as Isis"*.[269] Was she really devoted to Isis or had Arsinoe become convinced that she was an incarnation of Isis? Arsinoe was in effect deified. At Philae she appears five times and receives offerings from her brother-husband Ptolemy II and is treated

---

[269] *Attic Grave Reliefs that Represent Women in the Dress of Isis*, Walters, 1988:10

as if she was sharing the temple with Isis. On the Gate of Philadelphus, Ptolemy II is shown offering to Nephthys and Arsinoe and to Isis and Arsinoe. Whether this level of deification was acceptable to the priests and priestesses of the temple is not known. They may have acquiesced as they had no say in the matter. Arsinoe's devotion to and identification with Isis probably encouraged the cult to spread throughout Lower Egypt. At her court Isis was of paramount importance and the officials would have propagated her cult amongst the Greeks living in Egypt.

– Cleopatra III

All the Ptolemaic queens had a close bond with Isis but Cleopatra III (142-101 BCE) and Cleopatra VII (51-30 BCE) were particularly devoted. Both were strong queens who ruled on behalf of fatherless sons and came to believe that they were the living incarnation of Isis. Cleopatra III is shown as saying to Ptolemy VIII (170-161 BCE) *"trust in Isis, she is the mistress of men and women"*.[270] Cleopatra III was called *Rait, "female sun"*, an allusion to Isis in her Hathoric aspect. She particularly identified with Isis in her regal role as Queen Isis.

– Cleopatra VII

Cleopatra VII is one of the most famous devotees of Isis and she actively promoted the cult of Isis, learning Egyptian and honouring the traditional cults. Royal propaganda deliberately blended her features with the iconography of Isis. On her coins she is shown in the likeness of Isis with her epithets and crown. She appeared in public in the dress of Isis calling herself the *"New Isis"*.[271] It was rumoured that she dressed as Isis when she met Mark Antony. This was particularly appropriate as he considered himself the living Dionysus, who was often associated with Osiris and considered one of the Greek consorts of Isis. Much has been written about the death of Cleopatra VII but there were no eyewitnesses. All the reports were written a long time after her death. If she had used a cobra to kill herself then it was an appropriate choice. As a symbol of the *uraeus* it delivered a death befitting a living goddess. Some classical writers said it was a pair of cobras, the double *uraeus*.

---

[270] *Hymns to Isis in Her Temple at Philae*, Zabkar, 1988:62
[271] *A History of the Ptolemaic Empire*, Holbl, 2001:290

Royal Isis

Isis played an important role in kingship in Egypt as demonstrated by her throne crown. The Queen Mother may have once had an important role and the mother of the king could provide legitimacy in an inherited kingship. Was this another reason for the strong association between Isis and the throne? She was popular amongst queens, especially the Ptolemies, but was this just because they identified with her so much that they became convinced that they were her reincarnation? Viewing yourself as a goddess is not the same as worshiping her. To be fair, the Pharaonic kings believed they were the reincarnation of Horus. Excluding rulers, the Greco-Roman cult of Isis was more concerned with her saviour aspects and the spiritual development of cult members rather than her kingship aspect. Today Isis' role in kingship is not needed. Many would add that it is not wanted. We have no desire for rulers with delusions of divinity and alleged divine justification of their actions.

CHAPTER 13

THE GREAT MAGICIAN

"I am Isis the Goddess, Mistress of Magic who makes magic, glorious of speech."[272]

Great of Magic

Isis may have acquired attributes as she assimilated other goddesses but she was always Great of Magic. It is an essential part of her nature and she was considered to have the most *heka* of any deity with the exception of Thoth. Great magical power was essential, without this Isis would not have been able to resurrect Osiris or conceive and protect Horus. The myth of *Horus at Edfu* tells how *"Isis performed all the magic spells for driving back Be from Neref...and Thoth said 'therefore shall the songstress of this god be called Mistress of Magic'"*.[273] Be was another name for Seth. Medicinal knowledge and healing was an important and specialised part of magic and is covered in chapter 15.

The Differing Concepts of Magic

The Egyptians thought of magic in a completely different way to the Greeks and Romans. It was not considered sinister but was viewed more like a science to be used to maintain order and help people, an

---

[272] *The Metternich Stele*, Scott, 1951:201-217
[273] *The Myth of Horus at Edfu: I*, Fairman, 1935:26-36

important weapon in the war against the chaos and negativity that was always threatening creation. Egyptian magicians were famous and a 3rd century CE document states that *"Egypt is the mother of all magicians"*.[274] There was no clear demarcation between religion and magic. One definition of magic is the control of supernatural forces for one's own purpose whilst religion is worshiping and appealing to such forces. The Egyptian priests and priestesses did both using magical rituals to protect the king and country and to protect and assist the deities against the forces of chaos. In the New Kingdom, magical texts appear to play an increasingly important role. This might just be our perception though as older evidence is always scarcer due to lower survival rates.

The attitude of the Greeks and Romans to magic was very similar to the general perception held throughout history and in modern times. It was something dangerous used for malicious ends with the help of powers coming from an evil entity. This made it very appealing to certain types of people but not to the political and religious establishments. In the Greco-Roman Period Isis was very popular as the Great Sorceress. Her magical appeal seems to have grown when she was associated with the moon. To the Greeks and Romans a lunar aspect meant a strong magical and occult aspect. The Egyptians didn't hold this view but Thoth was a Lunar God and he had the greatest *heka* and magical knowledge of all the deities. In one magical papyrus the magician burns incense to the moon and invokes Isis under her various names. Another spell threatens the waning moon saying that the magician will destroy her light unless she obeys his will.[275]

Heka

Heka is one of the basic powers which was used to create and order the universe. It is an essential energy which flows between the sacred and secular world and between objects and people. All deities and supernatural beings possess *heka*. A ritually charged object will be able to contain and direct this energy. *Heka* is released and directed through the use of words, in particular the true names. A spiritual image is created and its true essence revealed when the name is

---

[274] *Egyptian Magic*, Raven, 2012:185
[275] *Isis, or the Moon*, Delia, 1998:548

pronounced correctly. The sound activates and engages with the *heka* so incorrect pronunciation renders the spell useless. Isis was the *"golden-tongued goddess; her voice shall not fail"*.[276] The spoken word was considered audible thought and script visible thought. Hieroglyphics was a sacred script, created by Thoth, and contained a great deal of power. What was written in them could become alive through that power. The myths themselves, being spoken stories, contained magic and Egyptian magic is built upon myths which tell of events surrounding the deities.

Weret Hekau, Great of Magic (or Greatest of Magic) is a common epithet of goddesses and especially of Isis. Weret Hekau could also be a Goddess in her own right, depicted as a cobra. Some have suggested that cobra-shaped wands represent her. Another magical force is that of *akhu*. It is particularly associated with afterlife deities and the blessed dead. Isis is referred to as using her *akhu*. Both *heka* and *akhu* are essentially neutral, like any natural force. It is the channelling for good or bad intent that is important.

The Power of the Name and of Speech

"I am Isis the Wise, the words of whose mouth of mine come to pass."[277] *Heka* will only work if the magician knows the true name and nature of an object, person or deity. If your true name was pronounced then you had no choice but to obey which is why it was essential to keep it secret. People were given special names known only to themselves and their parents. In spells the mother's name was often used as maternity is certain whilst paternity is not. If the wrong name was used the spell was useless. In funerary spells the deceased often says *"I know you and I know your names"* for this reason.[278] The powerful role of the name is emphasised by the fact that it is one of the essential components of a person that have to be reassembled after death before they can be reborn. It was as important as the body and soul. Your name was part of your identity, to forget your name was to incur non-existence. In one *Coffin Text* spell the deceased states *"I will*

---

[276] *Echoes of Egyptian Voices*, Foster, 1992:43
[277] *The Leyden Papyrus*, Griffith, 1974:31
[278] *The Ancient Egyptian Book of the Dead*, Faulkner, 1989:133 Spell 144

not forget it, this name of mine".[279] A spell against Apophis uses this concept where *"Horus obliterates thy name".*[280]

Obtaining the Sun God's Name

The story of how Isis obtained the true name of Ra comes from the New Kingdom. Isis, it is said, knew everything *"in the sky and on earth"* expect for the secret name of Ra.[281] Isis creates a poisonous snake using a mixture of soil and the saliva of Ra. We are told Ra was getting old and drooled as he walked, not a very dignified description of an important god. Perhaps it is a way of explaining imperfection in creation, the fact that a god can age and become decrepit like humans.

Saliva was considered to have magical powers as it came from the mouth which had uttered magical incantations. As a Creator God Ra's saliva would have been infused with his creative power. Only a creature created by Ra, however inadvertently, has the power to harm him. Isis placed the snake at a crossroads where she knew Ra would walk. The Egyptians probably viewed crossroads as we do, being liminal places where the veils are thin and hidden forces stronger. The snake bites Ra when he walks along the road, another reference to the failing power of Ra is that he didn't see the snake. The pain focuses his mind and Ra realises that he has been bitten by a creature that he doesn't know and therefore has power over him. Isis then tells Ra that she has a powerful spell which will release the poison but that she needs to know his true name. There follows a long list of epithets but not his true name. Eventually Ra is in such agony that he whispers his true name to Isis and she cures him.

Why did Isis need to have this power over Ra? Was it merely to enhance her own considerable powers? In the myths she is never in conflict with the Sun God except during the *Contendings of Horus and Seth* and here she resorts more to crafty thinking and shape-shifting. Isis uses the name of Ra to halt the Solar Barque when Horus lies dying after being poisoned by Seth (see chapter 15). By imperilling creation she forces the deities to assist her, perhaps she had some

---

[279] *The Ancient Egyptian Coffin Texts Volume II*, Faulkner, 2007:63 Spell 411
[280] *The Bremner-Rhind Papyrus: IV*, Faulkner, 1938:41-53
[281] *Conceptions of God in Ancient Egypt*, Hornung, 1996:88

foreboding that she would need this ultimate power in her fight against Seth. The secret name of Seth would have been infinitely more useful and as Seth seems easily tricked it shouldn't have been hard to obtain. Perhaps it would have unleashed a more chaotic power than Isis was prepared to deal with. The snake was a symbol of rebirth as well as being a symbol of goddesses in general. Is Isis asserting the power of the Goddess and forcing Ra to move on from his stasis as an aging god?

Power Over Life and Death

The highest magic after creation was that which gave life and Isis has this magic. Using her powerful magic Isis resurrects Osiris, and through Osiris everyone. The method of resurrection varies and is mentioned only briefly in the texts, after all it was the highest magic which no mortal could understand or emulate. It is discussed in more detail in chapter 14.

Isis gives the deceased, and Osiris, their heart back. *"I am Isis, and I have come that...I may place your heart in your body"*.[282] The heart was seen as the source of wisdom, memory and emotion so it was critical for survival in the afterlife. It could also reveal a person's true character, hence the weighing of the heart during judgment. A 19th or 20th Dynasty pectoral in the shape of the hieroglyph for *"heart"* shows Isis and Nephthys kneeling next to it. They protect and revive the heart of Osiris and the heart of the deceased.[283]

Not only can Isis resurrect the dead, but she can also make humans immortal. At the palace at Byblos the coffin of Osiris is encased in a pillar. Isis gains access to the palace via the queen' s servants and is employed as a nurse for the baby prince. *"At night she burnt round the mortal elements of its body, and, turning herself into a swallow, flew round the pillar and twittered a dirge."*[284] One night the queen hears the noise and comes to investigate. Her screams of terror at the sight of her baby over the fire halt the magic of Isis and the child is denied immortality. It was obviously a slow and complicated process

---

[282] *The Ancient Egyptian Coffin Texts Volume II*, Faulkner, 2007:152 Spell 526
[283] *Reading Egyptian Art*, Wilkinson, 2011:77
[284] *Plutarch: Concerning the Mysteries of Isis and Osiris*, Mead, 2002:199

as the mortal parts have to be burned away each night over a period of time. It is not clear why Isis wanted to make the baby immortal. Was it in exchange for the corpse of Osiris? Would the child have wanted to become immortal given his family and friends would have remained mortal? At one level it is through the magic of Isis that everyone can become immortal. Because she brought Osiris back to life everyone can be resurrected. This part of the story was probably a reflection of this. Isis' command over life can also be seen in the conception of Horus from the deceased Osiris. Like a Creator she can produce life without an active sexual partner, as discussed in chapter 5.

Magical Protection

Through her magical powers, as well as her sympathetic nature, Isis is an effective protector. She *"ended unspeakable mischief by the power of her spell"* while she protected the body of Osiris from Seth. She was his *"shield and defender"*.[285] Isis uses her power to assist Horus in his many battles. The myth of *Horus at Edfu* tells how he was *"a hero of great strength when he sallieth forth to battle with his mother Isis protecting him"*. She also gave some of her *heka* to Horus, *"I give thee power against those who are hostile towards thee"*.[286] Horus can use this magical power until it has dissipated, like a battery which needs recharging. He doesn't have the necessary *heka* of his own and Isis can, or will, only transfer some of her power on a temporary basis. Isis has an unending supply of *heka* herself. Without this constant protection and *heka* from Isis, Horus would have failed in his destiny to avenge the death of his father and to ascend his throne.

The magical power of Isis is essential in the nightly battle with Apophis. In the *Book of the Dead*, and the New Kingdom books of the underworld, the newborn sun is threatened by the powers of evil and chaos in the form of Apophis. Here Isis combines forces with Seth, their differences forgotten as they battle to save the reborn light. The Solar Barque *"sails by the magic of Isis and the Eldest Magician"*.[287] Seth does not have the magic and wisdom of Isis but he provides the power and

---

[285] *Echoes of Egyptian Voices*, Foster, 1992:43
[286] *The Myth of Horus at Edfu: II. C. The Triumph of Horus over His Enemies a Sacred Drama (Continued)*, Blackman & Fairman, 1943:2-36
[287] *The Egyptian Amduat*, Abt & Hornung, 2007:219

brute force. As a Chaos God he contains within himself the understanding and ability needed to repel the Chaos Serpent Apophis. He became a significant threat during the later periods. The *Bremner-Rhind* papyrus contains the *Book of Overthrowing Apep*. This ritual was enacted daily in the temples. "*Isis fells thee with her magic, she closes thy mouth, she takes away thy power of movement...thou shalt die, and not live, for Isis and Nephthys fell thee; together they avert thy rage.*"[288]

Magic was used to protect both the king and Egypt. Some have suggested that a major function of the temple of Isis at Philae was to create a powerful magical boundary with Nubia. The Nubians were feared as very powerful magicians. "*Isis is more powerful than a thousand soldiers.*"[289] There were many dangers to be faced in this world and many amulets and spells ask Isis for protection. "*Come to me, Great Isis, deign to guarantee my protection, save me from the reptiles and let their jaws be sealed.*"[290] To the Romans she was Isis *Victrix*, "*Isis the Victorious*". Her victory was over evil and so this name was used as a charm to repel evil and was inscribed on amulets. Like many deities Isis provides protection for the deceased in the afterlife. "*I have come as your protection.*"[291] This is covered in more detail in chapter 14.

Shape-Shifter

Isis is a shape-shifter when she needs to disguise herself, usually to trick Seth. In the *Contendings of Horus and Seth* Isis performed "*conjuration with her heka, and she turned herself into a girl beautiful in all her body*".[292] This allowed her to gain access to the Tribunal of the Gods who were deciding whether Seth or Horus had claim to the throne of Osiris, having been barred on the insistence of Seth. She also transfigures herself into an old woman to trick Seth into denouncing his own actions.

Her transformation into a kite has already been discussed in chapter 4. In another version of the *Contendings* she transforms into a

---

[288] *The Bremner-Rhind Papyrus: IV*, Faulkner, 1938:41-53
[289] *Magic in Ancient Egypt*, Pinch, 2006:29
[290] *Magic and Mystery in Ancient Egypt*, Jacq, 2002:157
[291] *The Ancient Egyptian Book of the Dead*, Faulkner, 1989:145 Spell 151
[292] *Through a Glass Darkly*, Szpakowska, 2006:82

headless flint statue after Horus attacks her.[293] Flint was considered celestial in origin and was associated with Hathor as a Sky Goddess. Two pieces of flint will produce a spark when struck, which confirmed its solar powers. Isis changing into a flint statue further emphasises her merging with Hathor and becoming solar. In the *Book of the Dead* there is reference to a flint staff called the Giver of Breath. This is a reference to the adze used to open the mouth of the deceased allowing them to breathe again, and Isis is the one who gives breath to the deceased.

A Ptolemaic manuscript from a temple library contains a spell for *"knowing the secret form which Isis assumed for concealing the god in his hiding place"*.[294] Isis hides the corpse of Osiris in a tamarisk grove near Busiris and transforms herself into the Sacred Cow, taking the Cow form of Hathor, but this time Seth is not fooled. We are told the colour of her hide gives her away but not what this colour is. In another Greco-Roman tale Isis is leading a campaign against Seth. She transforms herself into Sekhmet and hides on a rocky hill. She can do this because she has completely absorbed Hathor's aspects. In the myth of the *Destruction of Mankind* Ra sends Hathor to kill the rebellious humans and she does this by transforming into the dangerous Sekhmet. When Seth appears, Isis as Sekhmet sends a blast of fire at him. Seth recognises her as Isis, we are not told why but it is probably because Sekhmet has never attacked him before. Isis changes into a dog with a knife in her tail and outruns Seth. Finally she turns into a snake and bites and poisons Seth.[295] An echo of this shapeshifting occurs in *The Golden Ass*. Whilst tinkering with magic Lucius manages to transform himself into a donkey. He is unable to reverse the process and only Isis can help him.

The Magic of Knowledge

"Isis was a wise woman...more smart than an infinite number of gods. She was more clever than an infinite number of spirits. There was

---

[293] *Myths & Legends of Ancient Egypt,* Tyldesley, 2010:139
[294] *Another Hieratic Manuscript from the Library of Pwerem Son of Kiki (Pap. B.M. 10288),* Caminos, 1972:205-224
[295] *The Egyptian Myths,* Shaw, 2014:91-92

nothing she was ignorant of in heaven or on the earth."[296] There was no disconnection between science and religion for the Egyptians. All knowledge was deemed important as it was learning about creation and this knowledge could bring you closer to the deities. It was also prized for its own sake. Knowledge is power and learning and wisdom was considered part of magic. Indeed to the illiterate and uneducated knowledge and writing were magical. Medical knowledge and treatment were seen as a specialised branch of magic. Isis was the *"Magician with divine wisdom"*[297] and she is happy to share her wisdom and give advice being the *"Magician with excellent councils"*.[298]

Isis and the Magician

Sometimes the magician narrates the spell, at other times they assume the role of Isis or Thoth. Associating with such great magicians would, in theory, intimidate the forces they were attempting to control. Psychologically it would also strengthen their confidence in the power of their speech. A Greco-Roman document refers to a *"sacred scribe"* in Memphis who lived in a subterranean shrine for 23 years and gained his magical powers from Isis.[299] In the tale of *The Sorcerer's Apprentice*, written by the Roman Lucian (120-185 CE) the sorcerer Pancrates learns the art of magic from Isis.[300]

Magical Numbers

There is power and symbolism in many numbers but three and seven were particularly potent for the Egyptians. Three is an expression of plurality; from the earliest hieroglyphic writing three strokes indicated many. Unlike European cultures who have four seasons, the Egyptians had three with each month divided into three ten-day periods. The significance of three was carried on further. Rituals were carried out in the temples three times a day, at morning, noon and

---

[296] *Ancient Egyptian Magical Texts*, Borghouts, 1978:51
[297] *The Living Wisdom of Ancient Egypt*, Jacq, 1999:109
[298] *Gods and Men in Egypt: 3000 BCE to 395 CE*, Dunand & Zivie-Coche, 2004:237
[299] *Isis in the Ancient World*, Witt, 1997:187
[300] *The Secret Lore of Egypt: Its Impact on the West*, Hornung, 2001:59

evening and the Sun God had three forms. He was Khepri in the morning, Ra at noon and Atum on the evening.

In the New Kingdom divine triads, a grouping of three deities, became popular. They were usually family groups of god, goddess and child; Isis, Osiris and Horus being the best known. Family triads were the norm because the family was the main social unit in Egypt. People weren't viewed as individuals so much as members of an immediate family. Other triad groupings also occurred and deities could belong to more than one triad. Thus there is the triad of Isis, Osiris and Horus but also that of Isis, Nephthys and Osiris. Sometimes the deities in the triad have no logical link that we can perceive. There are two ways of looking at a triad. It can represent a closed system that is complete and internally interactive, or as one that can create tensions as with Isis, Horus and Seth. Horus and Seth represent the duality of opposites whilst Isis is an interweaving character who can alter the balance of power depending upon which character she chooses to support.

Seven is one of the most symbolic numbers and of major significance in magic. The actual meaning this number had for the Egyptians is hard to define but it is associated with perfection and effectiveness. Important spells are repeated seven times and there are seven scorpions who escort Isis. Multiples of seven are also important. The body of Osiris is cut into 14 pieces by Seth and it is thought that this may represent the 14 days of the waning moon. 42 is also important. There are 42 *nomes* (provinces) in Upper and Lower Egypt and 42 *ba's* of Ra. In a spell against scorpion poison, the Seven Hathors make seven knots in their seven hair bands and use them to drive out the poison. They appear to be a seven-fold form of Hathor and, unlike Hathor, have a strong magical aspect as well as being allied with fate. In *The Golden Ass*, Lucius bathes in the sea and then plunges his head beneath the waves seven times before he prays to Isis. Plutarch reports that at the winter solstice the priests "*carry the Cow around the shrine seven times, and the circuit is called the Seeking for Osiris*".[301]

---

[301] *Plutarch: Concerning the Mysteries of Isis and Osiris*, Mead, 2002:231

Divination

Divination was a popular form of magic and took a number of forms. One was using a vessel or lamp. Reference is made to Isis using divination when she sought the body of Osiris. *"For this vessel-divination is the vessel-divination of Isis."*[302] The magician assumed the persona of Isis to ensure they would get a correct answer. *"Tell me an answer...without falsehood therein, for I am Isis the wise."*[303] The answers appear to have been brought by a spirit which had to be controlled by the magician. *"I am Isis, I shall bind him."*[304] Another seeks a parallel in the myths. *"Let my vessel...go forth here today, because of the vessel of Great Isis seeking her husband."*[305] Skulls were also used, a more risky practice as a spell for a *"restraining seal for skulls which are not satisfactory"* suggests.[306] The spell was designed to prevent the skull from speaking or acting of its own accord. Amongst other things the mouth is blocked with mud and a crown of Isis placed over it.

The *Berlin* papyrus tells us that the *"number seven: it stands for Isis"*. However, the *Carlsberg* papyrus assigns this number to Horus. Both refer to strips of paper used for divination. Another divination method is given in the *Vienne* papyrus which represent questions asked by Isis. It is thought it involves some sort of number casting as the sections consist of three numbers which all add up to 4, 14 or 24.[307]

An icosahedron, a Greek die with 20 sides, was found near Deir el-Hagar. The names of deities are inscribed on each side. These include Isis, Nephthys, Osiris and Horus as well as the local deities of the area; Thoth, Amun, Mut and Khons. It was used as an oracle; ask a question then throw the die and the deities will provide the answer.[308] A spell for receiving an omen alludes to Isis using the same method of divination with the *"29 letters through which letters Hermes and Isis, who was*

---

[302] *The Leyden Papyrus*, Griffith, 1974:23
[303] *The Greek Magical Papyri in Translation. Volume One: Texts*, Betz, 1996:198
[304] *The Greek Magical Papyri in Translation. Volume One: Texts*, Betz, 1996:210
[305] *The Greek Magical Papyri in Translation. Volume One: Texts*, Betz, 1996:239
[306] *The Greek Magical Papyri in Translation. Volume One: Texts*, Betz, 1996:75
[307] *Through a Glass Darkly*, Szpakowska, 2006:183
[308] *Isis in Roman Dakhleh: Goddess of the Village, the Province and the Country*, Kaper, 2010:174

seeking Osiris her brother, found him".[309] Other spells were like a prayer, a direct appeal to her. "*Isis Holy Maiden, give me a sign of the things that are going to happen.*"[310]

A spell for a dream oracle tells the person to "*put around your hand a black cloth of Isis and go to sleep*".[311] A number of spells refer to a black Isis band. This was a piece of material that had been taken from the clothes used to dress the sacred statues. These would have absorbed the power of the deity as the *ba* of the deity resided in the sacred statue. There may have been a trade, sanctioned or otherwise, of such clothes that had been replaced. More probably it was ordinary fabric sold as sacred or ritually transformed into sacred cloth. Ritual clothing was also important. One spell for an oracle says the magician must be dressed as a priest of Isis in clean linen.

Spells in General

Referencing the deities and the myths gave a framework for the spell and the instruments and ingredients are associated with the deities. A number of spells use myrrh for anointing or writing with, and this is frequently allied with myrrh used by Isis to anoint herself and Osiris. One Greek spell includes an incantation during the preparation of the ink. "*Isis uttered it and wrote with it.*"[312]

– Love Spells

Love spells were very common. The ethics of removing another person's free will appears to be a modern preoccupation judging by the number of these spells. Most of these are addressed to Hathor as she was strongly associated with love and sex but Isis is invoked or referenced in some of them. "*Cause her to feel a love for him in her heart, the love that Isis felt for Osiris.*"[313] Horus also appears in some later charms. One Coptic love charm refers to a story where Horus complains to Isis that he has trouble attracting girls and Isis gives him a charm to help him. A spell to "*give favour to a man before a woman*

[309] *The Greek Magical Papyri in Translation. Volume One: Texts*, Betz, 1996:264
[310] *The Greek Magical Papyri in Translation. Volume One: Texts*, Betz, 1996:285
[311] *The Greek Magical Papyri in Translation. Volume One: Texts*, Betz, 1996:147
[312] *The Greek Magical Papyri in Translation. Volume One: Texts*, Betz, 1996:144
[313] *The Leyden Papyrus*, Griffith, 1974:107

and vice-versa" required a "little amulet of Isis".[314] Some are dark magic, one Greco-Roman spell demands the woman be bewitched, in effect the equivalent of drugging the victim before raping her. The spell references the adultery between Osiris and Nephthys and the grief of Isis. One phrase from a spell recited over a love potion contains an interesting phrase. "The blood of Osiris bore witness to her name of Isis when it was poured into this cup, this wine."[315] It is from a 3rd century CE manuscript and has strong resonance with the Christian communion rite.

– Spells for Success

A charm for "acquiring business" references Isis and Osiris despite its irrelevance. "You will be successful. For Hermes made this for the Wandering Isis."[316] Another spell for ensuring success in a business venture invoked Thoth. "Whereas Isis, the greatest of all the gods, invoked you in every crisis...so also I invoke you."[317]

– Curses

There are plenty of curses and threats from the New Kingdom onwards and one popular formula includes a triad who will send divine vengeance. Rather than using the name of Seth, or another aggressive deity, any deity could be invoked. Their nature appears irrelevant to the curse. "As to anyone who shall be deaf to this decree, Osiris shall pursue him, Isis his wife, and Horus his children, and the great ones, the lords of the Holy Land, will make their reckoning with him."[318] The furious victim of a crime wrote this on a curse tablet. "Isis Myrionyma, I entrust you with what has been stolen from me...take away the life of the man who did this theft... I ask you, Lady, by your majesty, that you punish this theft."[319]

---

[314] The Leyden Papyrus, Griffith, 1974:91-93
[315] The Leyden Papyrus, Griffith, 1974:107
[316] The Greek Magical Papyri in Translation. Volume One: Texts, Betz, 1996:81
[317] The Greek Magical Papyri in Translation. Volume One: Texts, Betz, 1996:145-146
[318] When Justice Fails: Jurisdiction and Imprecation in Ancient Egypt and the Near East, Assmann, 1992:149-162
[319] Cursing a Thief in Iberia and Britain, Tomlin, 2010:260

The Decline of Magic

Anti-social dark magic became increasingly popular, especially during the Greco-Roman Period. All deities were invoked regardless of their character and their likely opinions of such actions. Healing and other aspects of magic were no longer the remit of the priest-magicians. The Egyptians believed that humans were given magic to use as an instrument, a divine gift, so that they could look after themselves. By the Greco-Roman Period, and thereafter for many centuries, the predominant belief was that you could only be healed and protected through divine grace. Isis still retains her status as High Magician - it is just our emphasis that has changed. *"Cause me to come to you, goddess skilled in magic."*[320]

---

[320] *Traversing Eternity*, Smith, 2009:255

CHAPTER 14

ISIS AND THE AFTERLIFE

"You have gone, but you will return, you have slept, but you will wake, you have died, but you will live." [321]

The Beyond

Isis plays an important role in the afterlife. Initially it parallels her role in the Osiris myths but over time these expand as she absorbs the roles of other funerary goddesses and as new ideas are incorporated. Nephthys usually performs a similar function although they do have their own roles at times. Ideas about what we would call heaven varied but the goal of every deceased person was to be reborn to eternal life as an *akh*, a transfigured and imperishable spirit. The word *akh* has associations with light and also with divine power. The deceased acquire some of the power of the deities as they are reborn. Deities associated with the afterlife such as Isis, Osiris, Horus, Nut and Ra can all be described as an *akh* and they have the power to transform others into this state.

The Egyptians held parallel ideas about what would occur in the afterlife. Some options for the deceased were: to stay with Osiris in the realm of the dead, for their spirit to remain near their tomb, to share the lives of the deities, to sail in the Solar or Lunar Barques or to live in a place very similar to the one they had known on earth. As with many

---

[321] *The Ancient Egyptian Pyramid Texts*, Faulkner, 2007:285 Utterance 670

aspects of their theology the Egyptians were quite happy to have a number of theories even if they were contradictory. After all, no one knew exactly what would happen, these were simply the official best guesses. Although critical, Isis and Nephthys are not the only deities assisting the deceased. There are plenty of guides and protectors in the afterworld such as Hathor, Thoth, Horus and Anubis.

The *Pyramid Texts*

The *Pyramid Texts*, carved on the walls of pyramids, were reserved for the king. Until the end of the Old Kingdom even the other royals did not have them in their tombs. This means that we have no knowledge of what rituals and expectations the rest of the people had. Elite burial practices probably echoed those of the kings. We can only speculate on those of the ordinary people, who may have had completely different afterlife myths. Isis plays a major role in the *Pyramid Texts* as she guides the deceased king to his eternal life as an imperishable star. What she did for Osiris she can do for a deceased king.

Isis and Nephthys mourn and search for Osiris, often in the form of kites. "*Isis comes and Nephthys comes...one of them as a screecher, one of them as a kite.*"[322] They "*have come seeking their brother Osiris, seeking their brother the king...weep for your brother*".[323] Most importantly they retrieve the body and protect it. This protection is extended to the mummy and the tomb as the survival of the body was an important component in ensuring eternal life. "*The tomb of whom Isis respects and Nephthys protects.*"[324] Osiris is then brought back to life by Isis and Nephthys "*whom you have caused to be restored that he may live*".[325] Details are vague referring to "*restore*" and "*reassemble*" and "*make you hale*". In the *Pyramid Texts* the milk of Isis is viewed as restorative and there are many references to Isis nursing Osiris or the king. Isis and Nephthys then help the transfigured king ascend into the heavens. "*How pleasing to behold, says Isis, when you ascend to the sky.*"[326]

---

[322] *The Ancient Egyptian Pyramid Texts*, Faulkner, 2007:199 Utterance 532
[323] *The Ancient Egyptian Pyramid Texts*, Faulkner, 2007:203 Utterance 535
[324] *The Ancient Egyptian Pyramid Texts*, Faulkner, 2007:201 Utterance 534
[325] *The Ancient Egyptian Pyramid Texts*, Faulkner, 2007:46 Utterance 219
[326] *The Ancient Egyptian Pyramid Texts*, Faulkner, 2007:227 Utterance 572

The *Coffin Texts*

The *Coffin Texts* appear during the 1st Intermediate Period and were common throughout the Middle Kingdom. As the name suggests they were often painted on coffins and were available to anyone who could afford them, although this did restrict them to the elite. Isis and Nephthys play a similar role to that in the *Pyramid Texts*, looking after the deceased as they looked after Osiris, but some new concepts and roles were added. Now Isis uses her wings to create life-giving air. "*She made him shade with her feathers, brought air by fanning her wings. Performed the rites of his resurrection...made breathe her brother, put life in the slackened limbs.*"[327] A number of spells refer to the calls and speech of Isis which will have been imbued with her magical power. There is vast power in the divine voice; orders from the Goddess are hard to ignore. "*I am Isis; rouse up at the voice...I am Nephthys; wake up...stand up.*"[328] The power and effectiveness of her voice also drives away demons. "*Go away because of those two sentences which Isis spoke against you.*"[329]

The afterworld has become a more perilous place and divine assistance is needed against demons and other terrors. A number of deities are there to help and "*the power of Isis is your strength*".[330] As well as demons the deceased has to cope with a variety of terrors including that of walking upside-down. This is a strange fear to us but it probably alludes to the possibility that everything is confused and reversed in the afterworld. The deceased hope to join the deities in the Solar and Lunar Barques but those who do not attain this, for whatever reason, may be destined to stay in the inverted underworld. "*I will not walk upside down, for it is Isis who rows me every day.*"[331]

Knowing the true names of someone or something gave you power over them. The components making up the ferryboat and the fishnet are named as deities, Isis and Nephthys included. The deceased have to persuade the ferryman to transport them across the Winding Waterway (the Milky Way) and show their knowledge and power by naming all the components of the boat and assigning deities to them. Isis is aligned to

---

[327] *Echoes of Egyptian Voices*, Foster, 1992:44
[328] *The Ancient Egyptian Coffin Texts Volume I*, Faulkner, 2007:69 Spell 74
[329] *The Ancient Egyptian Coffin Texts Volume II*, Faulkner, 2007:84 Spell 453
[330] *The Ancient Egyptian Coffin Texts Volume I*, Faulkner, 2007:39 Spell 45
[331] *The Ancient Egyptian Coffin Texts Volume I*, Faulkner, 2007:152 Spell 181

the bow-warp and the bailer. The reasoning behind the allocation is not known. The fishnet is a major hazard for the deceased although it is not clear what the net does and why. Is it to catch the unworthy deceased who might try and escape justice or is it just one of the many hazards to be faced? As with the ferryboat the deceased lists its components and allies them to various deities including Isis and Nephthys.

The Book of the Dead

Isis becomes increasingly prominent in funerary literature in the 19th Dynasty due to her rise in popularity and her assimilation of Hathor. The *Book of the Dead* developed from the *Coffin Texts* in the New Kingdom and incorporated many elements of the two earlier funerary texts. One significant change is the importance of the solar theology of Ra which was incorporated into the life-rebirth theology of Osiris. Isis is called the *"Radiant Goddess"*[332] in spell 69 and in vignettes she stands in the Solar Barque. The Chaos Serpent Apophis and the punishment of Seth are emphasised. The concept of the judgement of individuals is introduced, and Isis is part of the council who judges the deceased. Osiris watches the proceedings flanked by Isis and Nephthys. The heart of the deceased is weighed by Thoth against the feather of *Maat* to verify that the deceased has been virtuous enough to enter the afterlife.

As in earlier texts Isis provides the air that enables the deceased to breathe again and is allied with the west and north wind. Spell 161, *Opening the Sky*, allows the deceased to breathe as well as giving them access to the sky. Here Isis is aligned to the west wind and Nephthys to the east. On one coffin inscription Isis says *"I have come...with the north wind...I have let your throat breathe."*[333] The north wind was a cooling healthy wind for the Egyptians in contrast to the desiccating south wind which was associated with plague and pestilence. Particularly in summer the air would have been suffocating, hot and dusty so fresh air was equivalent to the breath of life in a way we can rarely appreciate. The ritual of *Opening the Mouth for Breathing* served

---

[332] *How to Read the Egyptian Book of the Dead*, Kemp, 2007:90
[333] *Journey Through the Afterlife: Ancient Egyptian Book of the Dead*, Taylor, 2010:106

a similar purpose. The body had been restored (preserved as the mummy) and now it had to be animated by enabling it to breathe. A ceremonial adze was used to symbolically open the mouth.

The *"secret mysteries"* of Isis are referred to in the *Book of the Dead*. These are the mysteries of her power over life and death with the rebirth of Osiris and the conception and birth of Horus. *"I have come forth…to the secret mysteries. I have been conducted to her hidden secrets for she caused me to see the birth of the Great God."*[334]

The *Amduat*

During the New Kingdom a parallel funerary tradition developed, the *Books of the Netherworld*. The best studied is the *Amduat*. It gives a detailed description of the journey of the Sun God through the twelve hours of darkness as he travels through the underworld, the *duat*, and it unites the solar tradition of Ra with the death-rebirth tradition of Osiris. Although it provides essential knowledge for the deceased it was also recommended for study by the living and can be read as an inner or psychic process of transformation and renewal. Unlike the other funerary texts looked at so far it forms a coherent story and the texts and pictures relate to each other. Consequently many productive studies have been made of it. At its heart is the renewal of the Sun God. Osiris is present throughout but he never speaks and is rarely referred to for it is his regenerative powers which are important rather than his death and resurrection. The roles of Isis and Nephthys have changed considerably from those of the other funerary texts which ran parallel to the stories of Osiris and the Horus child.

The Sun God enters the *duat* at sunset in the form of a *ba*-soul (depicted as ram-headed) and until the 12th hour is without his protective *uraeus*. Each hour of the night has its own location and action, the first two being the Waters of Wernes and the Waters of Osiris. These represent fertility and the chaotic but fertilising powers of the inundation. The procreative but passive powers of Osiris are present in the annual agricultural cycle and it is this power that can be harnessed for the renewal of the Sun God.

---

[334] *The Earliest Version of Book of the Dead 78*, Buck, 1949:87-97

The *uraeus* serpent is depicted many times, its role being to illuminate, guide and protect. Isis and Nephthys are present in the Solar Barque as *uraeus* serpents. *"Shine great Illuminator...be radiant you on the head of Re! Drive away darkness in the hidden realm...Illuminate the Unified Darkness, that the flesh may live and be renewed by it!"*[335] This is a very alchemical quote hinting at the miraculous transformation which will occur at the 6th hour. The unified darkness is the union of the souls of Ra and Osiris. It is the action of heat and light on seeds which causes them to germinate and this mysterious process is also needed for the Sun God to unite with his corpse, represented by Osiris, enabling him to be reborn. The creative spirit or energy here is feminine because the *uraeus* is the Eye Goddess (see chapter 4).

The 5th hour occurs in the vicinity of the burial mound of Osiris and embodies all the elements of the *duat* as the realm of the dead. Isis is depicted in three forms during this hour. She and Nephthys are in their common form of two mourning birds perching on the side of the mound and Isis is referred to as the Goddess of the West. Schweizer suggests that in psychic terms the mystery is known only by Isis and Nephthys in their form of Wailing Women. It is through feelings and emotions that the inner world can be comprehended and the mystery sensed.[336]

Isis is also depicted as an uncrowned head emerging from the burial mound which creates the narrow Passage of Isis. *"The flesh of Isis who is upon the sand of the land of Sokar...this god stops over the head of this goddess."*[337] The deities accompanying the Solar Barque have to tow the barge through this narrow and dangerous passage. *"The secret way of the land of Sokar, which Isis enters on, to be behind her brother."*[338] Here is the beginning of the union of opposites and it is a potentially hazardous time because it is a critical process and thus there is plenty of scope for disaster. On the accompanying illustration the head of Isis appears to form a cave, a good representation of her now chthonic nature. Water has been introduced into the landscape and the presence of fire and water is an important feature. Isis is here

---

[335] *The Egyptian Amduat*, Abt & Hornung, 2007:67
[336] *The Sungod's Journey Through the Netherworld*, Schweizer, 2010:108
[337] *The Egyptian Amduat*, Abt & Hornung, 2007:158
[338] *The Egyptian Amduat*, Abt & Hornung, 2007:164-165

as the ruler of the elements and she simultaneously keeps them separate and together, that is physically distinct but able to combine and react with each other. The sacred and critical area is defended by Isis in her snake form and the cavern is *"filled with flames of fire from the mouth of Isis"*.[339] A scarab, the form of the rising sun, is emerging from the burial mound hinting at the start of the regeneration. Next to it is the text *"Isis belongs to your image"*.[340] Isis dominates this hour because it is she who can protect and nurture, preserve and renew. It is Isis more than any other deity who can heal body and soul.

The 6th hour occurs at midnight at the very depths of the *duat* where the waters of the *nun* seep into the waterholes. At this time the Sun God reunites with his corpse. At the deepest and darkest hour the sun is reborn and the Solar Eyes have been healed by Thoth. The cult mysteries refer to the initiate experiencing the shining sun at midnight and this is what they have seen: the mystery of the regeneration of the sun and with it all life. Isis is shown half seated next to two *wedjat* eyes representing the regenerated and complete sun and moon. *"The image of Isis-Tait is close to this divine eye."*[341] Isis is identified with Tayet whose most critical function was the provision of funerary linen. At this stage funerary linen is no longer needed but as death is a prelude to new birth so new clothes are an important symbol of rebirth. In the 8th hour there are representations of new clothes to symbolise this new birth.

The 7th hour brings great danger to the new-born Sun God where all the powers of evil and chaos, represented by Apophis, attempt to extinguish the new light. Isis joins Seth at the prow of the Solar Barque and they use their combined *heka* to fight him off. The Goddess Serket stakes Apophis after *"Isis and the Eldest Magician have taken his strength by their magic"*.[342] Seth is no longer the hated murderer of Osiris and enemy of Isis and his chaotic strength is critical to their survival. The rebirth of the sun is more important than an individual's revenge. In the 11th hour Apophis has one last chance to destroy the Sun God before dawn at the 12th hour. He is defeated and Isis and Nephthys are shown as *uraeus* cobras carrying the crowns of Egypt to

---

[339] *The Egyptian Amduat*, Abt & Hornung, 2007:165
[340] *The Egyptian Amduat*, Abt & Hornung, 2007:159
[341] *The Egyptian Amduat*, Abt & Hornung, 2007:187
[342] *The Egyptian Amduat*, Abt & Hornung, 2007:232

the Gates of Sais where the Goddess Neith waits. This is in deference to her role as the Creator Goddess who originally birthed the sun. The Sun God is now reunited with his Solar Eye and wears the *uraeus* cobra on his forehead as he returns to the world as the rising sun.

In summary then, the main role of Isis is not resurrecting Osiris and conceiving Horus to avenge his father. She is embracing the solar role of Hathor. This is not unexpected given that Hathor and Isis are becoming synchronised during the New Kingdom. What we do see is Isis taking on the chthonic regenerative role of the Earth Mother Goddess which was not a concept common in Egypt at the time. The mystery here is the continual renewal and regeneration in the underworld darkness. The dominance of snake symbolism underlies the regenerative, female powers of the dark and fertile underworld and can be seen to parallel birth from the dark of the womb. In the *Amduat* Isis is taking on parts of the role of the Earth Goddess who gives birth to all life in the darkness of the earth. Although not depicted in this way, she acts as a night-time counterpart to Nut the Sky Goddess who arches over the earth and protects the Sun God on his daily journey. Isis likewise protects the Sun God during his dangerous subterranean night journey. The underworld is dark in terms of fear and death but it is the only place where regeneration can occur. Isis is seen combining all the elements; air and water from herself, fire from Hathor and the earth and underground from the ancient chthonic Earth Goddess.

The Greco-Roman Period

The *Books of Breathing*, like all funerary literature, took concepts from the preceding literature although they were shorter and more succinct. The Egyptians believed that there were two such books, the first written by Isis for Osiris and the second copied by Thoth for use by everyone. Here the emphasis returns to the resurrection of Osiris and Isis and Nephthys take on their traditional roles to mourn, protect and resurrect the deceased. *"They will protect you, Isis and Nephthys...you will awaken...you will see the companions of Isis the goddess."*[343]

---

[343] *The Liturgy of Opening the Mouth for Breathing*, Smith, 1993:31

Funerary Textiles

Given the link between women and cloth in all its forms, from production to wearing, it is not surprising that Isis has some association with textiles. The production of cloth was time-consuming and labour intensive and so it was a very valuable commodity. In the myths there are references to Isis in the spinning house where she had been imprisoned by her brother Seth. Like any woman, Isis will have spun, woven and made clothes for her family. A spell in the *Leiden* papyrus refers to the "*byssus robe of Osiris...woven by the hand of Isis, spun by the hand of Nephthys*".[344] Isis is also said to make garments for the other goddesses. "*I have made raiment for the Fen-goddess, for Tayt, Sdt, Sothis.*"[345] In a hymn from the *Oxyrhynchus* papyrus Isis is said to have "*devisest the weaving of...*" but the rest of the text is missing so we don't know what type of textile is referred to.[346]

The most critical textiles were funerary ones, from the mummy bandages which preserved the corpse to the protective coverings for the bier. The linen mummy bandages are sometimes referred to as "*the tresses of Nephthys*".[347] In the *Coffin Texts* there is reference to the cloth provided by Nephthys and netting provided by Isis.[348] A 2nd century CE painted linen shroud for a young boy was found in Thebes. It is a composite of Roman and Egyptian styles. The hieroglyphs down the centre read "*I am the cloth of the Two Goddesses...my two arms extend to envelop Osiris Nespawtytawy forever*".[349] The power of the Goddess will be woven into the textiles she creates making them ideal protection for the deceased.

Linen shrouds were also painted and will have offered a more affordable alternative to the ornate sarcophagi of the wealthy. One Roman Period shroud depicts the physical revival of the deceased by Isis. She stands by the bier and in her falcon form hovers above the mummy creating the breath of life from her beating wings.[350] "*She*

---

[344] *The Leyden Papyrus*, Griffith & Thompson, 1974:53
[345] *The Myth of Horus at Edfu: II. C. The Triumph of Horus over His Enemies a Sacred Drama (Continued)*, Blackman & Fairman, 1943:2-36
[346] *The Oxyrhynchus Papyri*, Grenfels & Hunt, 1974:455
[347] *Egyptian Mythology*, Pinch, 2002:171
[348] *The Ancient Egyptian Coffin Texts Volume II*, Faulkner, 2007:197 Spell 608
[349] *Ancient Egypt and Nubia*, Whitehouse, 2009:118
[350] *Eight Funerary Paintings with Judgement Scenes in the Swansea Wellcome Museum*, Griffiths, 1982:228-252

made him shade with her feathers, made breeze by fanning her wings."[351]

Funerary Amulets and Decorations

There are many examples of Isis, Nephthys, Serket and Neith guarding the sarcophagus and canopic chests and reference to them is made in the *Pyramid Texts*. The sarcophagus was an ideal space to add protective spells and images alluding to the resurrection of the deceased by aligning them with Osiris. Isis is usually placed at the foot of the coffin. "*Recitation by Isis...I come and hover around thee, my brother Osiris...thou shalt not tire...thou mayest be brilliant in heaven, powerful on earth and justified in the necropolis.*"[352]

Pectorals were a necklace worn by the elite from the Middle Kingdom. A 21st Dynasty gold pectoral from a funerary context is full of solar imagery. The gold was inlaid with lapis lazuli, carnelian and turquoise. The deceased was identified with the reborn sun, a scarab, who is protected by Isis and Nephthys who kneel on either side. Their skin is turquoise, the colour of rejuvenation, and their dress carnelian, the colour of rebirth.[353] Another example is a blue faience pectoral of Isis dating to the 3rd Intermediate Period. Faience is a ceramic, its name means "*what is gleaming*" and it represents celestial light. This light-filled amulet was believed to assist in the rebirth of the deceased. Isis is depicted as a kneeling winged Goddess wearing the cow horn sun disc.[354]

In the Middle Kingdom name-beads were placed in the mummy wrappings. They are usually made of carnelian, like the *tyet*, and are engraved with the name of the deceased. One is inscribed "*Give light to Isis as the Brilliant One*". From the Saite Period is a miniature collar inscribed with spell 158 from the *Book of the Dead* which frees the deceased from the mummy wrappings. "*O my mother Isis, unswathe me!*[355]

---

[351] *Hymns, Prayers and Songs*, Foster, 1995:51
[352] *The So-Called Tomb of Queen Tiye*, Gardiner, 1957:10-25
[353] *The Quest for Immortality: Treasures of Ancient Egypt*, Hornung & Bryan, 2002:130
[354] *Gifts of the Nile: Ancient Egyptian Faience*, Friedman, 1998:147
[355] *Notes on Some Funerary Amulets*, Shorter, 1935:171-176

The Greeks and Romans living in Egypt often combined Egyptian beliefs and depictions with their own funerary practices. Isis is depicted in tomb decorations in several cemeteries in Roman Dakhleh. Here the images and inscriptions conform to the traditional Egyptian style and Isis is shown as mourning with Nephthys, adoring Osiris or taking part in funerary rites.[356] A 3rd century CE grave *stele* for Julius Valeris, a young child, shows Anubis as a jackal, Horus as a falcon and Isis-Nemesis, the protector of the dead child, as a griffin.[357] In some tombs in Alexandria figures are depicted with *situla* and this probably indicates that the deceased were cult members. In a tomb in Tigrane the deceased is shown with a palm-branch as are Isis and Nephthys.[358]

The Gift of Isis and Osiris

The afterlife was seen as a continuation of the cycle of life and death and rebirth was a critical time for both humans and deities such as Osiris and the Sun God. Although Isis is by no means the only important deity in the afterworld, in the rebirthing process she is essential. Without Isis and Osiris there would be no afterlife and no rebirth.

"To thee belongs the light of the Solar Disk...thy bones are assembled for thee, And thy senses are recovered daily; Thou comest in like Atum in his time, without being held back, And thy neck is made firm for thee...Open thine eyes, that thou mayest see with them; Drive thou away the clouds, Give thou light to the earth in darkness."[359]

---

[356] *Isis in Roman Dakhleh: Goddess of the Village, the Province and the Country,* Kaper, 2010:150
[357] *Egypt After the Pharaohs,* Bowman, 1986:188
[358] *Referencing Isis in Tombs of Greco-Roman Egypt,* Venit, 2010:109
[359] *The Bremner-Rhind Papyrus: I. A. The Songs of Isis and Nephthys,* Faulkner, 1936:121-140

CHAPTER 15

THE HEALING POWERS OF ISIS

"All the world is eager to bestow honours on Isis because she clearly reveals herself in the cures of disease." [360]

Medicine in Egypt

Magic was an essential component of medicine but it was combined with the best scientific and clinical knowledge of the time. Medical papyri from the New Kingdom describe the symptoms of the disease and the possible remedy, they also show that the physicians tried to understand how the body worked. The *Serapeum* in Alexandria acted like a training hospital. It was next to the Library and offered the best of both Egyptian and Greek knowledge and practice. Healers often specialised, as they do now, and there were varying levels of competence. Magic was viewed as a way of using natural forces to achieve a specific outcome. As such it was an integral part of medicine and one that was studied seriously. It was not the dubious practice which other cultures and ages viewed it as. Prayers to deities always helped but using magic showed that the patient and healer were making the effort to do something for themselves even if they really needed divine guidance and assistance.

---

[360] *Ancient Mystery Cults*, Burket, 1987:15

Causes of Disease and Injury

Some causes are obvious, even to an uneducated observer, such as seeing a person bitten or observing the injury as a consequence of an accident or attack. Many medical problems had no observable cause so the supernatural was invoked. Sickness was believed to be caused by demons or spirits known as *akhs*. One spell is for *"conjuring the akh from the belly"* and the spell invokes Isis, Nephthys and Horus.[361]

Plague and disease were believed to be brought by demons sent by deities. The five days on which the children of Nut were born were special days, outside the normal cycle of time, and during these days people were more at risk from the forces of evil and chaos. These days occurred at the end of the year which was a perilous time with the Nile at its lowest level, food supplies dwindling and infectious diseases very common amongst the weakened people. The *"plague of the year"* was considered to be a manifestation of Sekhmet and her demons and numerous amulets and spells were used for protection. Some spells advise the wearing of a linen bandage around the neck. Isis, Nephthys and Osiris were often drawn on the bandage, because, as they had been born during these days they had the powers to deal with their special dangers.

Healing Deities

The term for doctor is *sunu*. Isis, Thoth and Horus are referred to as *sunu*. All deities can be invoked for healing and all are at various times, but there was a degree of specialisation. The Egyptians tended to view the deities as we view professionals, one person specialising in midwifery and another in infectious diseases. The fact that some deities specialised in healing suggests that originally more people were cured when they invoked these deities, or went to their priestesses or priests, compared to others. Healers would have been attracted to such deities and a body of knowledge based on experience would have been built up. Isis is not the only goddess invoked for healing. Sekhmet controlled the demons responsible for diseases such as plague and so was invoked to cure them. Her priestesses and priests specialised in this and were renowned for their medical knowledge.

---

[361] *Religion and Ritual in Ancient Egypt*, Teeter, 2011:168

Isis as a Healer

There are two reasons why is Isis a good healer. She has had plenty of practice on Horus and has a vast magical and medical knowledge and power. *"Her speech is breath of life, her utterance removes a suffering, her words restore the one with an oppressed threat to life."*[362] She certainly has the compassion. *"Her greatest delight is to bestow cures on mankind."*[363] Thoth is an important healer and in some texts he is the one who taught Isis the art of healing. He also helps her when she is unable to cure the patient. As the Earth God, Geb has power over snakes and other poisonous creatures and he taught Isis, giving her the knowledge and power to *"repulse poison"*. On the *Metternich stele* Isis explains how she is *"driving away reptiles...every reptile who stings listens to me"*.[364] The Greeks associated Isis with Asclepius, their God of Healing. At Athens there was a temple to Isis within the sanctuary of Asclepius and dream incubation was practiced in both. Isis was also associated with the Goddess Hygeia who personified health.

Methods of Healing

The patient was not expected to take a passive stance in the healing process. They had a part to play, which would have had useful psychological benefits giving them some control over the healing process. One technique was for the patient to identify with a deity who had been in a similar predicament and was healed or with a deity powerful enough to fight back. *"You are Horus, no poison has power over your limbs."*[365] Isis and Horus are the deities most frequently referred to in this way. Horus because he has been healed many times and can rely on his mother to assist him and Isis because she has great *heka* and knowledge and can call on powerful allies such as Thoth.

Another principle used was that of transference. The problem was moved from the patient into a statue. One such spell transfers stomach ache from the patient into a clay statue of Isis. *"Anything he suffers*

---

[362] *Ancient Egyptian Magical Texts*, Borghouts, 1978:53
[363] *The Antiquities of Egypt*, Diodorus Siculus & Murphy, 1990:31
[364] *The Metternich Stele*, Scott, 1951:201-217
[365] *The Metternich Stele*, Scott, 1951:201-217

from in his belly – the affliction will be sent down from him into the Isis-statue, until he is healed."[366] It is more understanding to transfer the pain into an anonymous statue which could then be destroyed rather than into a statue of Isis. To us it is almost sacrilegious. Perhaps it was believed that only a statue of Isis had enough *heka* to deal with whatever was causing the pain.

Because of the potency of magical words the spell could be written on papyrus and then soaked in a liquid which the patient would drink. One spell for "*a complete destruction of the poison*"[367] gives the healer a choice. Either the patient ingests the written spell or it is written on a band of linen and tied around the throat. The spell is recited over images of Isis, Atum and Horus.

Incubation involves the patient sleeping overnight in a temple, or sacred area, in anticipation of healing or receiving advice through dreams and visions. "*Hovering near the sick while they slumber, she grants them succour in their afflictions.*"[368] It was often carried out at temples of Isis and Serapis and fees from this would have formed a significant part of the temple's income. The temple of Isis at Menouthis (near Alexandria) was famous for magical cures. One Greco-Roman letter refers to this. "*I was in the Great temple of Isis for healing, owing to the sickness from which I was suffering.*"[369]

Placebos

Modern medicine is dismissive of treatment which involves deities and magic, relying only on scientifically proven procedures. We are fortunate to live at a time where there is a large amount of medicinal knowledge and treatments available. The Egyptians had to work with what they had. Much as they believed in the deities and magic they would have adopted our skills and medicines without a second thought.

---

[366] *Daily Life in Ancient Egypt*, Szpakowska, 2008:129
[367] *The Wisdom of Ancient Egypt*, Kaster, 1993:65
[368] *The Antiquities of Egypt*, Diodorus Siculus & Murphy, 1990:31
[369] *Popular Religion in Graeco-Roman Egypt: I. The Pagan Period*, Bell, 1948:82-97

Any apparent effectiveness of prayers and magic is viewed as a placebo effect by mainstream medical practitioners. There is increasing evidence that placebos can work by utilising the brain's healing and painkilling abilities and in some cases they produce measurable physical changes in biochemistry. In one study the subjects knew they were taking a placebo but were told it would tap into the body's self-healing abilities and the placebo still worked. In other studies, if the practitioner had minimal interaction with the subject they got a much lower positive result from the placebo than when they spent a lot of time with the subject and sympathised with them. Not wishing to detract from the healing powers of Isis and her magic, the healer-magicians of Ancient Egypt could have achieved significant results without the benefits of modern medical knowledge.[370]

Medicinal Ingredients

By the Greco-Roman Period Isis was said to have discovered healing drugs and the elixir of life, becoming the patron Goddess of pharmacists. *"The Egyptians credit Isis with the discovery of many therapeutic drugs"* and also with the *"elixir of immortality".*[371] The Roman writer Galen said that Isis created drugs which could staunch bleeding, cure headaches and heal wounds and fractures.[372] A further reference to this comes in an invocation to be recited while picking medicinal herbs. *"You were given birth by Isis."*[373] In the Greek magical papyri there is reference to an *"amulet plant of Isis".*[374] There is also a *"footprint of Isis plant".*[375] Neither species has been identified. The leaves and fruit of the persea tree were said to be a cure-all and the tree was sacred to Isis. There is reference to a plant called the *"blood of Isis"* which has been identified as black horehound.[376] A spell for a dog bite from the *Leiden* papyrus gives the words to be recited as the medicine is made, the major ingredient being crushed garlic. *"I will do*

[370] *The Power of the Placebo.* Horizon (BBC). First broadcast February 2014
[371] *The Antiquities of Egypt,* Diodorus Siculus & Murphy, 1990:31
[372] *Isis in the Ancient World,* Witt, 1997:195
[373] *The Greek Magical Papyri in Translation. Volume One: Texts,* Betz, 1996:95
[374] *The Greek Magical Papyri in Translation. Volume One: Texts,* Betz, 1996:216
[375] *The Leyden Papyrus,* Griffith, 1974:81
[376] *Oils and Perfumes of Ancient Egypt,* Fletcher, 1999:52

for thee...like the voice of Isis, the sorceress...who bewitches everything and is not bewitched in her name of Isis the sorceress."[377]

Clay was very common in Egypt and widely used in medicine and to make healing artefacts. Obviously it was cheap and easily available but it was still considered a magical substance as both the land and human bodies were made from clay. Bodies were said to have been moulded by the Potter God Khnum. Isis used clay to make the snake that poisoned Ra.

The Horus Child

Treatment frequently involved referencing the deities and Horus was a useful example. He appears to have been a very sickly and accident-prone child, reflecting the hazards of childhood. In virtually all cases Isis is able to cure and help him. Horus suffers from many headaches. One headache spell from the *Budapest* papyrus states *"look she has come, Isis here, she has come...on account of the smashing of his head."*[378] A bandage soaked in ointment is applied to the head in another spell. The words are recited over the bandage which was said to have been spun by Nephthys and woven by Isis. In creating the bandage they would have imbued it with their healing *heka*. Another spell requires seven knots to be tied in the bandage beforehand. The *Berlin* papyrus dates to the New Kingdom but is thought to be based on a Middle Kingdom document. *"My head, says Horus...come to me mother Isis and aunt Nephthys, that you may give me your head in exchange for my head."*

Stomach ache was often blamed on intruders inside the body. Technically this is often true but they probably didn't mean bacteria or viruses. *"Come to me mother Isis and sister Nephthys. See, I am suffering inside my body...Do worms interfere?"*[379] Whether worms referred to intestinal worms as we would understand them or a more demonic agent is not clear. Horus was also mischievous and good at getting himself into trouble. He once ate the *abdu*-fish from Ra's sacred pond and suffered extreme stomach ache for his sacrilegious act which

---

[377] *The Leyden Papyrus*, Griffith & Thompson, 1974:123-125
[378] *The Egyptian Myths*, Shaw, 2014:87
[379] *Daily Life in Ancient Egypt*, Szpakowska, 2008:163

Isis had to cure. Burns would have been a regular occurrence with small children running around next to open fires used for cooking. A spell from the *British Museum* papyrus states that "*the boy was small, the fire was powerful*".[380] In one story Horus is alone in the desert and suffers burns. "*Would that I had the goddess Isis here...then she would set me in the right way with her powerful spell.*" Fortunately the ever-vigilant Isis is "*behind you with my spell*".[381]

There are even spells against recurring nightmares which the sufferer would recite ending with the optimistic "*Hail to you, good dream*". Horus was troubled by nightmares and would call yet again to his mother. She comforts him and advises him to talk about it "*so that your dream apparitions draw back*".[382] Egyptian healing magic continued into the Christian Period and the Horus stories continued to be a source of inspiration and guidance. An 8th-century Coptic manuscript refers to the story of Horus who eats raw the birds he's just caught rather than be patient and wait for them to cook. Isis recites an incantation to cure him. To keep it Christian, and the healer out of trouble with the church authorities, it then adds that it is really Jesus who is doing the healing.

Horus *Cippi*

Horus was considered a Healing God who had been taught by Isis. Given his fraught childhood he probably empathised with the pain and despair of those who sought his help. *Stelae* depicting Horus as the vanquisher of dangerous animals appear during the 19th and 20th Dynasties and became increasingly popular by the Late Period. He is depicted as a youth standing on the back of crocodiles. In his hands he brandishes animals such as snakes, scorpions and lions. These *stelae* are referred to as *cippi*. Texts on the back refer to the myths in which Isis cures Horus after his various mishaps. The best known is the *Metternich stele*. "*Fear not, my son Horus, I am around thee as thy protection, I keep evil far from thee and from everyone who suffers likewise.*"[383] Water was poured over the *cippus*. The magic from the texts would dissolve in the water which could then be drunk as a

---

[380] *The Egyptian Myths*, Shaw, 2014:87
[381] *Ancient Egyptian Magical Texts*, Borghouts, 1978:26
[382] *The Egyptian Myths*, Shaw, 2014:86
[383] *The Metternich Stele*, Scott, 1951:201-217

medicine. One statue of Nursing Isis has a Horus *cippus* at the back. The *stele* contained practical instructions as well, such as for poisonous bites: cutting the wound so that the poison would flow out with the blood, sucking out the poison, applying tourniquets to stop the poison from circulating in the blood stream, applying poultices and keeping the patient awake.

Healing amulets and statues were very common at all levels of society. One statue of Isis was brought to Antioch from Memphis by Seleucus IV (187-175 BCE) and used by him for healing purposes. He apparently came upon this knowledge in a dream.[384] Limestone *stelae* have been found at Amarna which show people worshiping Shed and Isis. Shed was a minor God closely associated with the Horus child in his healer aspect, his name meaning Saviour or Enchanter. Similar *stelae* have been found in private chapels at Deir el-Medina.[385]

Poisonous Creatures

Snake bite and scorpion stings were common hazards in Egypt and there is a large volume of spells both to prevent them and to treat them. Many deities are invoked but Isis is frequently referred to due to her experience. Nephthys quite often works with Isis in healing. On the *Metternich stele* is says that Isis spun and Nephthys wove a bandage for use as a tourniquet, to act against the poison. What they are doing is creating a web of *heka* to contain the forces of evil which reside in the poison and draw them out of the body.

– Scorpions

Scorpions were abundant in Egypt and most stings were painful with short-term effects but the venom could be fatal to small children as they received a higher dose in proportion to their body weight. Inevitably Horus was stung when he was playing in the marshes. "*May your mother Isis recite spells over you. All her words are effective.*" [386] One spell for a sting says "*I sat down and I wept. Isis my mother, sat*

---

[384] *Isis in the Ancient World*, Witt, 1997:196
[385] *Private Religion at Amarna: the Material Evidence*, Stevens, 2007:143
[386] *Egyptian Magic*, Raven, 2012:80

near me, saying 'do not weep".[387] Comforting words mean a great deal to someone who is not only in pain but fearing for their life. "*Nothing bad will happen to you...you will not die from the heat of the poison...the poison will have no power over your body.*"[388] When these words come from the loving and powerful Isis they will have brought relief to many a distressed patient.

– Snakes

The *Turin* papyrus describes the spell that Isis recited to heal Ra. "*Leave Re...flame of the mouth – I am the one who made you, I am the one who sent you – come to the earth, powerful poison...Re shall live, once the poison has died.*"[389] As Isis created the snake she knows its true identity and name and therefore can control it. Many snake-bite spells are based upon this myth as well as those of the Horus child being bitten.

Childbirth

Midwifery was a specialist area assisted by various Goddesses, the main ones being Hathor, Taweret, Meskhent and Heket. Taweret is the Hippopotamus Goddess, a popular Goddess who protected women during childbirth. Meskhent ensures a safe delivery and also determines the destiny of the new-born child. Heket, the Frog-headed Goddess also protects women during childbirth. According to the Greek *aretalogies* it is Isis who determined the nine-month pregnancy. Childbirth was hazardous, many women died in childbirth and many more would have suffered from long term complications. Infant mortality was high especially in the first year. Isis was not the primary Goddess dealing with childbirth, but because she had given birth herself the woman in labour could identify with her. In the *Leiden* papyrus is a spell dealing with protracted labour entitled "*for speeding up the childbirth of Isis*".[390] As in all magical healing the patient and the healer align themselves to characters in the myths. Convincing the other deities that it was Isis who was at risk would encourage them to make every effort to assist and also fooled the evil spirits, frightening

---

[387] *The Greek Magical Papyri in Translation. Volume One: Texts*, Betz, 1996:228
[388] *Ancient Egyptian Magical Texts*, Borghouts, 1978:69-70
[389] *The Egyptian Myths*, Shaw, 2014:49
[390] *Servants of Heket*, Sayell, 2012:10-15

them so they would leave the victim. In case this does not work the spell then lists the catastrophes that will happen if Isis does not give birth.

The Late Period *Westcar* papyrus tells how Isis was also involved in the mythical birth of triplets by Queen Ruddedet. Ra summons four Goddesses to help the queen who is in difficulty: Isis, Nephthys, Meskhent and Heket. Disguised as midwives they go to assist her, Isis standing in front of the queen and Nephthys behind her. Heket hastened the delivery while Isis greeted and named each child, Meskhent then announcing their destiny.

At Alexandria Isis had a temple dedicated to her in her role as protector of pregnant women. It was probably located on the Lochias promontory. A marble plaque dedicated to Isis-Lochia was found on Delos (Greece). It was a votive offering from a lady and her husband giving thanks for the safe birth of their daughter. Below the text is a carving of a *sistrum*.[391] The Greeks associated Isis with Artemis who has a strong midwife aspect (see chapter 11). She was also identified with Eilithyia, a Greek Goddess of midwifery. It is as Isis-Eilithyia that Isis was invoked by the Roman poet Ovid when his mistress was having complications due to an abortion.[392]

Human Fertility

Devotees may have prayed to Isis for a child but she doesn't have the same association with human fertility as other Goddesses such as Hathor and Bastet. This is less of a surprise as Isis did not conceive naturally. She had to use magic and only became pregnant after the death of her husband. Not something that many women would wish to emulate.

The Healing That Isis Cannot Do

One day Horus is stung by Seth who has transformed into a scorpion. Isis is unable to heal him and Horus is dying. Her anguished

---

[391] *Isis in the Ancient World*, Witt, 1997:113
[392] *Isis, or the Moon*, Delia, 1998:547

cries cause the Solar Barque to halt. To do this she must have uttered the secret name of Ra, only a name that powerful that could cause this universal standstill. Halting the course of the sun in effect suspends time and whilst time is frozen there can be no further deterioration in Horus' condition. It also threatens creation forcing Ra to act. Isis states *"it will be dark, and the light will be driven away until Horus is cured for his mother Isis"*. Ra sends Thoth to cure Horus. *"Thoth comes, equipped with magic, to exorcise poison...I come from heaven at the command of Re."* Thoth revives Horus using his words of power and great *heka*. *"Awake, Horus, your protection is strong."* Isis is able to deal with *"every reptile who stings"*[393] but Horus has not been poisoned by such a creature but by Seth and she doesn't know the true name of Seth. Thoth obviously does. But Isis if is all-knowing and great of magic why does she fail? Why couldn't she obtain the secret name of Seth? Perhaps part of the story is to impart the lesson that no cure can be taken for granted and that death is always a certainty.

The Gift of Healing

Isis always had a strong healing aspect and this increased in line with her power and popularity. Her devotees were eager to tell others about her skill and compassion. Diodorus tells of her miracle cures: *"She even saves many of those for whom...the doctors have despaired."*[394]   The author of the *aretalogy* of Kyme said that he composed it in gratitude, to thank Isis for her miraculous healing of his eyes. Similarly a Greek from Maroneia, cured of blindness by Isis, left a long hymn of praise on a *stele* telling the world of the *"greatness of the beneficial action"* which she performed.[395]

---

[393] *The Metternich Stele*, Scott, 1951:201-217
[394] *The Antiquities of Egypt*, Diodorus Siculus & Murphy, 1990:31
[395] *The Hellenistic Face of Isis: Cosmic and Saviour Goddess*, Gasparro, 2006:40

CHAPTER 16

PROTECT AND SAVE

"Hear my prayers, O One Whose Name has great power; prove yourself merciful to me and free me from all distress."[396]

Isis the Compassionate

Isis has the very strong protective and caring instincts of a loving mother and wife. Rather than being the Earth Mother Goddess who collectively gives and takes all life Isis brings a deeply personal, maternal approach to each individual who calls upon her. As Isis protects Osiris and Horus so she will protect all people from physical and magical danger. *"His sister served as his protector, drove off the enemies, put a stop to the misdeeds."*[397] Compassion without the ability to help is of limited use. Isis can act to save and protect by two principle means; her great magical powers and her ability to alter fate.

Protector

"Come to me in order that I may be your protection."[398] Unlike some protective deities, such as Sekhmet, it is her wisdom and magical powers rather than her ferocity which give protection. Isis is the

---

[396] *The four Greek hymns of Isidorus and the cult of Isis*, Vanderlip, 1972:19
[397] *Hymns, Prayers and Songs*, Foster, 1995:51
[398] *The Quest for Immortality: Treasures of Ancient Egypt*, Hornung & Bryan, 2002:130

"*possessor of Magical Protection*".[399] From the 3rd Intermediate Period Isis was particularly associated with magical protection. This was a time of upheaval and invasion and as there was no longer a strong state to protect people they turned to strong, benevolent deities. Her protective role was an important component of her cult in the Greco-Roman Period.

Travel in ancient times was very dangerous. There is graffiti at Thebes praising Isis as the protector of travellers. "*O you of all lands! Call to Isis...She listens at every moment, she does never abandon the one who invokes her in the road! I prayed to Isis and she heard my voice...we were safe at the command of Isis.*"[400] Traveling by river was common and with it came the risk of shipwreck or drowning. Attack by dangerous water creatures was ever present, anyone near or on the water being at risk especially from crocodiles. There are many magical spells for protection near or on water. From the *Tait* papyrus comes the wise advice "*O you who are in the rivers. Pray to Isis, and she brings you to the bank*".[401]

A 19th Dynasty *stele* identifies Isis with Meretseger, the dangerous but merciful Cobra Goddess who lives in the mountains near the Valley of the Kings. On it she is called by Meretseger's title Great Peak of the West "*who gives her hand to him that she loves, and gives protection to him that sets her in his heart*".[402] Does this imply that you have to know and love her before she will help you? This seems unlikely and certainly didn't apply to Lucius in *The Golden Ass*.

Malicious magic such as the evil eye and malevolent spirits were a constant threat, but they were sometimes treated with humour. In Pompeii a fresco on a corridor leading to a latrine depicts Isis protecting a man who is relieving himself.[403] "*Released is someone released by Isis...O Isis, great of magic, may you release me, may you deliver me from anything evil, bad or ominous.*"[404] This comes from a spell said whilst unwrapping a bandage but was probably used in a similar form as a general prayer or cry for help.

---

[399] *The Book of the Dead or Going Forth by Day*, Allen, 1974:119
[400] *Praising the Goddess*, Knockelmann, 2008:26
[401] *Praising the Goddess*, Knockelmann, 2008:33
[402] *Apuleius of Madauros – The Isis Book*, Griffiths, 1975:246
[403] *Life and Death in Pompeii and Herculaneum*, Roberts, 2013:263
[404] *Ancient Egyptian Magical Texts*, Borghouts, 1978:49

Protection was needed in the afterlife which Isis, along with other deities, provided. She gives the deceased the means to protect themselves. In one *Coffin Text* spell she hands the deceased her knife, the one she lent to Horus for his protection. In the *Book of the Dead* it states that *"Isis wraps you in her peace, the adversary is driven from your path".*[405] No wonder the deceased say *"I ally myself with the divine Isis".*[406]

The Saviour Goddess

"Isis the strong saviour...who rescues everyone whom she wishes."[407] Deities often fall into two basic types. There are those who are the aloof remote ones who issue orders but keep themselves apart from humanity, demanding worship but seldom granting requests. The other type are the saviour deities, who bridge the chasm between humans and the divine and descend to the world to assist us. A saviour deity is personally involved in the wellbeing of humanity. They have experienced and shared human suffering and act from a position of understanding, experience and empathy.

The Egyptians had a number of saviour deities, such as Thoth and Horus, but Isis is the supreme Saviour Goddess. As well as being a very human figure she is proactive and her actions result in the salvation of Osiris and, through him, everyone. She isn't a remote, unapproachable figure but a personal, sympathetic and caring Goddess who is happy to rescue those in need. She has experienced suffering for herself and wants to save people from theirs. Isis is the comforting example to those in distress. It was through her own courage in bearing her sufferings that she overcame her tribulations and was able to bring about the resurrection of Osiris and the birth and triumph of Horus, and because of this she has the wisdom and power to redeem suffering humans. In the magical texts Isis appears as a popular and sympathetic goddess. She is the deity most associated with the suffering which all people have to endure. Osiris is not a Saviour as he spends only a limited time in the world before moving on into the

---

[405] *Hymns, Prayers and Songs,* Foster, 1995:100
[406] *The Earliest Version of Book of the Dead 78,* Buck, 1949:87-97
[407] *Apuleius of Madauros – The Isis Book,* Griffiths, 1975:246

afterworld. He is more of a pioneer. As the first to be resurrected he paves the way for all to be resurrected.

"*The saviour...who comes at call.*"[408] Any deity will receive prayers but there are a few who are referred to as Hearing deities – that is they listen to the request and, more importantly, respond. Isis is one of these, other Hearing deities being Thoth and Amun. Isis is portrayed as constantly listening to and answering prayers. A hymn of Isidorus refers to those who are in the "*grip of death...if they pray to you they quickly attain your life*".[409] This could be read either way; they survive by her grace or die but are united with her. There are ear *stelae* from the New Kingdom dedicated to Isis. These were shaped in the form of an ear to encourage the deity to listen to the prayer inscribed upon them.

By Greek times Isis was the Saviour Goddess who redeems individuals, as was Demeter with whom she was closely aligned. Both Goddesses used their Mystery teachings and rituals to achieve this. "*She desired that the struggle, the danger and the wanderings, which she passed through, being so many acts of courage and wisdom, should not be forgotten. Therefore, she wove into the most secret initiations the images, indications and imitations of previous sufferings, and she instituted to men and women, who find themselves in the same misfortune.*"[410]

In *The Golden Ass* Lucius, in his abject misery, begs Isis "*by whatever name, and by whatever rites, and in whatever form, it is permitted to invoke, come now*". She replies saying that she was "*moved by your prayer*"[411] and goes on to help him. The Greco-Roman hymns to Isis constantly reiterate her Saviour aspect. "*Those who are weak; if they invoke you, they become strong...those who are hungry; if they call to you they become satisfied.*"[412] She is also the "*one who creates prosperity after poverty*".[413] Isis brings the concept of divine mercy. "*I decreed mercy to supplicants.*"[414]

---

[408] *An Ancient Egyptian Book of Hours*, Faulkner, 1958:13
[409] *Apuleius of Madauros – The Isis Book*, Griffiths, 1975:166
[410] *Isis as Saviour*, Bleeker, 1963:11
[411] *Apuleius: The Golden Ass*, Lindsay, 1962:178-179
[412] *Praising the Goddess*, Kockelmann, 2008:8
[413] *Praising the Goddess*, Kockelmann, 2008:33
[414] *Hellenistic Religions: The Age of Syncretism*, Grant, 1953:457

Ruler Over Fate

As well as her kindness, empathy and desire to help Isis has a very important aspect for a successful Saviour Goddess. As the *"ruler of fate and destiny"* Isis has control over fate.[415] This appears to have been a predominantly Greco-Roman aspect of Isis. In the Pharaonic Period a person's destiny was in the hands of Meskhent, Renenutet and Thoth. Isis acquired her control over fate from Renenutet (see chapter 10) and as Isis-Hermouthis she was associated with Tyche the tutelary Goddess who controlled the fate of the city. Fate was considered to be determined by the stars. As Isis has control over the course of the stars she has control over fate. *"I showed the paths of the stars...the stars do not move on their own course unless they receive commands from me."*[416]

It was this ability to control fate which made Isis so popular outside Egypt, especially with the Greeks and Romans. Fortune was powerful and frightening and she acted either maliciously or at random, ruling deities as well as people, but Isis was Isis *Victrix "whose orders destiny and fortune obey"*.[417] The Egyptians aimed for constantly renewed regeneration but the Greeks wanted a release from the forces of fate and morality, from the imprisonment of this world. The words *"I set free those in bonds"*[418] probably refer to her role as Fate, although it could also allude to her as the saviour of prisoners and slaves. Isis altered the lifespan of those who pleased her. *"Who prolongs the years of him who is submissive to her."*[419] She also directed the lives of people. *"Man lives on your order, nothing happens without your agreement."*[420] Unfortunately this does give a divine excuse for immoral and illegal behaviour. If whatever you did succeeds it must be the will of the Goddess because *"what I decide is also implemented"*.[421]

---

[415] *The Great Goddesses of Egypt*, Lesko, 1999:180
[416] *Apuleius of Madauros – The Isis Book*, Griffiths, 1975:323
[417] *The Hellenistic Face of Isis: Cosmic and Saviour Goddess*, Gasparro, 2006:71
[418] *Hellenistic Religions: The Age of Syncretism*, Grant, 1953:457
[419] *Egyptian Religion*, Morenz, 1992:74
[420] *The Living Wisdom of Ancient Egypt*, Jacq, 1999:109
[421] *Apuleius of Madauros – The Isis Book*, Griffiths, 1975:272

Helping All

In *The Golden Ass* Lucius calls Isis *"perennial saviour of the human race, you are ever-generous in your care for mortals, and you bestow a mother's sweet affection upon wretched people in misfortune"*.[422] She can even *"untwine the hopelessly tangled threads of the Fates...mitigate the tempests of Fortune and check the stars in the courses of their malice."*[423] This saviour aspect does align Isis closely with Christianity in the belief that victory over fortune and forgiveness cannot be achieved without divine aid. In an uncertain and dangerous world Isis is in constant demand. It would be unrealistic to believe that everyone who calls to Isis is released from their fate, no matter how unpleasant that is. The body of a girl was found in Pompeii clutching a silver statuette of Isis-Fortuna.[424] She is seated on a throne and carries a rudder to show her control over fate, but for the inhabitants of Pompeii their destiny remained unchanged.

If Isis determines fate and nothing happens without her agreement then in effect she saves us from Herself. Such is the contradiction of the All-Goddess.

---

[422] *The Golden Ass*, Apuleius & Walsh, 1994:235
[423] *Apuleius: The Golden Ass*, Lindsay, 1962:190
[424] *Life and Death in Pompeii and Herculaneum*, Roberts, 2013:300

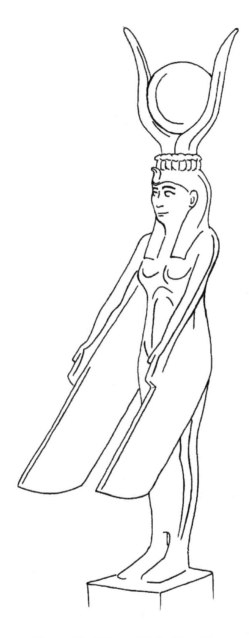

Figure 7 - Winged Isis Standing

CHAPTER 17

THE ELEMENT OF WATER

"I am Queen of the rivers and winds and sea."[425]

Water in Egypt

Water is essential to life everywhere but this dependency is particularly evident in desert lands. The Nile brought the life-giving water to virtually everybody in Egypt. Only in the sparsely populated desert regions did people have another source such as oases or springs. In the summer the river level fell dangerously low, making irrigation of fields and navigation impossible and reducing the water supply for people and livestock. It was also a time of infectious diseases. Little wonder then that the annual Nile flood was such a central event in religious and secular life. The inundation occurred at the height of summer, which is counterintuitive making the event more mysterious. Summer rains in the Ethiopian Highlands are responsible for the flood but this was unknown in both the Pharaonic and Greco-Roman Periods.

The rising floodwater drowned the land leaving settlements on higher ground as isolated islands. To the Egyptians this was an important annual reminder of how creation arose from the waters of the *nun* as well as the resurrection of Osiris. Given the importance of the Nile it is surprising that it was never personified as a deity. The inundation itself was, as the God Hapy, but he had no temples. He

---

[425] *Hellenistic Religions: The Age of Syncretism*, Grant, 1953:457

lived in a cavern at Elephantine which was considered the source of the inundation.

Sothis and the Inundation

The star Sirius is in the constellation of Canis Major (the Great Dog) and is also referred to as the Dog Star. It is the brightest star in the sky but, more importantly to the Egyptians, its heliacal rising coincided with the start of the inundation. A heliacal rising is when the star reappears in the east just before sunrise after being invisible for a period. In Egypt in 3,000 BCE this occurred at the summer solstice; now it is about six weeks later.[426] *"At the same time that the Dog-star rises...the Nile also in a sense rises, coming up to water the land of Egypt."*[427] The reappearance of Sirius brought the hot 'dog days' of the summer. From the earliest times New Year was considered to start with the inundation because it was so critical to the country.

The Goddess Sothis, Sopdet to the Egyptians, was associated with the star Sirius. She is an ancient Goddess; her earliest representation being on the 1st Dynasty ivory tablet of Djer from Abydos. It refers to *"Sothis, Opener of the Year, the Flood"*.[428] Here she is depicted as a reclining cow and worshiped as a Cow Goddess. Between her horns is a plant, probably representing the hieroglyph for *"year"*. In the Pharaonic Period Sothis was normally depicted as a woman with a tall crown surmounted by a five-pointed star. She was also shown wearing the hieroglyph used to write her name (an elongated triangle) or two long feathers from a hawk. There was no cult of Sothis nor any temples to her. Traditionally the inundation was said to rise from a cavern at the First Cataract and she was closely associated with Satet, a local Goddess of the region around the First Cataract. In the *Pyramid Texts* there are traces of an early astral cult. The king unites with his sister Sothis who births the morning star, which could be seen as the next king. *"My sister is Sothis and our child is the dawn."*[429]

Sothis was increasing merged with Isis during the Late Period, losing her autonomy but never completely losing her name. In the

---

[426] *The Egyptian Calendar: A Work For Eternity*, Bomhard, 1999:26
[427] *On the Characteristics of Animals Volume II*, Aelian & Scholfield, 1957:341
[428] *Men and Gods on the Roman Nile*, Lindsay, 1968:57
[429] *Hymns, Prayers and Songs*, Foster, 1995:29

Greco-Roman hymns Isis is *"she that riseth in the Dog Star"*[430] but there was still reference to Sothis *"who gives the flood each year...who gives the Nile from its cavern"*. The two Goddesses were seen as interchangeable as regards the inundation. In the Delta region one charm used for protection during floods was *"I invoke you, Lady Isis...Isis-Sothis, in your morning...protect me"*.[431] Plutarch said that *"they consider Sirius to be Isis's - as being a water-bringer"*.[432]

Isis and the Inundation

The constellation Canis Major is associated with that of Orion, the Hunter. To the Egyptians he was known as the god Sah, the husband of Sothis. As Osiris was an Agricultural God connected to the inundation and the ensuing fertility of the land it was easy for him to be associated with Orion. The star Sirius is invisible for 70 days which was the idealised duration of mummification. After 70 days Sirius is reborn as is Osiris and the deceased. In the *Lamentations* Isis describes herself as Sothis who will follow Osiris in his manifestation as Orion. *"You are Orion in the southern sky while I am Sothis, acting as your protector."*[433] In the New Kingdom Ramesseum, Isis and Orion are depicted standing in boats which face each other. *"Isis, Sopdet, she faces Orion."*[434] Sometimes the Goddess was depicted as Sothis but named as Isis. In effect it was to be read as *"Isis acting as Sothis to bring the inundation"*.

The Nile turned a red-brown during the flood due to the silt it carried. This was associated with the blood of the murdered Osiris. The inundation could also be viewed as the *"efflux of Osiris"* the fluids which leaked from his decaying body. This idea is seen in the *Pyramid Texts*. *"The canals are filled, the waterways are flooded by means of the purification which issued from Osiris."*[435] Texts in later periods echoed this. *"The Nile is the efflux of thy body, to nourish the nobility and the common folk, Lord of provision, ruler of vegetation...tree of life which*

[430] *Hellenistic Religions: The Age of Syncretism*, Grant, 1953:457
[431] *Men and Gods on the Roman Nile*, Lindsay, 1968:58-59
[432] *Plutarch: Concerning the Mysteries of Isis and Osiris*, Mead, 2002:218
[433] *Traversing Eternity*, Smith, 2009:189
[434] *The Egyptian Calendar: A Work For Eternity*, Bomhard, 1999:22
[435] *The Ancient Egyptian Pyramid Texts*, Faulkner, 2007:151 Utterance 455

gives divine offerings."[436] It was said that the Nile rose from the sacred island of Abaton at Philae, the place where Isis had buried Osiris.

Osiris is usually thought of as a God of the Dead and the Afterlife but he is also a Vegetation God who is life-giving through his death and rebirth. *"The grain which grew there, like Osiris on the Great Flood."*[437] As well as crops he was associated with wine. *"Osiris appears...is exalted at the first of the year...the lord of wine in flood."*[438] The inundation was also said to be caused by the tears that Isis wept over the death of Osiris. *"It is a common saying among the natives that it is the tears of Isis that cause the river to rise and water the fields."*[439] There is a pun between the word for inundation, *3gb*, and that for mourning, *i3kb*. It is thought that these words sounded the same during the Late Period.[440]

The Inundation in the Greco-Roman Period

Whilst Osiris represented water in the form of the inundation Isis could be said to represent the fertile earth and their union was the life-giving interaction of water and fertile land. Plutarch interpreted the Osiris myth as an explanation of the inundation with Isis as the fertile Earth Goddess. *"They hold the Nile to be Osiris' efflux...the earth Isis' body...the Nile covers, sowing her with seed and mingling with her."* He said that Nephthys was also associated with the earth but she was the infertile desert. *"When the Nile exceeds its boundaries and overflows... they call it the union of Osiris and Nephthys."* Proof of their infidelity is seen in *"the springing up of plants"*.[441] The adultery of Osiris and Nephthys is covered in chapter 7 but it is worth noting that Nephthys couldn't conceive a child with her husband Seth because he was not a Fertility God.

The earth-water polarity can however be reversed. In one annual festival for Osiris a jar of water was carried to represent Isis.[442] Here

---

[436] *The Great Goddesses of Egypt*, Lesko, 1999:174
[437] *The Ancient Egyptian Pyramid Texts*, Faulkner, 2007:175 Utterance 493
[438] *The Ancient Egyptian Pyramid Texts*, Faulkner, 2007:232-233 Utterance 577
[439] *Pausanias's Description of Greece Vol 1*, Pausanias & Frazer, 2012:550
[440] *The Nile, Euthenia and the Nymphs*, Kakosy, 1982: 290-298
[441] *Plutarch: Concerning the Mysteries of Isis and Osiris*, Mead, 2002:219
[442] *Symbol & Magic in Egyptian Art*, Wilkinson, 1994:95

she was associated with the watery *nun* from which creation began and also the waters in the womb where each individual's creation begins. This is a hint at her Creator role (see chapter 18). During the Greco-Roman Period the cause of the inundation remained the same but Isis was given increasing powers in line with her All-Goddess role. A failure of the inundation meant famine and too high a flood was equally disastrous. The kings were always aware of the importance of the inundation and the power of Isis to grant it. *"Isis of Behdet gives the king a high Nile."*[443] In the temple at Philae Ptolemy XIII (51-47 BCE) offers flowers to Isis and she says *"I give thee the Nile, verdant with flowers"*.[444] Isis was the *"Mistress of the Year's beginning"*.[445] The *Decree of Canopus* by Ptolemy III (246-221 BCE) stated that *"on the day when rises the star of Isis, the day recognised...as being the New Year"*.[446]

By the Roman Period Osiris was linked with Hapy and his consort was Isis-Euthenia who played an active part in the inundation and personified abundance and wellbeing. There are depictions of Isis-Euthenia on coins from Alexandria up to 272 CE and she occurs on reliefs on lamps and as statues. She is portrayed as a recumbent Goddess surrounded by eight children who represent the heights of the inundation. She wears Greek clothing with a very distinctive Isis knot at the breast. Her expression is one of sorrow, recalling Isis weeping for Osiris. What is given can also be withheld. The *Harris Magical* papyrus holds Isis responsible for the drying up of the Nile during her bitter despair over the death of Osiris. *"She closed the mouth of the river. She caused the fishes to lie down on the mud shoal."*[447] This seems to be an act similar to that of Demeter's when she caused the earth to become barren in her distress over the abduction of Persephone.

Isis and Rivers

As the cult of Isis spread outside Egypt she was associated with other rivers, particularly those in flood. The Nile inundation was

---

[443] *Men and Gods on the Roman Nile*, Lindsay, 1968:59
[444] *Apuleius of Madauros – The Isis Book*, Griffiths, 1975:132
[445] *Men and Gods on the Roman Nile*, Lindsay, 1968:59
[446] *The Egyptian Calendar: A Work For Eternity*, Bomhard, 1999:29
[447] *Ancient Egyptian Magical Texts*, Borghouts, 1978:88

beneficial and essential but floods in other rivers were usually destructive so her connection with the Nile flood must have outweighed the negative association with the damage caused. In the *Oxyrhynchus* papyrus there is reference to Isis controlling the river Eleutheros in Tripoli and the Ganges in India. "*Mistress of the Earth, you bring the flooding of rivers.*"[448] The Greeks and Romans often personified rivers as goddesses and water in general was regarded as a feminine element so Isis is likely to have ended up with such aspects regardless of her association with the inundation. In the Greek hymn of Isidorus she is the "*Creator of...all rivers, and very swift streams.*"[449]

The tradition of Isis as Mistress of the Nile continued into the Middle Ages. There is reference to a large statue of Nursing Isis near the el-Muallaqa church in Old Cairo which was held to have supernatural powers over the Nile and protected the district from flooding. It was said to have been destroyed in 1311 by a treasure hunter.[450]

Rain and Weather

The Egyptians didn't have a deity responsible for the weather, with the exception of Seth who brought storms. One reason may be the lack of variable weather compared to the Greek and Roman worlds. In the Greco-Roman Period, and outside Egypt, Isis is often a Rain Goddess. "*I am the mistress of rain.*"[451] The first use of the rainmaker epithet occurs at Philae, where rain is a very rare occurrence. It is not unheard of though, an inscription at Philae tells of rain in Nubia which made the hills glisten. In the calendar from the *Rhind Mathematical* papyrus it records that it rained on the birthday of Isis. In the hot dry climate of Egypt rain was vital and seen as a blessing. In *The Golden Ass* Lucius says "*at your nod breezes blow, clouds nurture the earth*".[452] The hymn in the *Oxyrhynchus* papyrus gives her "*dominion over winds and thunders and lightnings and snows*".[453] She was also associated with dampness. Plutarch says Isis was born "*in all moist conditions*".[454] In

---

448 *Men and Gods on the Roman Nile*, Lindsay, 1968:59
449 *The four Greek hymns of Isidorus and the cult of Isis*, Vanderlip, 1972:36
450 *The Nile, Euthenia and the Nymphs*, Kakosy, 1982: 290-298
451 *Hymns to Isis in Her Temple at Philae*, Zabkar, 1988:141
452 *The Golden Ass*, Apuleius & Walsh, 1994:236
453 *The Oxyrhynchus Papyri*, Grenfels & Hunt, 1974:456
454 *Plutarch: Concerning the Mysteries of Isis and Osiris*, Mead, 2002:195

the Greek hymns she was said to bring the benevolent north wind and the morning dew. A Greek magical spell for consecrating a ring refers to Isis as the dew.

Isis and the Sea

Despite having the Red Sea and Mediterranean Sea on their borders, and having sailed both for trade and military purposes since the Old Kingdom, the Egyptians never had a deity connected with the sea and it had no place in their theology. There are a number of reasons for this. The sea was at the extremities of the country, didn't belong to Egypt and, lacking a strong naval power, they had little control over it. The Egyptians were very inward-looking and the major centres of population and power were inland. Even in the populated Delta the emphasis was on its agricultural fertility not on its proximity to the sea.

The Greeks had the Sea God Poseidon and a number of goddesses associated with the sea so they looked for an equivalent deity in Egypt. Finding none they gave power over the sea to Isis. Perhaps depictions of Isis in the Solar Barque or in ceremonial barques suggested a Sea Goddess, but all Egyptian deities could be pictured in boats. For the sea-faring Greeks being without a Sea God or Goddess was unthinkable. The Greeks gave Isis a new role, Isis *Pelagia*, the Maritime Isis who was Mistress of the Sea and Shipping and Protector of Seafarers. She was hailed as the one who invented the art of sailing and navigation. One Greco-Roman legend tells how Isis discovered sailing whilst she was seeking the Horus child who had run off and got lost. An inscription from Delos (Greece) says she is the *"provider of good sailing"* while one at Corinth (Greece) calls her *"mistress of the open sea"*.[455] The lighthouse on the island of Pharos was dedicated to Isis *Pelagia* and was one of the seven wonders of the ancient world. *"Bringer to harbour...guardian and guide of seas."*[456] Isis, to the Greek and Roman mind, was so closely connected with the sea that it was almost inevitable that when she appears to Lucius in answer to his prayers she rises from the sea. Isis was also responsible for delimiting the

---

[455] *Attic Grave Reliefs that Represent Women in the Dress of Isis*, Walters, 1988:15

[456] *The Oxyrhynchus Papyri*, Grenfels & Hunt, 1974:455

extent of the land and the sea. *"I am...inspector of the limits of the sea and the land."*[457] Earthquakes and the accompanying tsunamis were not uncommon along the Mediterranean coast and people were well aware of the risk of incursion by the sea.

Sailing was a dangerous activity and a protector deity was essential. Those who *"sail on the Great Sea in winter when men may be destroyed and their ships wrecked and sunk...All these are saved if they pray that You be present to help"*.[458] There is a poem written by Philip of Salonica in honour of Isis where he tells of gifts of frankincense and spikenard being offered in gratitude by Damis after she saved him from a shipwreck.[459] In Pompeii in Italy there are votive paintings of Isis to give thanks for rescue from shipwrecks. Using the name of Isis gave added protection to a ship. One Roman writer described a large grain carrier which had paintings of *"the figure of Isis, the goddess the ship was named after"*.[460] One ship was called *"Isis of Geminius"*.[461] An anchor stock found underwater near Malta (ancient Melite) had the names of Isis and Serapis inscribed on its arms.[462] Roman depictions of Isis often refer to her maritime connection and there are many Greek and Roman coins depicting the Maritime Isis, which are covered in chapter 3. The festival for Isis as Lady of the Sea, the Isis *Navigium*, is covered in detail in chapter 22.

Sailing as a Metaphor

It is easy to see life as a journey, a voyage where the destination is a safe harbour. In the *Pyramid Texts* Isis is referred to as *"the Great Mooring Post"*.[463] This theme also occurs in the *Coffin Texts*. The deceased identify themselves with Isis and say *"I have gone forth from my house and my boat is at the mooring rope...I will travel as Isis."*[464]

---

[457] *Romanising Oriental Gods*, Alvar, 2008:51

[458] *The four Greek hymns of Isidorus and the cult of Isis*, Vanderlip, 1972:19

[459] *Isis in the Ancient World*, Witt, 1997:290 n 7

[460] *Ships and Seafaring in Ancient Times*, Casson, 1994:123

[461] *Isis in the Ancient World*, Witt, 1997:71

[462] *Serapis – Before and After the Ptolemies*, Mifsud & Farrugia, 2008:50-55

[463] *The Ancient Egyptian Pyramid Texts*, Faulkner, 2007:155 Utterance 466

[464] *The Ancient Egyptian Coffin Texts Volume I*, Faulkner, 2007:153 Spell 182

On a 18th Dynasty *stele* hymn to Osiris it says that Isis *"danced the Dance of Last Mooring for her brother"*.[465]

The Religious Significance of Water

Nile water was a sign of prosperity, fertility and wellbeing and it had long been exported both for sacred use and for drinking. Water is very precious in a hot dry climate and a true symbol of fertility and life. The Nile was the main provider of water and thus was life. For the Egyptians water was important in the afterlife hence the water libations to the deceased. In funerary art Isis or Hathor often greet the deceased with water. *"You will receive water from Isis and Nephthys."*[466] The *Pyramid Texts* frequently refer to *"cool water"* for the deceased. This association continued unchanged, a Greco-Roman text saying *"let Isis shed upon you the holy water of Osiris"*.[467] In most cultures water was essential for purification. *"I am purified with these four nmst-jars of mine which are filled to the brim from the Canal of the God in Iseion, which possesses the breath of Isis the Great."*[468] The priest who carried out cleaning duties was the *wab*-priest. The hieroglyph denoting this is a jar used for pouring out water.

Water and the Cult of Isis

There was a cult of Osiris at the First Cataract. An important ritual was the libation made by Isis at the tomb of Osiris. On the first day of the week she was said to cross from Philae to Biggeh, where his tomb was located, to pour out a water offering in the Abaton. The chief officiant was the *kbh.t*, a priestess taking the role of Isis.

In Isis cults outside Egypt water was used for ablution, purification and consecration but it was also a connection to the inundation and the Nile and hence to Egypt. Ideally it should have been Nile water. Servius said that *"the water used to sprinkle the Temple of Isis was supposed to be that of the Nile"*. There is written reference to priests in

---

[465] *Hymns, Prayers and Songs*, Foster, 1995:51
[466] *Traversing Eternity*, Smith, 2009:326
[467] *Men and Gods on the Roman Nile*, Lindsay, 1968:277
[468] *The Ancient Egyptian Pyramid Texts*, Faulkner, 2007:186 Utterance 510

Rome sprinkling the holy Nile water on the congregation.[469] Nile water was exported for such purposes but it would have been very expensive so it is likely that most water was subject to a ritual which turned it into Nile water for the purposes of subsequent rituals. At the temple of Isis at Pompeii there is a *purgatorium*, an area used for purification before worship, with a basin to hold the holy Nile water.

The satirical Roman poet Juvenal mocks her worshipers who "*bring back water from scorching Meroe, to sprinkle Isis' temple*". Excavations at Meroe uncovered a large temple of Isis with a number of objects associated with water offerings and purification. Deposits of cult objects suggested that this was a place of pilgrimage in the Greco-Roman Period. There was an inscription from someone who had travelled from Rome to meet "*the Lady Queen*".[470] In Greek and Roman portrayals of Isis her cult instruments often include a long-spouted *hydreion* which was filled with Nile water for ritual use.[471] A mosaic at Praeneste (Italy) shows Anubis beside the procession of the sacred vase which contains the water of new life.[472]

As with many cults, water played an important role in the Isis cult due to its symbolism. Water basins have been found in crypts of some Isis temples. Were they used for the ritual drowning of initiates during the rites of Osiris? Many temples to Isis or Isis and Serapis have basins for either ablution or storing Nile water. In the Greek temples these often imitated Nilometers (a device, usually consisting of steps, used to measure the height of the Nile) but the Roman ones didn't. There were also water channels in the temples and it is suggested that the inundation was symbolically created. Flowing water was a sign of the beneficial power of the deity. The Romans showed less interest in the inundation possibly as a consequence of their wetter climate. The cultures also differed in their interpretations. The Greeks saw the flood as a sign of the power of the deity whilst the Romans saw the water as a sign of the presence of the deity. The Greeks believed that the deities controlled the natural forces compared to the Romans and Egyptians who saw the divine immanent in nature. Outside Egypt all temples to Isis were built close to natural water sources, a spring or river,

---

[469] *Men and Gods on the Roman Nile*, Lindsay, 1968:268
[470] *Daily Life in Roman Egypt*, Lindsay, 1963:112
[471] *Isis in the Ancient World*, Witt, 1997:55
[472] *Men and Gods on the Roman Nile*, Lindsay, 1968:60

wherever possible. For some reason they were never sited next to lakes. Failing that, proximity to a well was critical. Water was essential in the performance of the rites. At Soli (Turkey) an Iseum was built at the same time as the adjacent sanctuary of Aphrodite. A channel of water ran between them.[473] On Delos (Greece) it was believed that the river Inopus was the Nile which had flowed under the Mediterranean Sea.[474]

All Water is Mine

Unlike in western cultures, the fertility of the land and vegetation growth was the responsibility of gods in Egypt. Indeed the earth itself was a God, Geb. Osiris, as the Grain God, was present in the grain. In the Egyptian mind the inundation was directly linked with the fertility of the land and the harvest. Too low or high an inundation meant famine. Isis was associated with the fertility of the inundation in the early periods through her connection with Sothis. As the waters receded the plants grew and it was *"Osiris of the Mysteries who springs from the returning waters"*.[475]   In a dry environment it is the water which is clearly seen as the fertiliser of barren ground. Add water to the desert and vegetation will grow. In the temperate, wetter climates of Europe there was not this clear distinction. The Earth herself is fertile and productive because rain and water in general are such an integral part of the environment and severe drought a rare occurrence. Isis' Pharaonic role of bringer of the inundation almost parallels her act of conceiving Horus from the inert but fertile Osiris. She is the active power which enables fertility to manifest. It is also worth noting how closely Osiris is linked to the element of water (see chapters 5). Yet Isis is not always associated with water. *Coffin Text* spells 48 and 49 refer to Isis as *"Lady of the Deserts"*. This is an unusual epithet for Isis, as it is Nephthys who is more likely to be aligned with the desert. Was this one of Hathor's epithets she adopted?

Although in Western thought goddesses tend to be associated with water, and water to be viewed as a feminine element, it was only in the Greco-Roman Period that this association comes to dominate. To the Greeks and Romans Isis was present in all forms of water and was

---

[473] *Water in the Worship of Isis and Sarapis*, Wild, 1981:14
[474] *The Oxford Handbook of Roman Egypt*, Riggs, 2012:428
[475] *Osiris. Death and Afterlife of a God*, Mojsov, 2005:8

particularly associated with the sea, which is not surprising for cultures so bound to the Mediterranean Sea. The *Book of Hours* refers to her as "*dwelling in the lagoon*"[476] alluding to the swamps of Khemmis where Horus was born. It also links her to the swamps of the Delta which was probably her original home and gives an older link with watery places.

---

[476] *An Ancient Egyptian Book of Hours*, Faulkner, 1958:12

CHAPTER 18

GRECO-ROMAN ADDITIONS TO THE CHARACTER OF ISIS

"Might One, I shall not cease to sing of your great power."[477]

Adding to the All-Goddess

As Isis increased in popularity and importance it was inevitable that she would acquire more attributes. Some were extensions to existing powers but the Greeks gave Isis two that appear to have had little or no connection with the Pharaonic Isis.

Lunar Isis

"For I knew that the Moon was the primal Goddess of supreme sway." [478]

In the Old and Middle Kingdoms Isis was associated with neither the sun nor the moon. She acquired solar attributes in the New Kingdom and to the Egyptians remained that way. Isis as a Lunar

---

[477] *The four Greek hymns of Isidorus and the cult of Isis,* Vanderlip, 1972:18
[478] *Apuleius: The Golden Ass,* Lindsay, 1962:177

Goddess is an entirely classical construct. By the middle of the 2nd century CE Isis was almost completely identified with the moon when she was outside Egypt. Although the Egyptian Isis had solar aspects, to the classical mind the moon was a goddess and this cultural association was too ingrained for it to be ousted by a foreign Goddess, no matter how important. Isis was *Regina Caeli*, the title given to the Moon Goddess when she appeared in the night sky. When Lucius sees Isis he addresses her as a Lunar Goddess for that is how she appears and it is also how his readers would expect to see her. Whilst he watched the full moon rising over the sea he became aware that "*the supreme goddess wielded her power with exceeding majesty, that human affairs were controlled wholly by her providence*".[479] In answer to his desperate prayers Isis appears out of the sea crowned with a lunar disc and wearing a black cloak studded with the stars and a full moon.

Diodorus states that Cleopatra called herself "*Isis or the moon*".[480] This clumsy epithet was also used by a writer from the Ephesus area who mentions that the festival of the Voyage of Isis was called the *Ploiaphesia* in honour of "*Isis or the moon*". The Greeks associated Isis with the Goddess Selene (the Roman Luna) who personified the moon and drove the Lunar Chariot. Other Greek goddesses associated with Isis had strong lunar aspects; Artemis, Hecate and Eileithyia. Artemis was also identified with Selene. "*The moon is called the eye of Artemis.*"[481]

The solar crown of Isis was changed into a lunar one by the Greeks. They shrank the sun disc to depict a full moon and portrayed the cow horns as the crescent moon. Diodorus said "*they put horns on her head...because of the appearance...when the moon is crescent shaped*".[482] Plutarch echoes this explanation. Depictions of Isis at Ephesus (Turkey) show her with a crescent moon or a lunar disc on her shoulders. This is not surprising as Selene is portrayed with a crescent moon on her brow or head. It is easy to interpret the cow horn sun disc as a symbol of the moon, especially when it aligns with your cultural interpretations. One Greco-Roman spell involves burning incense made

---

[479] *The Golden Ass*, Apuleius & Walsh, 1994:218
[480] *Isis in the Ancient World*, Witt, 1997:19
[481] *Apuleius of Madauros – The Isis Book*, Griffiths, 1975:117
[482] *Isis, or the Moon*, Delia, 1998:543

of sulphur and the seeds of rushes and offering it to the moon while calling upon Isis.

Lunar Goddesses have three main characteristics; magic, the sea, and generative powers, and Isis has strong associations with all three. She always possessed great magical powers, and she became closely associated with the sea in the Greco-Roman Period. The moon was believed to play an important part in plant growth. A Greek magical hymn to the moon states *"you have established every worldly thing, for you engendered everything on earth"*.[483] Through Demeter and Renenutet Isis is associated with fertility, especially that of crops.

Isis' marriage to Osiris, or Serapis, was interpreted as the union of the sun and moon, despite Osiris having no solar connection and no such tradition existing in Egypt. *"You took Serapis as your husband and after being joined in marriage, the world shone under your faces, you Helios and Selene, having opened your eyes."*[484] Ironically Osiris had lunar associations himself. In the Greco-Roman *Lamentations of Isis and Nephthys* he is addressed as *"in this your name of Moon"* and *"Lord-of-the-sixth-day-feast…Lord-of-the-fifteenth-day-feast"*.[485] These feasts were monthly lunar festivals.

Isis did not lose her solar aspect entirely when she left Egypt. She is depicted on some Syrian bowls wearing a winged sun disc as a crown.[486] In the *aretalogy* from Kyme the solar Isis is also present. *"I am in the rays of the sun."*[487] The *Oxyrhynchus* papyrus contains a long hymn to Isis which is largely a list of her names in different places including *"among the Thessalians, moon…in Tendros, name of the sun"*.[488]

---

[483] *Isis, or the Moon*, Delia, 1998:540
[484] *The Hellenistic Face of Isis: Cosmic and Saviour Goddess*, Gasparro, 2006:41
[485] *Ancient Egyptian Literature Volume III*, Lichtheim, 2006:118
[486] *Isis in the Ancient World*, Witt, 1997:289
[487] *Hellenistic Religions: The Age of Syncretism*, Grant, 1953:457
[488] *The Oxyrhynchus Papyri*, Grenfels & Hunt, 1974:455

Becoming the Creator and Controller

"I who control by my will the luminous heights of heaven."[489]

Neith is the principal Creator Goddess. She is a Pre-dynastic Goddess from Sais who rose from the *nun* as the Celestial Cow to create the universe. There are three other creation myths. The dominant one was from Heliopolis, in which the self-created god Atum arose from the *nun* and created light. At Memphis it was believed that Ptah created the universe through speech. The Hermopolitan theology is more complex. Here Thoth and the Ogdoad, four pairs of primeval gods and goddesses, were responsible for creation. Many local or popular deities were said to be Creator deities as well. There is no evidence from the Pharaonic Period for Isis as a Creator but by the Greco-Roman Period she is lauded as the Creator.

An important aspect of the hymns of this time is the stress placed on Isis as the omnipotent Creator. *"The one who was in the beginning, the one who first came into existence on earth."*[490] This is particularly seen in the hymns from the temple at Philae which were addressed to a largely Egyptian audience. Isis is the *"Lady of Heaven, Earth and the Netherworld, having brought them into existence"*.[491] She is the *"creator of the universe"*[492] and is described using terms reminiscent of those applied to Ptah, bringing it into existence through her thoughts. Her creation aspect is very prominent in the *aretalogies* which were written by Greeks for a Greek and Roman audience. For them Isis is the All-Goddess and so must have been the Creator. In the *aretalogies* there is an emphasis on her control of the cosmos and time. *"I am Isis, sole ruler of time...for I myself have discovered everything, all is my work...without me nothing has come into existence."*[493] The *Hymn to Isis* in *The Golden Ass* follows this theme, here she is *"mistress of the elements, the first child of time"*.[494] It is Isis who enables the sun to shine, who keeps the planets spinning and the universe in order. Isis is called the Mother of the Stars and she controls the stars and planets.

---

[489] *Imagining Isis*, Dousa, 1999:161
[490] *Apuleius of Madauros – The Isis Book*, Griffiths, 1975:170
[491] *The Complete Gods and Goddesses of Ancient Egypt*, Wilkinson, 2003:147
[492] *The Living Wisdom of Ancient Egypt*, Jacq, 1999:109
[493] *Romanising Oriental Gods*, Alvar, 2008:51
[494] *Apuleius: The Golden Ass*, Lindsay, 1962:179

In the Kyme *aretalogy* Isis says "*I divided the earth from the heaven*".[495] As the Mistress of the Sky she was the embodiment of cosmic order. The night sky is a reflection of her glory and the "*constellations are full of your beauty.*"[496]

Isis has become the Ruler of "*Heaven, Earth and the Netherworld*"[497] and what was once applied to Neith is transferred to Isis. An inscription at the temple of Athena-Isis at Sais says "*I am all that has been and is and will be*".[498] A hymn at Philae calls her She "*who gave life to all the gods*".[499] This epithet was originally given to Sky Goddesses such as Nut, Hathor and Neith and implies something much greater than being mother of one god, Horus. From Isis descends the life-force, she sustains everything she has created. "*She is called Mistress of life, because she dispenses life, men live by the command of her ka.*"[500] What is created can and will be destroyed and the Egyptians understood natural cycles at both the human and the cosmic level. They believed that eventually creation will sink back into the *nun* and only the Creator will survive to begin the process again. "*Whatever I please, this too shall come to an end.*"[501] Time will have ended. "*When I cease, the hours will cease.*"[502]

How This Changed Isis

To the Ancient Egyptians Isis becoming a Creator Goddess would be a natural extension of her powers. They always had a tendency to inflate and extend the powers of a favoured deity as a way of honouring them. Likewise the extension of her gifts to humanity. The fact that other deities were seen in the same way did not present them with a problem. What would have been hard for them to comprehend though would be her transformation into a Lunar Goddess. This would have been a shock and I suspect it would have been an aspect which they

---

[495] *Hellenistic Religions: The Age of Syncretism*, Grant, 1953:457
[496] *The Hellenistic Face of Isis: Cosmic and Saviour Goddess*, Gasparro, 2006:71
[497] *Religion and Magic in Ancient Egypt*, David, 2002:327
[498] *Apuleius of Madauros – The Isis Book*, Griffiths, 1975:170
[499] *Hymns to Isis in Her Temple at Philae*, Zabkar, 1988:119
[500] *Gods and Men in Egypt: 3000 BCE to 395 CE*, Dunand & Zivie-Coche, 2004:237
[501] *Hellenistic Religions: The Age of Syncretism*, Grant, 1953:457
[502] *Traversing Eternity*, Smith, 2009:89

would have ignored. If the Classical world automatically aligned the moon to goddesses then the Egyptians aligned it to gods and both cultural associations were deeply engrained. In their eyes Thoth, the major Lunar God, was too important and popular to cede his moon and lunar barque to Isis. If the Greeks and Romans hadn't turned Isis into a Lunar Goddess then we probably would have done it later. Today we tend not to see Isis as a Solar Goddess for her lunar aspects speak much louder given our cultural background. Women and goddesses are viewed as strongly aligned with the moon and lunar energy and there is often a reluctance to embrace a Solar Goddess.

CHAPTER 19

THE DARK SIDE OF ISIS

"I am the Queen of War. I am the Queen of the thunderbolt."[503]

Is There a Black Isis?

All deities can be dangerous if only because of their great powers but some do have a malevolent side, such as Seth, or an aggressive angry aspect, such as Sekhmet. How does Isis fit into this scheme? Does the benevolent Isis have a dark side?

Protector of Egypt

Protection is an ambiguous aspect that can easily slip into aggression depending upon your position. Isis, like many other deities, was invoked to protect the king and Egypt. Much of this involved smiting enemies and conquering territory. Fear of invasion was never far away and the southern border with Nubia was often of great concern. Here she was honoured as the patron of the army. Her temple at Philae protected Egypt from invasion from the south and was probably viewed partly as a magical fortress. *"Trust in Isis. She is more effective than millions of soldiers."*[504] Isis also has a protective function

---

[503] *Hellenistic Religions: The Age of Syncretism*, Grant, 1953:457
[504] *The Great Goddesses of Egypt*, Lesko, 1999:156

known as *"Bai"* in which she watches over cities. The word means punitive power and is similar to the word for leopard.

War Goddess

The Ancient Egyptians did not have a warrior culture but they had a civilisation which lasted thousands of years, a country which needed protection and at times an empire to expand and maintain. They had need of powerful war deities. All deities can be invoked during times of war or upheaval but some have specific war aspects, such as Montu the Falcon War God of Thebes. The Creator Goddess Neith has a war aspect and Sekhmet and the other Eye Goddesses are aggressive with strong protective instincts making them ideal deities to turn to in military matters. In the myths Isis fought against Seth and his followers and aided Horus in his many battles. It takes little to align the king with the righteous battling Horus, strongly supported by Isis, and his enemies with Seth.

The kings in particular allied themselves with this aspect of Isis and justified their conquests, saying that it was her will. Divine approval has always been used by military leaders, and always will be, regardless of the sensibilities of the deity in question. When fate was considered the will of the deities this is an inevitable attitude. Kings were believed to be semi-divine and as they ruled by divine assent the power of the deities became manifested in the king. As a supreme deity Isis determined the destiny of rulers and empires. At Philae Isis is depicted as giving Ptolemy II (285-246 BCE) victory over the North, South and Great Green (the Mediterranean).[505] In the hymns at Philae she is *"mistress of the battle"* and *"Monthu of the combat"*.[506] At Philae she encourages the king *"let your mace fall upon the heads of your enemies"*.[507] Indeed, all lands *"bow before her power"*.[508]

As Isis absorbed the attributes of the other goddesses it was inevitable, particularly when dealing with the Eye Goddesses, that their protective aggression was transferred to her. Statements such as *"I am*

---

[505] *Hymns to Isis in Her Temple at Philae*, Zabkar, 1988:23
[506] *Hymns to Isis in Her Temple at Philae*, Zabkar, 1988:149
[507] *Hymns to Isis in Her Temple at Philae*, Zabkar, 1988:64
[508] *Gods and Men in Egypt: 3000 BCE to 395 CE*, Dunand & Zivie-Coche, 2004:237

Queen of war" is a very un-Isis like statement but it appears in the *aretalogies* as well as Egyptian texts where she gives victory (presumably to whichever side she favoured). The Romans also appreciated the warlike aspects of Isis and she was equated with Minerva as a Warrior Goddess. In Rome Isis could be "*she who goes into battle*".[509] In the Petubastis cycle of stories, which was heavily influenced by Greek storytelling, Petubastis fights the Syrian queen, Serpot, who rules over a land of women warriors.[510] She invokes Isis "*mistress of the land of women*" before going into battle.[511]

Angry Isis

The Eye Goddesses are particularly prone to losing their temper but Isis has more self-control. She always comes across as very approachable and benevolent, but some incidents in the mythology don't quite fit with this view. When Isis is in Byblos and is finally given the coffin of Osiris her wails of grief are so intense and powerful that they kill the queen's baby. This was not intentional but is a demonstration of the power of Isis. Natural and supernatural power of any kind can be dangerous under certain circumstances. One assumes, indeed hopes, that if Isis hadn't been so wracked with grief she would have been aware of the child and tempered her power, conscious of its strength and the child's vulnerability.

In the later myths Isis is shown as the increasingly implacable enemy of Seth. One protective spell refers to the eternal punishments sent by Isis. This is more likely to be a reflection of society at that time than of Isis herself. In the *Pyramid Texts* there is a spell which at first reading hints at a negative side to Isis. "*If Isis comes with this her evil coming, do not open your arms to her.*"[512] The spell also refers to the evil of a number of other benevolent deities such as Nephthys, Horus and Thoth. It is not clear what the spell means. Perhaps it is directed at demons who have disguised themselves as benevolent deities.

---

[509] *Apuleius of Madauros – The Isis Book*, Griffiths, 1975:254
[510] *Praising the Goddess*, Kockelmann, 2008:38
[511] *The Routledge Dictionary of Egyptian Gods and Goddesses*, Hart, 2005:83
[512] *The Ancient Egyptian Pyramid Texts*, Faulkner, 2007:201 Utterance 534

Trickster

Although Isis is not a Trickster deity there are a number of occasions when she uses cunning to achieve her aims. Usually these are directed at Seth but the story of how she obtained the true name of Ra does hint at a ruthless streak. How she does this is covered in chapter 13 but why she does it needs to be considered in more detail. Ra isn't always presented in a good light. He orders the destruction of humanity when he suspects a plot against him but sends Sekhmet to do his dirty work. He did not create evil and chaos but they are present in his creation and when faced with their consequences he retreats to heaven and delegates responsibility. He argues with his Eye Goddess and behaves in a juvenile manner during the trial of Horus and Seth. The myths reflect life on earth when the king was all-powerful but not always competent or benevolent. Isis probably had a premonition of what would happen to Horus, despite the promised divine protection. Seth was cunning as well as dangerous. To defeat him and save Horus she needed the ultimate power; the ability to halt the sun and with it time. Only by uttering the true name of Ra could Isis guarantee to stop Ra in his circuit across the sky and force him to save Horus.

Dark Magic

Isis is invoked for black magic but she does not use it herself. Any deity can be invoked for malicious purposes but it doesn't mean that they have a malevolent aspect. A curse for a grave robber states that the "*sacred rites of Isis, which mean peace for the deceased, turned in rage against him*".[513]

Contemporary Comments

Ovid refers to Isis temples as places of prostitution and loose morals. This may have just been derogatory. Isis appears to have demanded chastity and restraint from her followers (as discussed in chapter 21) but humans are not always virtuous. Some of the scandals may have been true or may have just been a case of different points of

---

[513] *Ancient Mystery Cults*, Burket, 1987:26

view. People may have been abused, as they are under the cloak of any religion, but this does not mean that it is what the Goddess wants.

There were two contrasting elements of the cult, the spiritual and the erotic. However the evidence of the latter comes from unfriendly sources and may have been propaganda. Juvenal talks about the *"bawd of Isis"* and the Christians refer to Isis as *"that harlot in Tyre"*.[514] All religion has its dark side because all people have a dark side. Every religion and cult has been accused of sex abuse and orgies at some time, some without foundation and others quite rightly so. Personally I am inclined to treat such comments as unfounded and malicious. When writing in exile near the Black Sea Ovid writes about penitents near her temple who have sinned against her and been punished by blindness. Most people, including the physicians, believed that illness and misfortune were often retribution for offences against a deity. All deities have been blamed for some misfortune or other but we can only consider them as malicious or evil if they actually did cause the misfortune. Even today with our scientific knowledge it is still hard not to feel that fate, or the divine, is intentionally acting against you when something unpleasant happens.

Dark Isis?

Does Isis have a dark and dangerous side? Yes, in that any deity can be dangerous and also because she is prepared to fight for justice and the protection for her loved ones using all means at her disposal. Despite her battles with Seth Isis is not a naturally aggressive Goddess. She prefers to use reason and cunning rather than violence to deal with problems. Regardless of the claims of the kings, Isis is not a champion of war and violence. She is a reluctant warrior who prefers peace and *"greets the non-aggressor"*.[515]

Although Isis absorbed many Lioness and Eye Goddesses, such as Sekhmet and Bastet, she rejected their aggressive, angry sides and is not portrayed as a lioness. Despite being aligned with the Solar Tradition, through her assimilation of Hathor, Isis never really becomes an Eye Goddess because it is not in keeping with her fundamental character. She has self-control and is very focused unlike the volatile Eye Goddesses. Isis does take on the protective role of the *uraeus* as

---

[514] *Isis in the Ancient World*, Witt, 1997:85
[515] *An Ancient Egyptian Book of Hours*, Faulkner, 1958:13

this is in line with her character. She is a very powerful Goddess who will only display her power to protect those she loves, not to vent her anger.

Some authors have suggested that Nephthys is the shadow or dark side of Isis. I disagree. Nephthys has a different character to Isis but she does not have a malevolent or dangerous side. If you view Isis as the All-Goddess then she must have a dangerous and dark aspect for she embodies all energies and aspects. She contains everything and evil is part of this universe, unless you take the view that evil, like the Egyptians' chaos, exists outside creation. The original Great Mother Goddess was seen as both good and bad as she was both birth and death, giving and taking. Losing a loved one is hard but death is part of a natural cycle so should we equate death with evil? Slavery, torture, sexual abuse and the endless list of humanity's evils surely have no place in the All-Goddess.

CHAPTER 20

WORSHIP IN THE PHARAONIC PERIOD

"Goddess of Heaven, harken to me."[516]

Isis Before Her Cult

During the Pharaonic Period, state religion existed to serve the king and Egypt. The elaborate rituals and vast quantities of offerings had two functions. They pleased the deities and so kept the cycle of giving between this world and the divine realm. It also ensured that creation was preserved and chaos kept at bay, both in the divine realm and in Egypt. The spiritual life of the ordinary people was of little interest as long as it didn't pose a threat. Despite this, people were involved in their religion and there was no great divide between the sacred and the secular for anyone. During this period it was rare to have the focus of worship solely on Isis and as a result there is little information about her worship outside festivals. The temple calendars from the Pharaonic Period mention festivals for the inundation and for Osiris but none solely for Isis. In many ways this amount of information doesn't merit its own chapter but I feel that it is important to separate the Isis cult of the Greco-Roman Period from her worship in earlier periods as they are quite different. Temples and festivals for both periods are covered in chapters 22 and 23.

---

[516] *The Living Wisdom of Ancient Egypt*, Jacq, 1999:155

The Rise of Isis

Little is known about the worship of Isis in the Old Kingdom. At this time kingship was particularly powerful so her role tended to focus on that and her character was constrained by serving kingship and the throne. Isis and Osiris may have been important figures in the *Pyramid Texts* but were they well known by the ordinary people and those living away from the centres of power? Possibly not. The 1st Intermediate Period brought social and political change which slightly weakened the grip of the monarchy and Isis expanded her role and her worship began to spread throughout the rest of the population.

The popularity of Isis and Osiris grew in the Middle Kingdom, especially amongst the ordinary people. Abydos became the primary cult centre of Osiris. Isis' role in the Osiris cult at Abydos was marginal until the New Kingdom, when they became the divine family triad. The cult of Isis and Osiris continued to develop from the New Kingdom and was embraced by many foreign settlers. During the 3rd Intermediate Period the character of Isis changes. These were troubled and unstable times. It is then that her family aspect becomes emphasised. She is defined mainly as a wife and mother and as a result was venerated everywhere in Egypt by about 500 BCE.

The cult of Isis was introduced to Philae by the 26th Dynasty kings, who originated from Sais in the Delta. An important part of Isis' development occurred when Nectanebo I (30th Dynasty) claimed Isis as his tutelary deity. This strengthened her association with kingship and politics and the king built a large sanctuary for her at Behbeit el-Hagar as well as the earliest surviving parts of her temple at Philae. At the end of the Late Period many cults went into decline but others increased in popularity, especially those of Isis and Osiris. Chapels to them were built all over the country under the rebuilding program of the last Pharaonic king, Nectanebo II (30th Dynasty). To the Old Kingdom Egyptians Isis and her cult of the Late Period would have appeared unfamiliar but not as strange and unfamiliar as she would become in the Greco-Roman Period.

Temple Staff

There had always been priestesses from the Old Kingdom, and probably in the Pre-dynastic Period, but their roles became increasingly restricted over time. Female singers were always present in the temples. There are some *stelae* of women singers in the cult of Isis dating to the 19th Dynasty. These were found in the Valley of the Kings and at her cult centre at Memphis. A letter from the same period to the Chantress of Isis calls upon various deities *"to keep you alive, to keep you prosperous, and to keep you in the favour of Isis, your mistress"*.[517] For the *Lamentations of Isis and Nephthys* two women played the role of the Mourning Goddesses (see chapter 22). It is not known if these two women were priestesses, or other temple staff, or if they were specialists hired for the ceremony.

Encountering Isis

The Egyptians didn't learn about their religion through preaching and there wasn't a spiritual community that parallels those of modern religions. There was no authoritative body directing and protecting the doctrine and the orthodoxy of the worshipers. The sacred and the secular overlapped. The Egyptian texts don't tell the myth of Isis and Osiris only allude to it. This is because they weren't designed to tell the story, they merely referenced it to sanction the ritual. Oral storytelling will have been the way most people learnt about their religion. For ordinary Egyptians their experience of the divine came mainly via household or local shrines together with the continual telling of the myths. In the Egyptian texts Isis, Hathor and Neith are all called Mistress of Women but we will never know if more women than men worshiped Isis.

Processions

The public face of the cult was the processions and pageants. Dramas about the myths of Isis and Osiris would have educated the people in much the same way as the medieval mystery plays did. The cult statues would have been taken out of the sanctuary during festivals and carried on sacred barques for the general population to see, although they were often veiled. *"This beautiful day on which you have gloriously appeared."*[518] This was the only time that people would

---

[517] *Letters from Ancient Egypt*, Wente, 1990:34
[518] *Hymns to Isis in Her Temple at Philae*, Zabkar, 1988:120

have had contact with the statue of their deity. Nakht-Thuty, the Superintendent of Carpenters and Chief of Goldsmiths, left details of his work in his 18th Dynasty tomb in Thebes. It lists the portable barques he made, including one for Isis, and states that he "*adorned them with gold, silver, real lapis-lazuli and turquoise*".[519] People could request oracles from the deity. These were read to the statue and the subsequent movement of the barque was interpreted by the priest. A 19th Dynasty limestone *stele* from the temple of Min at Qift illustrates this. Isis is shown making her processional voyage in a boat carried by 12 priests. The shrine is wrapped in cloth and shaded by large fans. In front of the procession a priest worships Isis and makes an offering to her. The texts records the answer to a question asked by Penre, the Overseer of Works at the temple, regarding a promotion he is seeking. He got the promotion he desired and praises Isis whose "*action cannot be opposed*".[520]

Mirrors where of ritual importance since the Old Kingdom and were mostly associated with Hathor. There is reference to a procession in honour of Isis in a Late Period text where women carry mirrors. They used these to reflect images of the statue of Isis being carried in the procession.[521]

Worship at Home

There is very little information about private worship from this period. Pendants depicting Isis in various forms were popular amulets. Some show her as standing but the majority are of her nursing Horus. The latter form appears in the 19th Dynasty but becomes increasingly common from the 3rd Intermediate Period An unusual blue-green glazed amulet of Isis dates to the 3rd Intermediate Period. A figure of Isis is protected by the winged arms of an identical figure. It is thought that this was a way of emphasising her protective function. One gold cylinder contained an amuletic decree. "*Words recited by Isis the great, mother of the god, who dwells in Coptos; may she protect S3k, the*

---

[519] *Nakht-Thuty: Servitor of Sacred Barques and Golden Portals*, Kitchen, 1974:161-167
[520] *Ancient Egypt and Nubia*, Whitehouse, 2009:89
[521] *An Inscribed Mirror in Athens*, Bird, 1986:187-189

justified."[522] He wore it during life and it was buried with him. It is thought to date to the New Kingdom or 3rd Intermediate Period.

The heretic king Akhenaten (18th Dynasty) could be considered an intolerant monotheist. He accepted only the god Aten and attempted to establish him as the sole deity. Many other deities had their images defaced and their names erased in temples. Excavations at his city of Amarna are inconclusive as to how effective his forced monotheism was. There is a lot of evidence of domestic worship at all levels of society and this couldn't all have been carried on in secret. It is probable that he didn't think that domestic deities were important enough to worry about and certainly not worth the effort and risk of trying to eliminate. It also shows that if a few major gods such as Amun and Ra were removed it had little impact on the majority of the population. People didn't feel obliged to worship state gods, Isis carried on regardless. About 30 copper-alloy figurines of Isis, Isis and Horus and Osiris have been found in Amarna.[523]

Offerings

All deities received offerings of food, drink, incense and flowers but some were specifically dedicated to a deity. Some offerings to Isis would be totally unacceptable today, those of mummified sacred animals. They were offered to the deities often with prayer requests or complaints. At the animal necropolis at Saqqara many *ostraca* (sherds of pottery used as a writing medium) were inscribed with prayers to the Apis or his mother Isis. Many are dedicated to Horus, Thoth and Isis. One bowl has an inscription on the lid *"to Isis, on the day of supplication"*.[524] This form of offering was most common during the Late Period. Statues of Isis were also given as offerings. Excavations at Saqqara have found numerous caches of bronze statues which appear to be associated with the construction or refurbishment of cult buildings. The majority are of Osiris but 157 are of Isis and Horus and seven of Isis.[525] An *ostracon* from the 19th Dynasty has a drawing of a

---

[522] *Two Further Decree-Cases of S3k,* Bourriau & Ray, 1975:257-258
[523] *Private Religion at Amarna: the Material Evidence,* Stevens, 2006:79
[524] *Excavations in the Sacred Animal Necropolis at North Saqqâra, 1971-2: Preliminary Report,* Martin, 1973:5-15
[525] *Gifts for the Gods: Images from Egyptian Temples,* Hill, 2007:178

kneeling Isis. It was *"made by the scribe Nebnefer and his son Hori"* and would have been a votive offering.[526]

Prayers

If you felt unable to approach Isis directly there were others willing to do it on your behalf, acting in a similar way to Christian Saints who convey prayers to Heaven. An inscription on a statue of a priest in the forecourt of the sanctuary of Isis as Coptos tells of one. *"I am the messenger of the mistress of the sky...tell me your petitions so that I can report them...for she hears my supplications."*[527]

Isis and Osiris

Isis was certainly worshiped during the Pharaonic Period at all levels of society but she didn't have her own cult as far as we can tell. The cult of Osiris was strong and she was worshiped as an integral part of this. But the lack of a formal cult does not equate to a lack of devotees. She may well have been one of the most popular of the domestic deities worshiped by ordinary people. Certainly the increasing volume of amulets and statuettes of Isis testify to her popularity. The Greco-Roman cult of Isis was built on very sure foundations.

---

[526] *Egyptian Drawings*, Peck, 1978:118-119
[527] *Egyptian Religion*, Morenz, 1992:102

CHAPTER 21

THE CULT OF ISIS

"I have come and adored the very great goddess Isis." [528]

The Rise of the Cult of Isis

Most of the information we have about the worship of Isis comes from the Greco-Roman Period. As with all religions there will have been varying levels of participation. Some people will have been highly devoted to Isis and very active in her cult, whilst to others she will have been just another deity to invoke in healing or another festival to celebrate. People will also have joined her cult for social and political reasons. Isis had become increasingly popular during the Late Period but what caused her massive surge in popularity and the development of her own cult in the Greco-Roman Period? Both the country and the state religions were in decline during this period and invasion and foreign rule brought dangerous and uncertain times. Many people turned to Isis and Osiris because their message of love, justice and resurrection brought comfort and hope. Isis in particular offered salvation and a mother's love. The Ptolemies actively encouraged a revival in the Egyptian religion and Isis was one of their favoured deities. Her cult was thus set for rapid growth.

---

[528] *Gods and Men in Egypt 3000 BCE to 395 CE*, Dunand & Zivie-Coche, 2004:229

The Followers of Isis

According to Apuleius the priestesses and priests of the cult came from the elite classes. They differed from their Egyptian counterparts who were there solely to serve the deities and carry out sacred rituals. The Isis clergy taught the mysteries and gave spiritual guidance to the congregation. There is little information about the priestesses of Isis. We don't know what proportion of the clergy and temple staff were women.

The high-level clergy were trained professionals and those at the most senior levels were meant to live austere and disciplined lives. The overseas cults usually had priestesses and priests from the native population but there was an Egyptian priest of Isis at Demetrias (Greece). There were a lot of specialist roles, similar to those of the traditional Egyptian temples. There are references to holders of the keys, cleaners, dream interpreters and those in charge of the wardrobe. Part of a work contract from 9 CE was for the services provided by performers including a two-day festival of Isis.[529] Below the official clergy came the guilds of lay helpers. From the descriptions these arrangements seem very similar to those of the early Christians. However there was no central authority, just a loose-knit network. There was a guild of *pastophers* who carried replicas of Isis shrines in processions. These were physicians who had learned the six medical texts, said to be the ones which Isis taught Horus, and the texts of Thoth. There is mention of a *collegia* of Isiac priests, or believers, in a number of Roman provinces. A specialist guild of lamp-makers for the cult is mentioned on a statue of Isis, depicted as a River Goddess. It was found in Pratum Novium in Spain.[530]

Although anyone could join the cult the majority would have come from the wealthy elite and middle classes. Initiation was expensive and so excluded the poorer members of society. People might have had to be sponsored or nominated which would have helped keep the cult confined to certain social groups. There is a reference to the Finance Minister of Ptolemy II celebrating a four-day Isis festival in Memphis.[531] Studies of grave reliefs in Athens suggest that the women of the cult belonged to the prosperous middle class and the elite. Two inscriptions

---

[529] *Daily Life in Roman Egypt*, Lindsay, 1963:168
[530] *The Isiac Jug from Southwark*, Griffiths, 1973:233-236
[531] *Cults and Creeds in Graeco-Roman Egypt*, Bell, 1957:59

refer to the dedication of daughters from important Athenian families to the Isis cult. It was prestigious and a mark of social status; the most eminent magistrate of Athens was a member of the cult.[532] The social makeup of the cult was a major reason for its acceptance and rise to prominence. All the Oriental cults began as private cults but were often absorbed into the public life of the city. Many of them, such as those of Isis and Cybele, were relatively wealthy and had land donated by local councils. Not everyone had to join the cult to be involved, for many of the important rituals were processions which could soon become part of everyday life.

One major attraction of her cult must have the fact that both men and women could attend and, unlike the official religions, the congregation could take up positions in the cult and participate in the rituals. For people who wanted to become actively involved with their religion, rather than observe (or sometimes not even that) the rituals carried out by official priestesses and priests, the cult of Isis offered the ideal opportunity. One aspect of the cult which is very Christian in its way, is the fact that Isis bestows her love on everyone from king to slave. There are references to slaves being emancipated in her name. At Valencia in Spain there is an inscription referring to an Isiac association of slaves.[533]

Wearing linen rather than wool was adopted from the Egyptian practice and seems to have been a way of showing membership of the cult. A *"crowd with linen clothes and shaven heads"* was a standard phrase used to describe the worshipers of Isis.[534] Devotees were referred to as *Isiakoi* (Greek) or *Isiaci* (Latin). Plutarch says that true *Isiakoi* were made by their pious and philosophical attitude rather than by their outward appearance of linen clothes and shaven heads. Political graffiti from Pompeii urges *"all the followers of Isis"* to vote for Helvius Sabinus for the post of *Aedile*.[535]

---

[532] *Attic Grave Reliefs that Represent Women in the Dress of Isis*, Walters, 1988:63
[533] *The Isiac Jug from Southwark*, Griffiths, 1973:233-236
[534] *Ancient Mystery Cults*, Burket, 1987:39
[535] *Ancient Mystery Cults*, Burket, 1987:47-48

Women in the Cult of Isis

"I am she that is called goddess by women."[536] The cult of Isis was popular with women as Isis was a Goddess who befriended women. They could identify with her struggles to raise her son and understand her grief over the murder of her husband. In the myths Isis appears very much as everywoman. She was also a mother figure, which was important at a time when many would have lost their mothers at an early age often through childbirth. The hymns emphasis the female divine and Isis' love of women. This does not mean that the cult was similar to the Goddess worship of today. It was very much a masculine world and all religions and cults reflected that.

Women in Egypt had higher status than women in the other surrounding cultures, even though this had declined since the Old Kingdom. Egyptian cults tended to accord women higher status as a result and this enabled them to play an active part in the cult. Details from the Isis *Navigium* in Eretria (Greece) were recorded in 1st century BCE. It includes a list of the 'captains' who launched the ship. These included a number of women; Isigenea, Parthena, Isidora, Theopompis (meaning lady of the sacred procession), Isias, Demetria and Paedeusis (meaning lady professor).[537]

The Mysteries

Mysteries hold the fascination of secrecy and the promise of exciting, life-changing revelations. An individual's initiation was at the heart of the Greek mysteries. The idea was to change the person through their experience of the sacred. The Egyptian religion didn't have this concept of individual initiation. The traditional view was that the divine was to be encountered at festivals, at prayer and after death. The higher orders of the priests and priestesses may have gone through what we would view as initiation, to enable them to further understand the rituals they were carrying out and to bring them closer to the deity, but that wasn't available to most of the temple staff.

The mystery religions all tend to involve divine suffering; Persephone is abducted and Dionysus, Attis, and Osiris die. Mourning

---

[536] *Hellenistic Religions: The Age of Syncretism*, Grant, 1953:457
[537] *Isis in the Ancient World*, Witt, 1997:178

and despair are followed by joy. "*Be confident, mystai, since the god has been saved: you too will be saved from your toils.*"[538] The concept of the mysteries was that the initiate gained esoteric wisdom, but only after enduring ordeals as they waited for enlightenment in the darkness. Training taught them silence, persistence and perseverance but they were guided only by blind faith. Initiation offered a foretaste of the vision and understanding revealed to the deceased. This differs from the Egyptian idea where guidance came through knowledge and magic. Once reborn the individual could join the ranks of the chosen elite. The theme of the mysteries was the eternal springing of life from death.

There were three degrees of initiation into the Isis mysteries. Apuleius is the most important source and although he revealed very little, what he did tell had an important impact on subsequent understanding and lore about the mysteries. The initiate experiences a symbolic death. How close to the real thing we don't know. It isn't recorded if any initiate encountered an actual death by mistake. The initiate sees the deities and gains an understanding of the workings of the universe and their own soul. The decisive moment was to see the shining sun at midnight as this confirmed the certainly of overcoming death. This is similar to the nightly journey of the sun in the *Books of the Netherworld* where the sun is renewed at midnight and its light rekindled. Similar concepts are found in some of the Greek magical texts. The aim here was to encounter the deities and to overcome fate.

As the rites are secret we only get the barest of details from Apuleius in *The Golden Ass* but we are told that "*the act of initiation itself was performed as a rite of voluntary death and salvation attained by prayer*".[539] It was expensive, thus restricting the cult to the more affluent members of society. Lucius said that he made all the necessary arrangements regardless of the cost. On the day he bathed then was sprinkled with holy water by the priests for purification. He was escorted to the temple where he sat at the feet of the statue of Isis and was given "*secret charges, too holy to be uttered*". He had to promise to abstain from wine and flesh for 10 days. That evening he dressed in a new linen garment and was led into the sanctuary. As with all mystery religions "*I would tell you if it were permitted to tell*". Lucius does tell us that he "*approached the confines of death. I trod the threshold of*

---

[538] *Ancient Mystery Cults*, Burket, 1987:75
[539] *The Golden Ass*, Apuleius & Walsh, 1994:232

Proserpine; and borne through the elements I returned, at midnight I saw the Sun shining in all his glory."[540] He had stood in the presence of the divine and had been transformed.

The following morning he was dressed in 12 garments, including an elaborately embroidered linen tunic and a cloak which was covered in multi-coloured animals including snakes and gryphons. He was dressed to represent the sun. A garland of palm leaves was placed on his head to symbolise the rays of the sun and he was given a lit torch to carry. Like the weary Sun God he had been rejuvenated and reborn in splendour. He stood like a statue and the curtains were drawn back to reveal him to the congregation. Then followed three days of celebration including a sacred banquet. This explains why the initiation rite was a costly affair. On an epitaph from Bithynia (Turkey) a priest of Isis states that he had travelled not to "*darkest Acheron*" but to the "*harbour of the blessed*" as a consequence of the secret rites he performed.[541] (Acheron is the river in Hades in the Greek underworld.) There is a reference to the "*oath of the Isis mystai*" but not to what it actually is.[542] The larger temples had areas that could be used as living space for pilgrims and for initiates. The latter was needed as the initiation took several weeks. Examples have been found at Memphis, the *Iseum Campense* in Rome and Philippi in Greece.[543]

Conversion to the cult didn't mean a withdrawal from the world. Isis doesn't want people to reject the world and its comfort and happiness. She can grant salvation in the form of a better life and this can be a prosperous life. In *The Golden Ass* Lucius becomes a successful lawyer after his conversion, due to her guidance and support.

Temple Rituals

A normal cult ran parallel to the mystery cult with daily services and yearly festivals. Initiation into the mysteries seems to have been an optional extra. It appears that the non-initiated were allowed into the temple but they may have had certain restrictions placed upon them.

---

[540] *Apuleius: The Golden Ass*, Lindsay, 1962:189
[541] *Ancient Mystery Cults*, Burket, 1987:26
[542] *Ancient Mystery Cults*, Burket, 1987:71
[543] *The Oxford Handbook of Roman Egypt*, Riggs, 2012:430

We also do not know what percentage of the congregation were initiated or in the process of doing so.

At their heart, the daily rituals of the temples would have been the same almost everywhere. The size and wealth of the temples would have dictated the number of staff involved and the quantity and quality of the offerings. All rites were accompanied by huge volumes of incense. The cult outside Egypt stressed the importance of its relationship with Egypt. *"To worship the gods of the fathers with the rites from home."* There is a reference to an Egyptian being needed to perform the rites *"with experience"*.[544] Their daily service would have paralleled those in Egypt. The morning rite unveiled the statue of Isis so that the faithful could gaze upon it. This was a major departure from the protocol in the Egyptian temples where only the highest ranking priests and priestesses could view the unveiled sacred statue. The statue was dressed and covered in jewellery and there was a cleansing ceremony which would have included dance and music. A fire was lit on the altar and hymns and prayers offered to Isis. During the day Isis was honoured with music and prayer. There was an afternoon service and at the end of the day the sacred statue was undressed and shut away for the night.

Worshipers could pray within the temple, unlike their Egyptian counterparts. It was considered a privileged and effective place to pray as you were in close proximity to the sacred statue and hence the presence of the deity. Prayers were uttered in front of an altar upon which was burning incense. Ovid and Tibullus both refer to women loosening their hair to pray to Isis. In Roman society, and many others, unbound hair was acceptable during mourning but at other times it was unacceptable because it was considered a sign of sexual attractiveness and thus availability (in the eyes of predatory males). Was praying with loose hair a way of abasing yourself, of showing how unworthy and miserable you were? Was it a defiant show of equality or pride in femininity? We shall never know. But this practice is one explanation as to why the Christian Paul was so obsessed with women covering their hair to pray and the prohibition about praying without a hair covering.

---

[544] *Ancient Mystery Cults*, Burket, 1987:39

Figure 8 - Isis Mourning

Frescos and mosaics sometimes depict services. One from Herculaneum in Italy shows a priestess and priest. The priestess wears a flowing shawl and carries a *sistrum* and *situla*. More women than men are present in the congregation. A text from about 200 BCE references some of the rituals held at Priene in Greece. There were torchlight processions in honour of Isis and only full-time native Egyptian priests were allowed to perform the special ceremonies.[545] All-night vigils were held at certain times. The writer Propertius complained that his girlfriend spent ten successive nights at services at the temple.[546] Rituals would have varied considerably. Pausanias says that on the way to Acrocorinth in Greece there were two shrines to Isis, one to Isis *Pelagia* and one to Isis the Egyptian. There were also two shrines to Serapis. Each temple appeared to have its own character and the rituals varied. They were close together so it was unlikely that they reproduced the same rituals in all four.

There is conflicting documentary evidence as to who was allowed in the temple and who could see the sacred statue. This may reflect different conventions over various places and times. Pausanias writes about many temples in Greece. He said that there are temples to Dionysus, Apollo and Isis at Phlius. *"The image of Dionysus may be seen by everyone, and so may that of Apollo; but only the priests may behold the image of Isis."*[547] He says the same about the Isis temple at Aegira. *"They pay the highest reverence to the Heavenly Goddess, but people are not allowed to enter her sanctuary."* Later on in the text he adds that certain people can enter *"on stated days but they must observe certain rules of purity, especially to diet"*.[548] Pausanias recounts a local story from Tithorea. No-one could enter the temple of Isis in Tithorea unless invited by Isis in a dream but one stranger ignored this, went in and found the temple full of ghosts. When he returned to the town he fell down dead. One assumes that this was after he had told someone of his misdemeanour. Pausanias adds *"I have heard a like story from a Phoenician man"*. In this story a Roman official bribed a man to go to the shrine of Isis at Coptos and report back to him. *"After he had told all that he had beheld he...immediately expired. Thus it*

545 *An Unexpected Turkish Delight*, Walker, 2009:36-37
546 *Isis in the Ancient World*, Witt, 1997:92
547 *Pausanias's Description of Greece Vol 1*, Pausanias & Frazer, 2012:91
548 *Pausanias's Description of Greece Vol 1*, Pausanias & Frazer, 2012:369

appears to be a true saying of Homer's that it is ill for mankind to see the gods in bodily shape."[549]

Praising Isis

Whilst there was no need for a creed or a public recitation of belief in Isis, many hymns and prayers come close to this. Eight hymns to Isis are inscribed on the temple walls at Philae. Although dating from the Greco-Roman Period they are composed by an Egyptian for an Egyptian audience and follow on from the established religious literary tradition. The author has drawn on older works to create devotional hymns dedicated to his Goddess. A complete translation and commentary on these hymns can be found in Zabkar (1988). Each hymn emphasises a different aspect of Isis. The first focuses on her role as the mother of Horus and the second as the wife of Osiris. She is praised as a Goddess of nature and as the supreme deity. In two of the hymns the imagery is very solar and Hathoric with Isis described as the *uraeus* of Ra. The seventh hymn portrays her as the Universal Goddess assuming the roles of other Goddesses through the epithets used. Lady of Imu from Hathor, Mistress of Biggeh from Satet or Anuket, Lady of Buto from Wadjyt and Lady of el-Kab from Nekhbet. The final hymn emphasises her pre-eminence as the All-Goddess, creator and provider.

There are about 12 known Greek hymns to Isis, the earliest being four composed by the Greek Isidorus who lived in the Fayum. They date to the 1st century BCE and were inscribed on the gate of the temple of Isis-Hermouthis at Medinet Madi. A translation and commentary on these hymns can be found in Vanderlip (1972). In these hymns Isis is addressed as Hermouthis, Demeter and Agatha-Tyche. The underlying theme is that of Isis as Divine Mother and beneficial saviour and protector. To Isidorus there is only Isis. *"Ruler of the highest gods...most sacred...bestower of good things...hearer of prayers...the merciful...healer of all ills."*[550]

The Greek hymns were written by Greeks who wanted to spread the cult of Isis among other Greeks and appear to all be variations on a Greek text from Memphis. The author of the Kyme *aretalogy* said it was

---

[549] *Pausanias's Description of Greece Vol 1*, Pausanias & Frazer, 2012:550
[550] *The four Greek hymns of Isidorus and the cult of Isis*, Vanderlip, 1972:50-51

copied from a *stele* in the temple of Ptah at Memphis. Isis appears more as a Greek Goddess than an Egyptian one although in one hymn she concludes *"Hail, O Egypt, that nourished me"*.[551] The authors adapted their work to suit the specific needs of the worshipers and the religious and social environment of the area. The *aretalogies* emphasise her omnipotence and role as creator as well as her more personal saviour aspects. Her speech in *The Golden Ass* focuses more on her saviour aspect. *"I am come to you in your calamity. I am come with solace and aid...through my providence shall the sun of your salvation rise."*[552]

"Hear my prayers, O one whose Name has great power."[553] Prayers in the Greco-Roman cult had changed from those of earlier periods. These took two main forms: either a peon of praise or the offer of a transaction - or sometimes both. The petitioner asks for a request (healing, lover or business issue) and undertakes to repay the deity in some way if the request is granted. The Egyptians tended to view their relationship with the deities as that of a servant towards a master, a reflection of their strongly hierarchical society, but the deity was usually a helpful or friendly one. The Greco-Roman prayers were different. The petitioner often stresses their wretched humility and the omnipotence of the deity. The prayers to Isis emphasise her closeness to her worshipers. One document refers to Isis as *"to whom one prays in all places"*[554] another states that *"she is not far from you at any hour"*.[555] A prayer fragment from the *ostracon* archive of Hor says *"Come to me, Isis! Your praise is among men, your glory is among the gods, for you give the food to man in his lifetime and when he dies it is you who buries."*[556] Many merely ask Isis to be with them rather than having a specific request. A lot of the graffiti at Thebes consists of *"come to me Isis"* followed by her various epithets.[557] Offerings and prayers were closely intertwined. This is an inscription from Philae. *"To Isis, very great goddess: Kasyllos, wife of Herculanus, centurion of the*

---

[551] *Hellenistic Religions: The Age of Syncretism,* Grant, 1953:458
[552] *Apuleius: The Golden Ass,* Lindsay, 1962:179
[553] *The four Greek hymns of Isidorus and the cult of Isis,* Vanderlip, 1972:19
[554] *Praising the Goddess,* Kockelmann, 2008:38
[555] *Praising the Goddess,* Kockelmann, 2008:64
[556] *Praising the Goddess,* Kockelmann, 2008:14
[557] *Praising the Goddess,* Kockelmann, 2008:18

cohort Flavia Cilicum, with her children, has dedicated this offering for a blessing."[558]

Worship at Home

There is only fragmentary evidence of the domestic worship of Isis. Wealthier followers will have left more material evidence than poorer but more devoted ones. Excavations of a large house dating to the 2nd century CE at the village of Ismant el-Kharab were carried out. The largest room was decorated with images of Isis and there were fragments of various plaster statues, several of which were of Isis.[559] Wall paintings depicting Isis nursing Horus have been found in a few Greco-Roman Period houses in Karanis in the Fayum. They are a mix of Greek and Egyptian styles. Small statues of the deities would have been common in homes and these were mass produced, as evidenced from moulds found. Some have a hook on the back to hang on a wall, others would have stood on altars or in niches. A large number of terracotta figurines of Isis testify to her popularity. One letter from the Ptolemaic Period addressed to two sisters reminds them not to forget to light a lamp for Isis on the altar.[560]

Cult members often held feasts at the temple rather than in their homes. There is a reference to this and an invitation to a meal in honour of the Lady Isis.[561] Large gatherings would have necessitated this but it was probably more expensive and thus prestigious to dine at the temple, as well as being in the presence of the cult statue of Isis. An echo of our annual festive trauma is seen in a letter dating to 110 CE from a Roman veteran who requests *"buy us some presents for the Isis Festival for the persons we send them to...buy the birds for the festival two days beforehand"*.[562]

Pendants depicting Isis in various forms were popular amulets. Some show her standing, but the majority are of her nursing Horus.

---

[558] *Pagans and Christians in Late Antiquity*, Lee, 2000:27

[559] *Isis in Roman Dakhleh: Goddess of the Village, the Province and the Country*, Kaper, 2010:173

[560] *Gods and Men in Egypt: 3000 BCE to 395 CE*, Dunand & Zivie-Coche, 2004:302

[561] *Cults and Creeds in Graeco-Roman Egypt*, Bell, 1957:21

[562] *Daily Life in Roman Egypt*, Lindsay, 1963:263

Semi-precious stones engraved with deities became popular in the Greco-Roman Period. Yellow agate ones depicting Isis nursing Horus are common. Another example is a square of carnelian in which Isis is depicted as Tyche and holding a cornucopia, while the Horus child holds a sword and adores his mother.[563]

Geographical Variations in the Cult

The cult of Isis showed considerable variation geographically and not only between Egypt and the other countries but also in the local religious landscape of Egypt. Her name remains constant but Isis in one cultural context can differ considerably from Isis in another. A study of tombs in Greco-Roman Egypt found that in Alexandria Isis appears in virtually every tomb which is decorated and she plays a major role in the scene depicted. In the same period at Tuna el-Gebel her role is very much reduced whilst in the Dakhla Oasis she appears frequently but remains true to her traditional Pharaonic roles. There were no references to the Isis mysteries in the tombs outside Alexandria.[564]

The variation can be noticeable even over a small area. A study of Isis in the Roman Period was carried out in the Dakhla Oasis area. Depictions of her in the temples of this region varied as did her roles. The local cults placed a different emphasis on her aspects depending upon what was important to the local community. This isn't just a feature of the Isis cult. The Egyptian cults were always tied to a specific location and their characteristics adapted to the local needs as they changed over time. Even the major deities have strong local idiosyncrasies. That is not to say these people took a shallow and provincial view of Isis. They appreciated her multifunctional complexity but what use was Isis *Pelagia* to someone who lives far from the sea? In addition, there might have been a strong local deity with an aspect normally taken by Isis. In that case the two Goddesses could be merged or the shared aspect downplayed in Isis. Outside the Oasis area Isis is renowned for wisdom, healing and magic. There is little evidence for these aspects within the study area. Even within the local area there

---

[563] *A Collection of Gems from Egypt in Private Collections*, el-Khachab, 1963:147-156
[564] *Referencing Isis in Tombs of Greco-Roman Egypt*, Venit, 2010:91-96

was a distinct variation. In Dakhla her role as Mother of Horus was paramount, in Dush it was seldom seen. Likewise, the agricultural aspects of Isis as Demeter and Isis-Sothis were prominent in Dakhla, in Kharga they weren't important.[565]

Isis Demands

Isis comes 'in person' to those who call to her. The only condition is that they must be loyal to her. After restoring Lucius to his human form Isis tells him that the rest of his life "*must be dedicated to me*". She promises Lucius that his life will be blessed and after his death he will be with Isis as long as he gives her diligent service. However "*nothing can release you from this service but death*".[566] The picture presented by the cult of Isis can appear severe and puritan with shaven heads and linen clothes. There is no overt sexual symbols and a prominent feature is sexual abstinence required in preparation for rituals.

– Confession

"*I have sinned; Goddess forgive me; I have turned back.*"[567] This utterance by a minister of Isis, once a consul, is very Christian in its essence. Isis appears gracious but strict. No one can be initiated unless she deems them worthy and calls them. A classical author suggested that people should openly confess offences against her regulations at the entrance to her temple, hence the "*wailing penitents*" whom the Romans complained about.[568] Misfortune and illness were both seen as a consequence of personal wrongdoing. Rituals of public and private repentance were needed to purge the faults and restore good fortune and health.

– Obedience

"*Dedicate yourself today in obedience to our cult and take on the voluntary yoke of her service.*"[569] This has a very Christian ring to it, where you are told that true freedom is actually doing as the church

---

[565] *Isis in Roman Dakhleh: Goddess of the Village, the Province and the Country*, Kaper, 2010:180
[566] *Apuleius: The Golden Ass*, Lindsay, 1962:180
[567] *Isis in the Ancient World*, Witt, 1997:286 n 59
[568] *Isis as Saviour*, Bleeker, 1963:14
[569] *Romanising Oriental Gods*, Alvar, 2008:179

tells you. The cult of Isis did not want social change. They were not there to change conditions or to overthrow the existing social order. The *aretalogies* tell how Isis devised the social order and created marriage. Trying to alter these would go against her wishes.

– Chastity

Chasity became an important part of the cult. An inscription near Delphi (Greece) tells of a young virgin who vowed herself to Isis for her earthly life.[570] Propertius complains about the 12 nights on which his girlfriend "*Cynthia has given to her religion*". He utters "*a curse upon the rituals...a goddess who so often keeps ardent lovers separated*".[571] This is a long way from the attributes of Hathor and Aphrodite as Goddesses of love and sex whom Isis absorbed. The Egyptians didn't appear to have had such an obsession with virginity and chastity. However, identifying Isis with Artemis will have introduced the chastity element. Artemis is very much the Virgin Goddess. She is virgin by choice because she doesn't wish to take a partner, she is not a virgin to keep herself pure for another's belief system.

The poet Tibullus gives some idea of the worship of Isis in this piece where he thinks on his mistress, Delia, whilst ill and alone on campaign. He refers to "*the bronze instruments so often clashed in thine hands...in dutiful observance of her rites thou didst bathe in clean water and...slept apart on a chaste bed.*" He then asks Isis to heal him saying "*that thou canst heal is shown by the crowd of painted panels in thy temples. Then my Delia will pay the debt of her vow, sitting all clad in linen before thy door and twice a day chant thy praises.*"[572] This is a very churlish request for help and all he can offer Isis is that his mistress will say thank-you. Perhaps his grumpy demands for healing were not answered a previous time. Sexual abstinence for a specified duration was required for certain rituals. It was viewed as a mark of piety, giving up pleasure and devoting oneself to the Goddess rather than self-indulgence, and it was seen as a technique to attain moral purity.

---

[570] *Isis in the Ancient World*, Witt, 1997:66
[571] *Isis Among the Greeks and Romans*, Solmsen, 1979:70
[572] *Isis Among the Greeks and Romans*, Solmsen, 1979:69

On a Path Towards Monotheism?

Is the cult of Isis the All-Goddess, who demands such loyalty and obedience from her followers, starting on the road towards monotheism? "*Pray to Isis; do not pray to another god*" urges one demotic hymn. The archive of Hor echoes this. "*You shall not pray to another deity but Isis.*"[573] A worryingly monotheist trend for a pagan religion. Does this injunction merely emphasise the fact that to her devotees Isis is the only deity in their hearts? I believe this is as far as the monotheist trend goes within the cult. The other deities are never denied, they are just not held to be as great as Isis. In her One you could see All rather than the jealous Only God of the Old Testament who desired to remove all traces of any others. Apart from women not being allowed in the Mithras cult, there was no prohibition of belonging to more than one cult. Many of those in the Isis cult had been initiated into other cults. An inscription from Paulina, a priestess of Isis, states that she was initiated at Eleusis to Dionysus, Demeter and Kore.[574] In Athens a priest of Isis also belonged to the Eleusinian cult whilst a priestess of Isis instituted a festival of Dionysus. There is theological justification for this according to Plato, as "*envy stands outside the divine cosmos*".[575] A great pity that the aforementioned jealous god didn't read Plato.

---

[573] *Praising the Goddess*, Kockelmann, 2008:33&35
[574] *Isis in the Ancient World*, Witt, 1997:67
[575] *Ancient Mystery Cults*, Burket, 1987:49

CHAPTER 22

FESTIVALS FOR ISIS

"Glorious are the great feasts when many festivals are celebrated for you."[576]

A Year of Festivals

The Egyptians had two calendars, one civil and one religious. Dates for religious festivals were usually set by the lunar calendar, and it was important that these coincided with key astronomical events and important points of the agricultural year. Timings for festivals will have varied over the country and also at different periods. *"The festivals of Heaven have their appointed day, in accordance with tradition."*[577]

Festivals in General

Festivals were popular, and frequent, events throughout the year. Even if you weren't particularly religious or a devotee of that specific deity they offered a break from daily routine as well as enjoyment. Feasting was often a key element of the festival; major temples gave out food and drink. Known as reversion offerings, they were removed from the temple after being offered to the deities and the sanctified food was then shared with the people. Festivals were the one time in which people could see and interact with their deity as most included a

---

[576] *Hymns to Isis in Her Temple at Philae*, Zabkar, 1988:80
[577] *The Living Wisdom of Ancient Egypt*, Jacq, 1999:166

procession of the sacred cult statue. The deity was believed to reside temporarily in this statue, which was carried in procession in the sacred barque.

The festivals were designed to celebrate the sacred and bring people closer to their deities. For some people it could be a time when the veil thinned and normal time aligned itself with cosmic or divine time. Some festivals involved the re-enactment of sacred drama such as the Osiris story. This taught the myth as well as involving the onlookers. It is probable that such dramas would have incorporated local events and landmarks bringing the sacred story into everyday life. The festival of a particular deity was never exclusive. For example one feast of Hathor at Edfu included *"taking out in processions, Isis the Brilliant...residing in Behdet...resting in the barque-sanctuary; every good thing is offered to her"*.[578] The lunar cycle had its own set of festivals. There is mention of offerings made in Heliopolis to Isis on the Feast of the Sixth Day, though this is probably because it was considered an important day on which offerings should be given to many deities.

The Festival Route

The route taken by the procession would be marked by *stelae* and shrines. There were resting places on processional routes and they seemed to have functioned in a similar way to the Christian Stations of the Cross. There is mention of a *pausarri* of Isis at Arles (France) and also references to ones in Rome. The Emperor Commodus (180-192 CE), a very faithful follower of Isis, shaved his head and carried an image of Anubis in the procession and it is said that he completed all the *pausarri*.[579] At each place they stopped and sang hymns to Isis. The *pausarri* may have also have a deeper significance, in *The Golden Ass* Lucius begs Isis to grant him rest (*pausa*) and peace.

---

[578] *Temple Festival Calendars of Ancient Egypt*, el-Sabban, 2000:172
[579] *Isis in the Ancient World*, Witt, 1997:182

The Festivals of Isis

- August: the month of Djehuti, the 1st month of Akhet (Inundation)

The New Year festival was celebrated at the start of the inundation and with it the promise of harvest and plenty. Amongst many other rituals the king stood before the deities and recited sacred texts designed to protect him, and thus Egypt and the people, from the risk of the evils of the old year carrying on into the new. Many events were celebrated at this time including *the Rising of Sothis, the Feast of Osiris* and *the Marriage of Isis and Osiris*. The Greco-Roman temple calendar from Esna refers to a procession of Isis "*in order to present offerings to her brother Osiris.*"[580] This was held on the 10th day of *Djehuti*.

Lychnpasia, the *Festival of Lights*, is recorded in the 4th century CE Roman calendar of *Philocalus* and also in texts at Dendera. It was held on the 12th August to commemorate Isis searching for the dismembered body of Osiris by torchlight. Its other names are the *Burning of Lamps* and the *Night of Sacrifice*. Herodotus attended this festival while at Sais. "*On the night of the searches everybody burns a great number of lamps in the open air around houses.*"[581] He also mentioned that this was done throughout the country. The mourning for Osiris was traditionally held in November so it is possible that the search for his body was appended onto another festival or just misunderstood by those reporting it. Sais was the cult centre of Neith so it could have originally been her festival. The date is close to the birthday of Isis so some have suggested that the lighting of lamps was in celebration of this.

– September: the month of *Paope*, the 2nd month of *Akhet*

The Greco-Roman temple calendar from Edfu records the 6th day of this month as the "*festival of Isis the great, Lady of the Two Lands. It is the beginning of writing for her (of her annals) by her mother Tefnut, as for her elder brother Osiris.*"[582] Nut is normally considered the mother of Isis. Tefnut is the mother of Nut and she is one of the Eye Goddesses.

---

[580] *Temple Festival Calendars of Ancient Egypt*, el-Sabban, 2000:160
[581] *The Histories*, Herodotus & Selincourt, 2003:120
[582] *Temple Festival Calendars of Ancient Egypt*, el-Sabban, 2000:174

– November: the month of *Koiakh*, the 4th month of *Akhet*

The *Festival of Koiakh* was a re-enactment of the Mysteries of Osiris and was celebrated throughout the country. Dendera texts refer to the festival of *Koiakh* and tell of a model of a cow which was said to carry the mummy of Osiris inside it.[583] Corn mummies were made to replicate the mummy of Osiris. They contained sand and grain bound in linen. Texts on the temple walls at Dendera give detailed instructions on their manufacture. They were made by a woman who took the role of Shentayet (see chapter 10). Some were kept for a year then ritually burnt, others were kept by individuals as part of their future funerary equipment.[584]

This festival is also noted in the calendar of *Philocalus* which describes a six-day festival to commemorate the search and discovery of the body of Osiris. This ended on the 3rd November with the *Hilaria* which entailed a procession to the sea. There is no description of the festival but as it lasted six days it would have been an elaborate one. An image of a cow, shrouded in black linen, was carried as part of the rituals. Plutarch describes such a festival. *"Priests perform both other melancholy rites, and, covering a cow made entirely of gold with a black coat of fine linen as a mask of mourning for the goddess – for they look upon the Cow as an image of Isis and as the earth – they exhibit it for four days from the seventeenth consecutively."*[585] He then says that on the night of the 19th the priests go to the sea with a small golden vessel which is carried in a sacred chest. Fresh water is mixed with soil and then mixed with spices and incense and moulded into moon-shaped images.

Herodotus tells how both men and women joined in the mourning rites held at Busiris. The Greeks will have been familiar with similar mourning rites held for Demeter and Persephone and to commemorate the death of Adonis. The mourning was taken seriously. In about 180 BCE a priest at Philae received a letter castigating him. *"You have committed an outrageous act against Isis, because you have drunk the wine of the night, when the divine Ladies were mourning."*[586] There were

---

[583] *Apuleius of Madauros – The Isis Book*, Griffiths, 1975:220
[584] *Religion and Ritual in Ancient Egypt*, Teeter, 2011:62
[585] *Plutarch: Concerning the Mysteries of Isis and Osiris*, Mead, 2002:220
[586] *At Empire's Edge*, Jackson, 2002:121

variations in the ways of celebrating the festivals. In some parts of the Aegean the procession centred on the carrying of torches.[587] During the *Great Festival of Isis* at Busiris animals were sacrificed and crowds of worshipers beat their breasts in mourning.[588]

The Festival of the Two Kites

The *Bremner-Rhind* papyrus, which dates to the 30th Dynasty, contains the *Songs of Isis and Nephthys* which consist of a series of hymns sung by two priestesses who take the roles of Isis and Nephthys. In the instructions they are referred to as the "*long-haired ones*". It was part of the Osiris Mysteries and the papyrus tells us that the ritual was performed in the temple of Osiris at Abydos from 22nd to the 26th of this month. It consisted of a series of alternating duets and solos interspersed by prayers and rituals performed by the lector-priest. The instructions are very specific. Before the ritual the entire temple was purified and sanctified. The two priestesses had to be virgins, they were purified and had all their hair removed. The names of Isis and Nephthys were written on their arms. Accompanied by tambourines they sang the lamentations in front of the sacred statue of Osiris.

Isis and Nephthys castigate Seth for "*the evil which he has done. He has disturbed the order of the sky; He has constricted thought for us*". They mourn repeatedly for Osiris throughout the hymns. "*Our eyes are weeping for thee, the tears burn.*" The sentiments expressed by Isis resonate deeply with anyone who has been bereaved. "*Darkness is here for us in my sight even while Re is in the sky; the sky is merged in the earth and a shadow is made in the earth to-day. My heart is hot at thy wrongful separation.*" Egypt itself was in turmoil over the death of Osiris. "*The Two Regions are upheaved, the roads are confused...The countries and lands weep for thee.*"

The two Mourning Goddesses constantly call upon Osiris to come to them and to return to temple. This calling is part of the resurrection magical sequence. "*Raise thee up...provide thyself with thy shape...Ascend into Life.*" They also address him as the Living God

---

[587] *Romanising Oriental Gods*, Alvar, 2008:303
[588] *The Histories*, Herodotus & Selincourt, 2003:120

because to refer to him as anything else would act against the magic of rebirth. The phrases *"come in peace"* are repeated many times and in one stanza is the phrase *"cease from thy wrath"*.[589] Osiris is unhappy at being murdered and may inadvertently turn his anger towards his mourners and worshipers.

– December: the month of *Tobe*, the 1st month of *Peret* (Emergence)

Plutarch records that *"they make offerings on the seventh of the month Tybi...and they mould on the cakes a bound hippopotamus"*.[590] This was to celebrate the *Arrival of Isis from Phoenicia*. One calendar carries a warning about the 14th day of this month. *"Weeping of Isis and Nephthys. It is the day when they mourned Osiris in Busiris...Do not listen to singing or chanting on this day."*[591]

– March: the month of *Parmoute*, the 4th month of *Peret*

This was the time of the Greek and Roman Isis *Navigium* – the sailing of the ship of Isis. It celebrated Isis as the protector of shipping and hence of trade. The festival also recalled Isis' voyage in search of Osiris. It was held on the 5th March to inaugurate the start of the sailing season. Sea travel was avoided wherever possible during winter due to the often treacherous conditions. The origins of the festival are unknown.

This festival is described in *The Golden Ass*. Although it is fiction it is believed that the novel gives a reasonably accurate description of the procession. It is led by a priest carrying a gold, boat-shaped lamp with a large flame. He is accompanied by two other priests, one carrying the staff of Hermes and a palm branch and the other a *situla*. Behind is *"Anubis, the awesome go-between of the gods above and the subterranean dwellers"*.[592] The priest wears a jackal mask in black and gold and also carries the staff of Hermes and a palm branch. We know that at least one of the priests carried roses as these are eaten by Lucius, in his donkey form, on instruction from Isis. When the procession reaches the sea, a ship is laden with offerings from devotees

589 *The Bremner-Rhind Papyrus: I. A. The Songs of Isis and Nephthys*, Faulkner, 1936:121-140
590 *Plutarch: Concerning the Mysteries of Isis and Osiris*, Mead, 2002:229
591 *The Egyptian Myths*, Shaw, 2014:151
592 *The Golden Ass*, Apuleius & Walsh, 1994:225

and the general public. It is then consecrated and set to sea. The procession returns to the temple where prayers are recited for the well-being of the empire and its seafarers. The festival will have had a carnival atmosphere celebrating the arrival of spring.

Rome was dependent upon the grain harvest brought from Egypt and so a safe passage across the Mediterranean was closely linked to the grain supply, hence the popularity of the Isis *Navigium*. There are many representations of Isis standing in a boat. A lamp in the shape of a ship with a regal-looking Isis accompanied by Serapis and Harpocrates was found in Puteoli (Italy).[593] In the Roman calendar the *Greater Holiday of Minerva* was held from 19th to 23rd March. The Isis festival of *Pelusuia* was superimposed onto the last five days of this festival.[594]

– April: the month of *Pashons*, the 1st month of *Shemu* (Harvest)

The *Harvest Festival* of Isis-Hermouthis was the third great festival of the Isis cult. One of the hymns of Isidorus refers to this festival where *"sacrifices, libations and offerings"* were made to Isis. The 20th of the month was the day when taxes were paid to the temple, and Isidorus refers to *"bringing a tenth for you"*.[595] In this hymn Isis is the Goddess of the Harvest granting a bountiful harvest to those who please her. One worshiper describes how celebrants *"return home reverently after celebrating your festival, full of the beneficence that comes from you"*. He then adds *"Grant a share of your gifts also to me, your supplicant, lady Hermuthis"*.[596] Diodorus said that the *"first-mown ears"* were dedicated to Isis. *"They do this to render praise to the goddess for her gifts."*[597]

– July: the Epagomenal Days

The 27th to 31st July were the Epagomenal Days, the days outside time which Thoth created so that Nut could give birth to her five children. The 4th day was the birthday of Isis *"that good feast of the sky*

---

[593] *Isis in the Ancient World*, Witt, 1997:81
[594] *Isis in the Ancient World*, Witt, 1997:123
[595] *The four Greek hymns of Isidorus and the cult of Isis*, Vanderlip, 1972:51
[596] *Apuleius of Madauros – The Isis Book*, Griffiths, 1975:325
[597] *The Antiquities of Egypt*, Diodorus Siculus & Murphy, 1990:14

and the earth". This consisted of *"Going out in procession, resting in the place of the first Feast...offering is made for the purification-feast. Every instruction for robing is carried out."*[598] Another inscription about the birth of Isis refers to the *"feast of the 'revealing the face' of this goddess"* so it must have involved taking the cult statue in procession. It then lists the offerings which included; bread, beer, milk, wine, pomegranate wine, ducks, pigeons and other birds, gazelles, oryx, fresh vegetables and fruits. It ends by saying *"it is so sweet to serve the Beautiful One with right offerings"*.[599] On the 5th day was a feast to celebrate the birthday of Nephthys and *"there is performed all the ritual of the day, as is appointed for the feast"*.[600]

The Greek Spring and Autumn Festivals

The Greeks held two major three-day festivals for Isis, one in spring the other in autumn. They seem to be a fusion of the rites of Isis and Demeter.[601] Details of one of these festivals come from Pausanias. They were held at the sanctuary in Tithorea which was in an uninhabited area. On the first day the sanctuary was cleared of the previous year's sacrifices, which were buried a short distance away, and the temple cleansed. On the second day there was a fair, and on the third day animal sacrifices were made. These consisted of cattle and deer from the wealthy or geese (for Isis) and guinea-fowl (for Artemis). The sacrificed animals were wrapped in linen bandages, in an echo of the Egyptian sacred animal votive offerings, and taken in procession to the shrine. At the end of the festival the booths from the fair were burnt.[602]

Gather Together in My Name

As well as being a way of worshiping Isis, and contemplating her role in the myths, her festivals brought people together. This could be either for celebration as in the Isis *Navigium* or for mourning and

---

[598] *Temple Festival Calendars of Ancient Egypt*, el-Sabban, 2000:172
[599] *Temple Festival Calendars of Ancient Egypt*, el-Sabban, 2000:178
[600] *Temple Festival Calendars of Ancient Egypt*, el-Sabban, 2000:172
[601] *Romanising Oriental Gods*, Alvar, 2008:303
[602] *Isis in the Ancient World*, Witt, 1997:66

consolation in the *Lamentations for Osiris*. Isis' festivals united her worshipers with each other in moments of sorrow and joy as well strengthening their ties to her. *"Everyman shall prosper who shall come to enrich the festivals and the acts of praise which Isis has made great."*[603]

---

[603] *A Pious Soldier: Stele Aswan 1057*, Ray, 1967:169-180

CHAPTER 23

THE TEMPLES OF ISIS

"Honour Isis in the temples, it is she who founded the sanctuaries and fashioned divine images."[604]

Isis Temples

For most of the Pharaonic Period Isis is not associated with any particular locality and she did not have any temples of her own. She will have shared temples with other deities. This was common practice, all deities can be present in each other's temples. It is sometimes referred to as *syn naos "associated with the sanctuary"*. This chapter is thus focused mostly on the Greco-Roman Period. Appendices I and II list all the known temples of Isis.

Egyptian Temples

The temple was considered the house of the deity and so was kept sacred and segregated. High encircling walls emphasised the importance of the temple and acted as a barrier between the sacred area and the mundane world outside. The normal design was an open courtyard leading into a colonnaded hall, the *hypostyle*. Beyond this were smaller halls and sanctuaries. As you progressed towards the most sacred area the levels of lighting dropped until the holiest place, the inner sanctuary, was in complete darkness. It was here that the

---

[604] *Hymns to Isis in Her Temple at Philae*, Zabkar, 1988:152

deity dwelt when on earth and only the High Priest and Priestess were permitted to enter and serve the sacred statue. Temples often had open outer courtyards where the public were permitted to enter on special occasions and to make offerings. They also contained workshops and storage areas. Large temples were major landowners and the temples were centres of administration, teaching and trade. Some had specialised roles such as centres of healing.

Major temples contained a House of Life. These acted as a library, scriptorium, archive and centre for learning. Scripts for all the rituals would have been stored there. The one in Abydos is described as having four walls *"they are Isis, Nephthys, Horus and Thoth...It shall be very hidden and very large. It shall not be known, nor shall it be seen; but the sun shall look upon its mystery. The people who enter into it are the staff of Re and the scribes of the House of Life."* The House of Life alluded to the mysteries of Osiris and the rebirth of the sun. Isis was the *"lady in the House of Life"* because of her great magical powers and her critical role in rebirth.[605]

Although all deities were believed to live in heaven they were numinously present in their temples on earth. Each day they were believed to descend and unite with their sacred images. This is the major reason why the cult statue was not to be seen by any but those of the highest rank. An invocation calls upon Isis to enter into her temple at Philae and to *"join her image, her radiance inundating the faces, like the radiance of Re when he shows himself in the morning"*.[606] The *stele* of Horemkauf, a 13th Dynasty priest, tells how he was commissioned to collect a new cult statue of Horus of Nekhen and his mother Isis. He made the trip by boat to collect it from the *nome* capital, Itj-tawy.[607]

Larger temples had a sacred lake with an island in the centre, an allusion to the island of Khemmis where Horus was born. Rameses III (20th Dynasty) said that he restored the House of Horus and *"caused it to bloom with papyrus clumps within a Chemis"*.[608] It is suggested that the temple at Heliopolis had a sacred lake with an island in it to represent the swamps of Khemmis which probably had a statue of Isis

---

[605] *The House of Life*, Gardiner, 1983:157-179
[606] *Temples of Ancient Egypt*, Shafer, 2005:213
[607] *Ancient Egyptian Literature Volume I*, Lichtheim, 2006:130
[608] *Horus the Behdetite*, Gardiner, 1944:23-60

nursing the Horus child. Herodotus said he'd been to the island "*called Chemis...This lies in a deep, broad lake by the temple, and the Egyptians say it floats.*" He wasn't convinced saying "*I never saw it move*".[609]

The Ptolemies embarked on vast temple-building programmes. Some of this was for political reasons but it still had the beneficial effect of developing and invigorating the religion of Egypt even though they did alter it. A number of the Ptolemies were personally involved in the cults. Temples built in the Greco-Roman Period do have their own style which takes the Pharaonic style as its basis. *Mammisi*, or birth-houses, became a standard feature of the temple precinct. These are small temples which celebrate the marriage of Isis, or Hathor, and the birth of the child-gods. In later periods they were also used to depict the divine birth of kings.

Pilgrimages

Pilgrimages were important in the Greco-Roman Period as a way of showing devotion as well as being an excuse for travel and adventure. Isis pilgrims would have travelled to Philae or Memphis in Egypt as well as to other important sites in Europe. At her temples in Delos (Greece) and Benevento (Italy) were carvings of footprints. It is thought that they represent pilgrims walking the path of Isis.[610] The Greeks and Romans had the concept of the 'sacred way' of the deities.

The Great Temple of Philae

A lot has been written about Philae and this is a short summary. The Island of Philae is now lost below the waters of Lake Nasser and the temple complex was relocated to the nearby island of Agilkia. The Egyptian name means "*island of the time of Re*"[611] and alludes to creation when the dry land rose out of the waters of the *nun*. However, the earliest evidence of religious buildings dates to the reign of Nectanebo I (30th Dynasty). Until the Ptolemaic Period the cult of Isis

---

[609] *The Histories*, Herodotus & Selincourt,2003:160
[610] *Isis in the Ancient World*, Witt, 1997:196
[611] *The Complete Temples of Ancient Egypt*, Wilkinson, 2000:213

here was a minor one and probably had little influence outside its immediate area. The Ptolemies promoted the cult of Isis and invested heavily in the temple at Philae. All of them were involved to some degree in building, decorating and remodelling with the main work starting with Ptolemy II (285-246 BCE) and Ptolemy III (246-221 BCE). The Ptolemies may have been worshiping Isis but they were also recording their power and staking their claim over the southern territories. The Roman Emperors were not always so enthusiastic about the Isis cult but saw political advantage in being seen to be supporting it. Augustus (27 BCE -14 CE), Claudius (41-54 CE), Trajan (98-117 CE), Hadrian (117-138 CE) and Diocletian (248-305 CE) all added to the temple complex.

There are many buildings in the complex, the largest being the temple of Isis. Just as Isis found a home in the temple of Hathor at her cult centre of Dendera, so Hathor was welcomed at Philae. The *mammisi* has scenes of Isis nursing Horus in the marshes as well as scenes of the triumphant adult Horus. One temple has an Osiris room with scenes of the deities mourning his death. A gateway leading to the river depicts the death and resurrection of Osiris. There are temples to Horus and to the Nubian gods Arensnuphis and Mandulis. The Ptolemies may have incorporated the Nubian gods into the cult as a way of strengthening ties with Nubia.

At Philae Isis usually wears a vulture cap and the cow horn sun disc crown and there are many depictions of the deified Arsinoe (see chapter 12). The Ptolemies and many of the Roman Emperors are shown making offerings to Isis. Ptolemy II offers wine to Isis, in another scene he offers linen, necklaces and eye paint and receives eternal life. Ptolemy XII (80-51 BCE) offers incense and pours water before Isis, Osiris and Horus. Trajan burns incense before Isis and Osiris and offers wine to Isis and Horus. Augustus offers a crown to Isis and flowers to Nephthys and refers to himself as the beloved of Isis and Ptah. Hymns to Isis are engraved on the temple walls; these have been translated by Zabkar (1988).

Philae became an important cult centre for Isis, a holy city and a place of pilgrimage. Pilgrims travelled very long distances and endured many hardships and dangers to adore Isis in her favourite temple. Graffiti on the walls record some of these visits. The graffiti is in hieroglyphs, demotic Greek, Latin, and pictographs (from the local desert tribes). "Act of adoration of Eutychos...and all of his relatives, *before the sovereign Isis of Philae."* Theonestor records *"I have come and adored Isis of the ten thousand names".*[612] Philae was particularly sacred for the Meroites and many priests and delegations of the elite made the hazardous journey. *"I have come to Egypt, having sung a song of triumph over the desert, thanks to the care and protection of Isis, the great goddess, because she heard our prayers and brought us safely to Egypt...O my lady...see to me that I be brought back to Meroe...keep me in good health in this fierce desert."*[613] This was recorded by the king's son who led a delegation bringing tribute to Isis.

The temple of Philae had amassed great wealth by the 3rd century CE. One Merotic envoy donated 10 talents of silver and some gold coins which were melted down into a vase for the temple.[614] A talent is a weight of silver or gold, and the Egyptian talent is thought to have been about 27kg. Silver was of a comparable price to gold in antiquity so this would have been a very generous gift. Petiesi was a soldier and priest of Isis at Philae who left a *stele* describing offerings he made to the temple. These include *"a doorbolt for the temple of Philae".*[615] Although this does not sound much, a pair of double bolts for the main door of a major temple would have been an ornate and expensive object.

Isis was embraced by the people who lived in the south of Egypt and Nubia despite not being a native Goddess. She became the *"Queen of the southern people".*[616] The territory between Aswan and Maharraqa in Nubia was viewed as her personal estate. Ptolemy II gave the temple all the tax revenue from a 12-mile area around the temple and this grant was confirmed a number of times during the Roman Period.[617] Reliefs on the temple walls shows local leaders bringing tribute to Ptolemy VI (180-145 BCE) and his wife Cleopatra II who then offer it to Isis. A long procession of people are shown with distinctive gifts; such as milk from Biggeh, malachite from Ta-Wadjet and gold from Napata.[618]

---

[612] *Gods and Men in Egypt: 3000 BCE to 395 CE,* Dunand & Zivie-Coche, 2004:231
[613] *At Empire's Edge,* Jackson, 2002:120-121
[614] *A Pious Soldier: Stele Aswan 1057,* Ray, 1967:169-180
[615] *A Pious Soldier: Stele Aswan 1057,* Ray, 1967:169-180
[616] *Isis in the Ancient World,* Witt, 1997:61
[617] *A History of the Ptolemaic Empire,* Holbl, 2001:86
[618] *Landmarks in Cushite History,* Haycock, 1972:225-244

In 451-452 CE the nomadic tribe called the Blemmyes were defeated by the Romans after continual raids on southern Egypt. The peace treaty allowed them access to worship at Philae and to borrow the cult statue of Isis in return for 100 years of peace. When Theodorius I (379-395 CE) made a decree against pagan worship Philae was exempt. Obviously he realised that the strength of feeling towards Isis in this region would make such a prohibition dangerous and impossible to enforce. She was one of the most important deities of the Meroites and their successors. Until 535 CE they made an annual pilgrimage to Philae to fetch the sacred statue of Isis which was then processed around their country to ensure the blessing of the crops. Qasr Ibrim was one of the chief stations of the route. The agreement was only broken when the Christians moved south and closed the temple.[619]

The Differences Between Egyptian and Greek Temples

Temples in Pharaonic Egypt were used in very different ways compared to the ones that the Greeks and Romans knew, and to modern places of worship. To the Egyptians the temple was the earthly home of the deity, it did not exist to serve the needs of the worshipers. The word for temple is *pr netjer* and it uses the same hieroglyph *pr* as that for a domestic house. Only the temple staff and the elite were allowed into the temple proper and only the privileged few were allowed to see the sacred cult statue. Greek and Roman temples were much more like churches. The congregation saw and participated in the rites and looked upon the statues. This moved private worship into a public sphere. For ordinary Egyptians worship was conducted in their homes or at small shrines. During the Greco-Roman Period temples built in Egypt for a predominately Greek or Roman population will have been used in the Greek fashion but those serving the native population are likely to have kept to the traditional Pharaonic practice.

---

[619] *At Empire's Edge*, Jackson, 2002:123

Pompeii

The best-preserved temple to Isis is at Pompeii in Italy. Parts of the temple date to 2nd century BCE but others to 61-62 CE. It had suffered damage in the past and had been extensively repaired and rebuilt. This was done in the name of Popidius Celsinus, a six-year-old boy from a wealthy family; his dedication plaque being found over the entrance.[620] The temple was fully functional when it was destroyed in August 79 CE. It was small but had a prime position next to two theatres. The site is 60 by 80 meters and was enclosed by a high wall. A roofed colonnade ran around the wall.

Opposite the entrance was the *purgatorium*, used for purification rituals. The main altar was to the right and in the open. On the altar Isis is addressed as Isis Augusta.[621] The temple itself was a 10m square building which stood on a podium. Seven steps led up to it and it was edged by six columns. It consisted of an outer *pronaos* and an inner *naos*, which was the sanctuary and contained the cult statues of Isis and Osiris. In the *pronaos* there were niches for statues of Dionysus, Anubis and Harpocrates with their own altars. Behind the temple was an assembly hall where meetings and banquets were held and a small treasury room. Having the main temple raised on a podium was a Roman style but other features were similar to Greco-Roman Egyptian temples, such as the open outer courtyard and subsidiary chapels for other deities.

The inner wall and columns were plastered and painted and the floor was tiled. The colour scheme was predominantly red. There are paintings of Isis and her priestesses, depictions of Isis are in the Roman style and only the *ankh* she holds hints at her Egyptian origin. The paintings are well executed but were done to a limited budget. The very expensive purple and Egyptian blue are not used. The landscape isn't Egyptian, the painter had probably never been to Egypt so had to use what he knew and could imagine. It contains some Egyptian objects and fauna and flora but the decoration is a mixture of general Greek motifs and items specific to the cult, most of which have nothing to do with Egypt. It is thought that some of the paintings were used to instruct new members of the cult. At the temple there was a sculpture

---

[620] *Egypt at Pompeii*, Walker, 2013:33-47
[621] *Apuleius of Madauros – The Isis Book*, Griffiths, 1975:157

of a large hand with an open palm. It was a votive offering, but for what is not known. There were also representations of ears; acknowledgment of the fact that Isis had heard their prayers and answered them.

Evidence of the worship of Isis was found outside her temple. In front of one bakery was a niche containing a statue of Isis-Fortuna. Here Isis was identified with Luna and has a globe at her feet (symbolising Panthea). Several pendants of Isis-Fortuna have been found in Pompeii. In the House of the Marriage a wall painting shows a procession at a festival of Isis. A pilgrim wrote graffiti on a temple wall *"in the presence of the Lady"*.[622] In the House of the Golden Cupids is a sacred area. The wall paintings show Isis with Serapis, Harpocrates, Anubis and snakes. On another wall are symbols connected with Isis, such as cobras and *sistra*.[623]

Honour Isis in the Temples

The vast majority of Egyptians will not have had the opportunity of visiting the temples to worship in the proximity of Isis, or indeed any of their deities, although this changed in the Greco-Roman Period with the development of her cult. The deities are present where they chose to be regardless of human dictates and Isis was, and still is, worshiped in homes, in transit and outdoors. Worship in a temple had distinct advantages in the beliefs of the Egyptians, Greeks and Romans. Temples were sacred places and through location and ritual had become infused with divine power. Sacred statues and images allowed the residual energy of the Goddess to be held here on earth and over time a patina of divine energy would have permeated the building. This, combined with the energy built up through innumerable prayers and rituals, made the temple the ideal place for personal communication with Isis.

---

[622] *Isis in the Ancient World*, Witt, 1997:82
[623] *Life and Death in Pompeii and Herculaneum*, Roberts, 2013:99

CHAPTER 24

OUT OF EGYPT

"Isis and the gods related to her belong to all men and are known to them; even though they have not long since learnt to call some of them by their Egyptian names, they have understood and honoured the power of each god from the beginning."[624]

The Traveling Goddess

Isis had travelled beyond Egypt before the Greek conquest. Egyptian diplomats, merchants and other travellers spread her cult overseas. Foreign visitors to Egypt would also have encountered the cults, become attached to them and brought them home on their return. Other deities will have spread in a similar way but what was exceptional about Isis is the fact that her cult was so widespread outside her country of origin. Because Nubia is so closely connected with the history and culture of Egypt I have not included it in this chapter but dealt with it as if it was part of Egypt, which it was at times. Appendix II gives a list of all places outside Egypt and Nubia where there is evidence of the worship of Isis.

The Cultural Environment

Isis could not have spread outside Egypt unless the people of those lands were receptive to her presence. There are two main factors which

---

[624] *The Hellenistic Face of Isis: Cosmic and Saviour Goddess*, Gasparro, 2006:44

encouraged the spread of her cult and her assimilation, particularly into the Greek and Roman world; Isis was Egyptian and hers was a mystery cult. It also helped that the Roman Empire was multicultural, people had become used to a number of ways of doing and understanding things.

– The Egyptian Factor

Egyptian civilisation was being discovered for the first time during the Greek and Roman Periods, and there was a fascination and hunger for all things Egyptian. An Egyptian mystery cult would have held more immediate appeal for this reason alone. The Greeks in particular were in awe of Egypt's civilisation in terms of its great age and knowledge. Herodotus visited Egypt in the middle of the 5th century BCE and gave the Greeks an extensive account of the country and its religion. At that time there was Greek settlement in the Delta which resulted in multi-lingual people who had insights into each other's cultures. Heliodorus said "*whatever can be heard or told about Egypt is most alluring to Greek ears*".[625] This is just as true today, regardless of our nationality. What the Greeks and Romans perceived as Egyptian religion was highly selective and was constantly being reinterpreted, very similar to the pagan tradition today. They imposed their own religious concepts upon the Egyptian religion but the Egyptian connection was still seen as very important. Isis might represent anything to everybody but she was still the Egyptian Goddess. If the context said Isis it also said Egypt and vice versa. Typical Egyptian animals, such as crocodiles and ibis, may have been kept in the temples. The Isis temples in Rome and at Benevento in Italy had a display of Egyptian antiquities for both devotees and visitors to admire.[626]

– The Appeal of the Oriental Mystery Cults

The mystery cults became popular at a time of change in the Roman Empire. Changes in society generate anxiety and the official Roman religion couldn't offer comfort or reassurance. It was very politicised and focused on the city of Rome, regimented and mainly

---

[625] *Isis in the Ancient World*, Witt, 1997:244
[626] *The Oxford Handbook of Roman Egypt*, Riggs, 2012:430

concerned with ritual. It could offer little in the way of emotional involvement, escapism or the promise of the afterlife. The exotic mystery religions could meet these needs and had the added allure of being foreign compared to the pedestrian home religions. The cults differed considerably in that they had congregations of adherents who were admitted after some level of teaching or initiation. Rituals were no longer public, they were performed inside the temple to the congregation and the congregation participated.

The mystery cults didn't see themselves as offering an alternate cultural and social model. They weren't aiming to take over, in fact they preferred to maintain a degree of exclusivity. If the mysteries were known to everyone then what was their appeal? Becoming common knowledge would debase them. As well as the established cults of Demeter and the rites of Dionysus there were plenty to choose from. The Romans had imported the Great Mother from the Aegean, Cybele from Phrygia, Atargatis from Syria and Tanit from Carthage. They obviously felt a lack in their own pantheon. The Greeks had long worshiped Demeter and both she and her mystery cult were very popular. Initiates from all over the Greek and Roman world travelled to Eleusis for the Mysteries. They were such an important event that a truce was always upheld between the warring Greek city states for the 55 days around the event. The entry requirements were apparently straightforward. You had to speak Greek and not have committed murder or manslaughter. Demeter's cult was never eclipsed by Isis in Greece. We do not know how popular the cult of Isis was in terms of the percentage of the population involved compared to that of the other cults.

Why Isis?

Out of all the deities in Egypt why was it Isis who made such an impression on the Mediterranean peoples? Why was Isis so acceptable to these cultures, some of whom had little if any knowledge of Egyptian religion? It must be remembered that by the time Isis left Egypt she had been transformed into a largely Greek Goddess making her a lot more appealing and understandable than she would have been in her pure Egyptian form. There is no doubt that Isis was popular. By the time Christianity became a deadly threat to paganism in the Roman Empire only the cults of Isis and Mithras were serious rivals. There are a number reasons why Isis was so appealing to the Greco-Roman world. Firstly she offered something which the standard Greek and Roman religions couldn't. The cult of Isis offered life after death, as did the Egyptian religion in general. This was very appealing to the Greeks and Romans whose religion was vague about this and what was offered wasn't very appealing.

Then she was kind. Her capacity to feel deeply and to express that grief, and thus empathise with her suffering followers, enabled her to win people's hearts and minds – both in Egypt and beyond. This kindness was an alien concept to most of the Olympian gods. The appeal of Isis was that she was a loving and tender-hearted wife, mother and sister and everyone at various stages of their lives could do with one or the other. She was a Saviour who would help people in distress and this almost guaranteed her popularity. In a dangerous, uncertain world people needed a friendly, divine figure to turn to in the knowledge that she would help and support them.

Of all the Oriental deities Isis established the closest contacts with the Greek and Roman traditions because she could be identified with their major goddesses. She was able to adopt new forms to suit her new followers without losing her identity. She was refashioned for her new worshipers and dressed in local attire but still managed to remain as Isis. Her fusion with Demeter and her relationship with Osiris, Serapis and Dionysus gave Isis a combination of very desirable qualities. She was majestic yet close and benevolent, powerful and attractive. She could appeal to different people for different reasons. Isis was responsive to the needs of the local area and took on new roles easily, such as Mistress of the Sea for seafaring cultures.

Other Goddesses and cults were able to offer some of these but I think it was her mobility and adaptability which gave her the edge over the competition. Demeter's rites, for example, were tied to Eleusis. If people had to travel there for initiation it would have restricted the number willing and able to join her cult. Initiation into the Isis cult was held at the local temple making her much more accessible.

Isis and the Greeks

Isis was deliberately refashioned by the early Ptolemies and this was done for a serious purpose. Egyptian and Greek priests and theologians worked together to create deities which would be meaningful to both the Greeks and Egyptians living in Alexandria and its vicinity. Why did the Greeks choose Isis over the other goddesses? The main reason was because she was a major Goddess in the Delta area and so they had got to know her and were able to understand her through her resemblance to Demeter. Many of the Egyptian deities were dropped from her myths and cult making the components easier to understand. Isis herself got more complex though as she absorbed, or joined with, the other Goddess cults of the Mediterranean area. Isis and her associated deities wore Greek clothes, this modernised them and made them approachable. Gods, such as Anubis, were often depicted as legionaries in the Roman Period.

Isis was transformed into a Hellenistic Goddess by the Greeks living in Egypt, rather than by the native Egyptians taking on Greek ideas. This transformation was possible because the Greeks had started translating and interpreting the religion and culture of the Egyptians, however inaccurate some of their understanding was. In the *aretalogies* Isis states that she is an Egyptian Goddess, which gives her a worthy and ancient origin, but she uses Greek speech and concepts and adopts their dress code. It was this that allowed her to become universal. Greek and Roman rituals took in some Egyptian aspects but remained faithful to their roots. Her Egyptian mysteries became Greek mysteries. To be fair to the Greeks, the Egyptians held the majority of their practices secret so if the Greeks wanted to worship Isis and partake of her mysteries they were compelled to use the only sources available to them. They would have witnessed public ceremonies and festivals and these will have been comparable to some of their own festivals.

How cultures reacted to Isis and the myths will have varied. The Greeks viewed myths as stories which were not to be accepted as fact. They were allegories concealing truths. The Romans tended to react more to the content they heard finding hope or courage in the myths. The central role of the king was of no interest to the Greeks, or to other cultures, and this steered the cult of Isis in a different direction to that in Egypt. In Egypt Isis had a strong personality and distinct attributes; such as her love of Osiris, the inundation and magic but when she went to Greece she took on the characteristics of a Greek Goddess. In the Egyptian mysteries Isis was important as the grieving widow of Osiris but to the Greeks her main appeal was that of saviour. Of all the Greek goddesses Demeter was the only one to whom this term applied.

Osiris held less appeal to the Greeks, possibly he was too inactive, although he was still important in the Isis mysteries. Serapis was more popular because he had been designed with a Greek audience in mind.

In the 6th century BCE there was a lot of Greek settlement in the Delta making it easy for the cult of Isis to spread back to Greece. Greek merchants and settlers were attending her temple at Naucratis in the 5th century BCE. Ptolemaic Egypt was a trading nation which spread the cult of Isis. The ruling Ptolemies had links with Greece and they would have set up and encouraged temples to Isis and Serapis for political reasons. The spread of the Isis cult into Greece was not always politically motivated. Soldiers serving in the armies of the Ptolemies would have spread the cult. There is a sanctuary for Egyptian deities at Thera on the island of Santorini. This was hewn out of the rock by sailors at the naval base there. The expansion of the Isis cult out of Egypt started in the late 4th century BCE and reached a peak during the 3rd century BCE. Initially it spread through the harbour cities. During the 2nd century BCE the cult had reached the remoter Aegean Islands and the hinterland of mainland Greece and modern Turkey. New sanctuaries developed in urban areas first and often shared cult centres with the local Goddess.

Because Isis identified with and assimilated many of the Greek goddesses the majority of Greeks felt comfortable with her, even if they didn't worship her. The Isis cult may have been well-known but it did not dominate the area. The late 2nd century CE guide to Greece by Pausanias references 19 temples dedicated to Isis or Isis and Serapis. In contrast Demeter has over 50. Whilst Isis was largely welcomed in Greece not everyone was happy with this imported cult. At Thessalonica and Delos attempts were made to stop the cults but they were unsuccessful.[627]

Isis in the Roman Empire

The Romans were a lot more suspicious of Isis than the Greeks were. Conservative tendencies in Rome were very strong. Native tradition was valued and guarded and foreign ideas viewed as suspect. The Romans did not have the same interest in Egyptian civilisation as

---

[627] *Isis in the Ancient World*, Witt, 1997:68

the Greeks had. They had no concept of spiritual transformation within their own religion, possibly the reason why the Oriental mystery cults had such an appeal. Such cults were seen as very un-Roman. There was a lot of anxiety in case the cult would become a political threat. Were they going to try and change society and politics either intentionally or otherwise? The fact that Isis was Mighty in Magic might have contributed to resistance from the Roman authorities who viewed all magic as black and suspect. The popularity of Isis swung wildly in the early days depending upon the feelings of the emperors towards her.

At the start of the 1st century BCE an Isis guild of *pastophori* was founded in Rome. In 56 BCE altars to Isis on the Capitol were destroyed by the consuls Piso and Gabinius. The Senate voted for the destruction of the Iseum and Serapeum but the workers were afraid to destroy the sacred buildings so in 50 BCE the consul Paulus attacked the temple doors. After the conquest of Egypt by Octavian in 31 BCE the cult of Isis and Serapis began to be established in Rome.[628] In 43 BCE Octavian decided to build a new temple to Isis and Serapis. There was a state-funded temple on the *Campus Martius*, a very prestigious place, by the late 30's. Octavian became the Emperor Augustus (27 BCE – 14 CE). Egyptian shrines were banned in the centre of the city of Rome by Augustus; this is the same Emperor who was depicted on the walls of Philae as the beloved of Ptah and Isis and offering them wine and myrrh. His edict can't have had much impact as the ban had to be restated seven years later. Maybe they detected how uncertain he was about her cult.

Caligula (37-41 CE) was a devotee of Isis and built himself a temple of Isis and thus gave the Isiac cult state recognition. By the time of Vespasian (69-79 CE), only 50 years after the death of Augustus, there was a link between the imperial cults and the Isis cults. Vespasian and his son Titus kept an evening vigil in the Iseum as part of a triumph for the capture of Jerusalem.[629] The younger Domitian (81-96 CE) once escaped his enemies disguised as a priest of Isis wearing an Anubis mask. During his reign the Iseum of Benevento was built, employing Egyptian craftsmen to work on the decoration. He also renovated the Iseum of *Campus Martius* and donated Egyptian statues. Hadrian (117-

---

[628] *A History of Pagan Europe*, Jones & Pennick, 1995:57
[629] *Isis in the Ancient World*, Witt, 1997:233

138 CE) commissioned a statue of Isis-Sothis-Demeter where she wears a lotus flower on her brow. Commodious (180-192 CE) was very attached to the cult of Isis. He shaved his head and carried the Anubis statue in procession, stopping at the stations to sing hymns to Isis.[630] Caracalla (198-217 CE) was also a devotee and raised the status of the Isis cult in Rome. He built many large sanctuaries for Isis, Serapis and Mithras. During his reign Isis enjoyed imperial patronage. The patronage of the emperors eventually declined but Isis was still important to the ordinary people and philosophers.

Some of the Romans found plenty of things to upset them about the cult of Isis. In 80 BCE the College of Servants of Isis was founded in Rome but there were a lot of complaints by the public against the sight of wailing penitents.[631] Juvenal mocks a society lady who leapt into the Tiber at the bidding of Isis and those who went on pilgrimages to Egypt.[632] Tiberius (14-37 CE) closed the temple of Isis in Rome following a scandal. It didn't matter if it was true or not, what mattered was that it was believed to be true. A noble lady, Paulina, spent the night in the temple of Isis with the approval of her husband. Her lover, Mundus, bribed the priest to adopt the role of Anubis and the couple spent an illicit night together. Tiberius had the temple pulled down and the priests executed. This seems an overreaction given the daily level of scandal in Rome but he was probably looking for any excuse as he abolished all foreign cults and forced the adherents to destroy their cult objects and garments. The temples of Isis were destroyed four times in ten years but they offered something the official cults couldn't and the cult of Isis proved unstoppable by political pressure and gradually became acceptable. Once established in Rome her cult spread into the western Mediterranean and north of the Alps following the expansion of the Roman Empire.

Different cultures place more emphasis on different aspects of a religion. The Romans in particular liked Isis as the upholder of marriage. She was a role model for their own wives and daughters. This is possibly why the cult in Rome developed such an obsession with chastity. It was the demand of the Roman male not of Isis.

---

[630] *Isis in the Ancient World,* Witt, 1997:237
[631] *A History of Pagan Europe,* Jones & Pennick, 1995:57
[632] *Cults and Creeds in Graeco-Roman Egypt,* Bell, 1957:70

Isis in Britain

There is a small amount of evidence for the worship of Isis in England. An altar stone was found reused in a wall in London. It tells how Marcus Martiannius Pulcher "*ordered the restoration of the temple of Isis which had fallen down due to its antiquity*". The location of the temple is not known.[633] The most famous object connected with Isis found in Britain is the Isiac jug from Southwark inscribed with the words "*Londini as fanum isidis*". Griffith suggests that it reads "*in London for the use of the shrine of Isis*" rather than the alternate interpretation of "*near the shrine of Isis*". The inference is that there was a temple of Isis at Southwark. There are a number of European parallels for the jug. A bronze drinking cup was found inscribed "*the cup of the shrine of Isis the great of the island of Paos*". Fragments of a jug found in Delos in Greece bore graffiti with the name of Isis as did one from Emporiae in north-east Spain and another from Cologne in Germany.[634] Apart from the jug there have been few objects found which are definitely associated with the Isis cult. A bone hairpin was found in Moorgate Street in London in the form of a hand holding a bust of Isis. A spiral snake bracelet was carved on the wrist.[635] A bronze steelyard weight in the form of a bust of Isis was found in London and a bronze ring with a glass intaglio of Isis-Fortuna.[636]

Outside London there is another bronze steelyard weight in the form of a bust of Isis, thought to have come from York.[637] A bronze figurine of Isis was found near the Roman-Celtic site of Thornborough and a statuette of Isis was found in Dorchester.[638] An amulet of haematite was found at a villa site near Welwyn. It was inscribed with Isis, a lion and the god Bes (the dwarf god associated with childbirth) enclosed by the *ouroboros* (a snake swallowing its tail). Haematite amulets were used to relieve labour pains.[639] In Wroxeter a poor quality intaglio was found. It shows Isis, or her priestess, with a *sistrum* and *situla*. A similar depiction occurs on the bezel of a large gold ring from

---

[633] *Roman Towns in Britain*, Bedoyere, 2004:204
[634] *The Isiac Jug from Southwark*, Griffiths, 1973:233-236
[635] *The Jewellery of Roman Britain*, Jones, 1996:141-142
[636] *The Oriental Cults of Roman Britain*, Harris, 1965:81 & 92
[637] *The Oriental Cults of Roman Britain*, Harris, 1965:80
[638] *The Gods of Roman Britain*, Green, 2003:25
[639] *Women in Roman Britain*, Allason-Jones, 2005:155

Silchester. A fragment of a faience *sistrum* was found in Exeter and an amulet of Isis in Gloucester.[640]

It is worth noting that the majority of these finds are from cities with a strong Roman presence. It is believed that the cult of Isis played a modest role in British religion, as did the cults of Mithras and Cybele. They were associated mainly with people and units from overseas. But we don't know if any local people participated even if it was just taking part in processions.

The Limits on Isis

Pagan religion on the whole is accepting and tolerant of other cults. Once established, the cult of Isis flourished largely as a private cult with state recognition and support. There were no missionaries as we understand the term, bringing organised propaganda and forceful persuasion. The cult of Isis may have spread rapidly but what did Isis mean to the majority of the population and how much was she welcomed? This is something that we will never know. Many could have found reasons to dislike her. The animal-headed deities aroused disgust in some areas and the secrecy of the cult created suspicion and made it an easy target.

"I am Isis, the ruler of each land."[641] Isis and her cult were ready and able to adapt to the religious climate of any locality but archaeological evidence suggests that her worship didn't extend beyond the Roman Empire and within the Empire it was concentrated in urban areas. This suggests that her worship wasn't taken up outside Greece and Italy by the local populations unless they were Romanised. I don't think that Isis will have made many inroads with the locals in places like Britain unless they were the urban elite who had adopted the Roman lifestyle. The cultural gap would have been too great. The cult of Isis spread across the Mediterranean because she was a pan-Mediterranean symbol that they could all understand. The Roman Empire was multicultural and well-connected. Evidence of her worship has not been found outside the Roman Empire and in the Near East. She went as far as Egyptian influence. For other cultures, such as the Celts, she wasn't needed or understandable and the Egyptian link was unfathomable. The Greeks and Romans adopted the Oriental mystery

---

[640] *The Oriental Cults of Roman Britain,* Harris, 1965:81 & 92
[641] *Egyptian Religion,* Morenz, 1992:249

cults because they filled a gap in their religion but there may not have been this need with other religions. It is hard to prove exactly who worshiped Isis. Even if a temple to Isis was found in countries such as Britain we still would not know who worshiped there unless a detailed register of the cult members was found. It would have to wait until the modern period for Isis to continue her journey over the earth so that she could finally be *"in every place where her ka desires to be"*.[642]

---

[642] *An Ancient Egyptian Book of Hours*, Faulkner, 1958:13

CHAPTER 25

CHRISTIANITY AND BEYOND

"Isis is with you and will not forsake you."[643]

The Rise of Intolerance

The unhappy story of the annihilation of pagan religions is well documented so I am not going to cover it in great depth. Although her cult was flourishing in the Roman Empire, Isis was not looking to oust her rivals. Pagan religion was tolerant and on the whole the various faiths coexisted without any problem until Christianity came along, with the missionary fervour of a new religion and backed by the intolerant monotheism of a jealous god. It is worth remembering that even if Egyptian paganism had flourished alongside Christianity, it would have been destroyed by the Islamic conquest. My interest is in Isis of Ancient Egypt and of the Greco-Roman Period. For completeness I have included a brief summary of the revival of interest in Egyptian religion and the worship of Isis. There are plenty of specialist works available in these areas for those who wish to study it in more detail.

Animosity Towards the Cult of Isis

Christianity aimed to destroy all pagan religions but there were a number of features of the Isis cult which they particularly disliked, the most important being the worship of a Goddess. Paul in particular

---

[643] *The Ancient Egyptian Book of the Dead*, Faulkner, 1989:184 Spell 183

hated the power of the Goddesses in the areas that he travelled in, especially that of Artemis and Isis. Clement of Alexandria gives a quote from the *Gospel of the Egyptians* in which Jesus says *"I have come to destroy the works of the female"*.[644] As Isis could be all things to all men she was a very direct threat to Christianity, especially the women and Goddess-hating elements within it. Isis was a healer which upset the Christians as only Jesus was meant to cure the sick. There were statues in the Serapeum at Alexandria which were said to hold miraculous healing powers. These were destroyed by the Christians. Christianity was innately hostile to magic and the fact that some people, and often those in power, distrusted the secret lore of Egypt helped the Christian cause. Isis was a Saviour bestowing divine grace on her follows in direct competition with Christ.

Similarities Between the Two Religions

The 3rd century Christian Minucius Felix asked what solace was to be found in the cult when Isis annually bemoaned the loss of Osiris then celebrated his rebirth.[645] A strange criticism given that each year Christians mourned then celebrated the death and rebirth of their god. It is easy to see many of the features of Christian worship in the Oriental cults such as doctrines of morality, salvation, initiation and baptism. The dangerous difference was that Christianity demanded exclusive power and encouraged a hatred of competing religions and non-adherence to their world view. Virginity was never an obsession for the Ancient Egyptians but it was with the Greeks and Romans and was incorporated into the Isis cult. This was one aspect which the Christians were very happy to adopt. An inscription near Delphi records that a young virgin dedicated herself to Isis for her earthly life which was very similar to vows taken by young Christian women.[646]

The Advantages Christianity Possessed

In the war of faith and souls Christianity had a number of advantages over the other pagan religions. Solsem calls Christianity

---

[644] *Isis in the Ancient World*, Witt, 1997:278
[645] *Gods with Thunderbolts: Religion in Roman Britain*, Bedoyere, 2002:171
[646] *Isis in the Ancient World*, Witt, 1997:66

"less refined but superior in dynamic".[647] It was young and full of zeal and better equipped for the role of a military, expansionist religion. Christians were originally a persecuted community which forced adherents to become close-knit and organised. The church developed a hierarchy with central control. Christians moving to a new community would have carried letters of introduction to their new church. In comparison the Isis cult, like the other pagan cults, never developed an integrated theology and so was very loosely bound compared to Christianity giving them all a distinct weakness in the battle. The Isiac community had no overall organising body only individual temples and groups of worshipers. From about the 7th century BCE the Isiac communities, particularly in the north, were in the hands of self-appointed and hereditary priestly families.

In paganism there was a gulf between the priests and the lay people and only a few cults had what we would understand as a congregation. There was no sacred book to unite them or educate them. Pagan cults weren't unified and there was no concept of a general pagan religion that we have today. The closed shop of the cults offered their adherents the advantage of contacts and the ability to pull rank over outsiders. Christianity offered this for free. Cults such as those of Isis and Mithras were exclusive and expensive to join. Christians held no distinction between rich and poor. The purpose of their cult was conversion and their sacred texts were a tool for this.

The Takeover

The single event which sealed the fate of all pagan religions was the conversion of Constantine (306-337 CE). Once Christianity had become the official religion of the Roman Empire it developed such a strong institutional structure that it outlived the empire. Once the political and social elite had converted to Christianity, the ordinary people had very little choice but to follow. It wasn't possible to stamp out the cults overnight so they usually 'converted' the temples to Christianity depriving people of their place of worship. Otherwise the temples were destroyed. The authorities appear to have turned a blind eye to the temple of Philae which remained open a lot later than the other

---

[647] *Isis Among the Greeks and Romans*, Solmsen, 1979:112

temples. This was probably for political reasons; they did not want to upset the stability of the southern border by antagonising the Nubians. It was finally closed in the reign of Justinian (527-565 CE) and rededicated to St Stephen and the Virgin Mary in 553 CE.[648] Julian the Apostate (361-363 CE) tried to reverse this destruction. He was a devotee of Isis and reopened the temples and revived the rites of Isis, and of the other deities, but unfortunately failed to change history.

Not all the followers of Isis gave up easily. At the end of the 4th century CE there is reference to a sanctuary of Isis at Menouthis being full of young men working as priests. The temple was converted into a church in 391 but the cult moved to another building and continued to worship discretely. The Patriarch of Alexandria had the building and all its images destroyed.[649] The Temple of Isis as the Mother of Heaven at Carthage was turned into a church in the early 5th century. In 440 bishops noticed that the congregation were continuing to worship Isis so had the church demolished.[650] During the 4th and 5th centuries Coptic texts speak of "*stamping out heathen rituals*" which were still being practiced in the temples and those from the 5th century speak of the destruction of sacred pagan texts.[651]

In the 5th century CE there is reference to the existence of pagan temples in Egypt and of the festival of Isis being celebrated by peasants in the north of Italy.[652] Isis and Horus continued to appear in Coptic spells for centuries after the official end of paganism.[653] The temple of Philae officially closed in the middle of the 6th century but medieval historians writing in the 10th century said that local villagers still gathered at Philae for the annual feast of Isis.[654] A medieval Arabic manuscript called the Great Circular Letter of the Spheres refers to the rites of Osiris, who as a king decays and engenders himself so he can live again. It also refers to a text called "*Isis the Prophetess to her son Horus*" and the New Year festival.[655]

---

[648] *The Complete Temples of Ancient Egypt*, Wilkinson, 2000:51
[649] *The Oxford Handbook of Roman Egypt*, Riggs, 2012:466
[650] *A History of Pagan Europe*, Jones & Pennick, 1995:73
[651] *The Oxford Handbook of Roman Egypt*, Riggs, 2012:466
[652] *Osiris. Death and Afterlife of a God*, Mojsov, 2005:119
[653] *Magic in Ancient Egypt*, Pinch, 2006:171
[654] *Osiris. Death and Afterlife of a God*, Mojsov, 2005:119
[655] *Osiris. Death and Afterlife of a God*, Mojsov, 2005:122

From Isis into Mary

For ordinary people who had worshiped a Goddess all their lives, like their ancestors before them, the loss of their Goddess was a painful one. Much of society wasn't ready or able to reject the feminine divine. The Christian hierarchy suspected that this might become a dangerous issue so the cult of Isis was superseded by that of the Virgin Mary. The Great All-Goddess was transformed into *"the Hidden One"*.[656] She was no longer hidden solely by her own veil but by the walls of the monotheist patriarchy.

Mary shares many titles with Isis such as Mother of God and can be called *"sister and spouse of God"*. She wears a diadem and is linked to agricultural fertility, being referred to as *"the earth"* and *"the cornucopia of all our goods"*. A hymn from the Greek Orthodox Church calls her *"the heifer who has brought forth the spotless calf"*. She is *"mistress of the world"* and is asked to be *"our haven and anchorage on the sea of troubles"* and in a very significant parallel with Isis she is called the *"throne of the king"*. A Marion *aretalogy* from Cologne, dating to 1710, calls Mary the *"power that heals the world"*. She is a protector of sailors and is identified with the moon and stars.[657] Isis statues could easily become Black Madonnas. Some authors have suggested that it was memories of Isis that led to the veneration of the Black Virgins in central and southern France. Figures of Isis were preserved and worshiped in a number of places, such as Metz and Ranville. In the abbey church of St-Germain-des-Pres (Paris) there was an image of Isis until 1514 when it was destroyed.[658]

An edict in Rome in 389 CE banned pagan festivals but the Isis *Navigium* outlived the edict. It was perpetuated at Les Saintes-Maries-de-la-Mer (France) and in the chapel of Notre Dame in the Morbihan (France).[659] In the 6th century there is a quote saying that it was still the favourite festival of sailors. Festivals blessing ships and sailors continued under Christianity and still occur today in the Roman Catholic Church. The carnival of medieval and modern times is the successor of the Isis *Navigium*. The carrying of ships in procession was particularly popular in the Rhineland and Italy. Some have suggested

---

[656] *A Saite Figure of Isis in the Petrie Museum*, Thomas, 1999: 232-235
[657] *Isis in the Ancient World*, Witt, 1997:272-273
[658] *The Legacy of Egypt*, Harris, 1971:4
[659] *The Legacy of Egypt*, Harris, 1971:4

that the name carnival derives from *carrus navalis*, the carriage of the ship, but this is disputed by others.

A few tantalising traces of the original Isis cling on into the Medieval Period. In the church of St John the Divine on Ios (Greece) is a *stele* invoking *Isis Pangaea*, Mistress of the World. In the church of Ara Coeli in Rome is a reference to Isis as the Bringer of the Harvest.[660] There is an ivory carving of Isis in the *ambo* (a raised stand used to hold a book for reading) of Henry II (1547-1559) at Aix-la-Chapelle in France, where she is in the Greek style and holds a boat.[661]

Other Borrowings from the Isis Cult

Christianity took a lot from pagan Egypt: the afterlife as a fiery place, the miracle birth, descent of Jesus into the underworld and his rebirth. The Holy Family also fled to safety in Egypt. One story from the Coptic Church tells how a palm tree bowed to Mary so that she could eat its fruit, very similar to the Tree Goddess feeding the deceased. Christians in Alexandria interpreted the *ankh* as an anticipation of the cross. In my opinion it is a pity that they did not also take Egyptian theology to build upon rather than the intolerant and often aggressive Old Testament. I feel that it would have produced a kinder religion.

A black cassock and white surplice was worn by Isiac priests and this description of the priest in the temple of Isis at Kenchreai (Greece) sounds very Christian. He stands in a pulpit and recites prayers for the emperor, senate and state, the Roman people, sailors and shipping.[662] A rattle, derived from the *sistrum*, is used in Ethiopian church services. Other similarities include the use of stations for prayers, the public confession of sins, fasting and holy water. However, we should not read too much into this. The Christians would have developed their religion using their surrounding culture as a basis or point of reference.

---

[660] *Isis in the Ancient World*, Witt, 1997:275
[661] *The Legacy of Egypt*, Harris, 1971:339 & plate 21
[662] *Isis in the Ancient World*, Witt, 1997:90

The Renaissance and Enlightenment

The Renaissance revived an interest in antiquity and Egypt, even though they had to rely solely on Classical accounts. Hermetic literature was also rediscovered at this time. The books of the *Corpus Hermeticum* consist of a dialogue between Hermes and his son or Hermes and his pupil. There is also a dialogue between Isis and Horus in the book *Kore Kosmou*, the Virgin of the World. It is considered an edited version of a Hermetic text which was changed to introduce a dialogue between Isis and Horus where Isis teaches Horus who asks the pertinent questions. Isis says *"I am initiated into the mysteries of the immortal nature; I walk in the ways of the truth and I will reveal all to thee without the least omission."* Horus concludes *"thou hast given me admirable instruction"*.[663]

Giovanni Nanni (1432-1502) was secretary to the Pope and wrote a book on the history of humankind in which he included Isis and Osiris giving the gifts of civilisation. She is also depicted teaching science and law in a fresco by Pinturiccio (1454-1513) in the Vatican.[664] Pope Alexander VI (1492-1503) commissioned a fresco for the Vatican apartments showing Hermes Trismegistus with Moses and Isis.[665] A bronze tablet called the *Mensa Isiaca* was acquired in Rome in 1527. It is believed to have been made in the 1st century CE as a decoration for a Roman Isis temple. Isis sits enthroned at the centre with other deities such as Thoth, Anubis, Ptah and Bastet. There are hieroglyphs used as decoration but they are incomprehensible, being produced by someone who didn't understand them.[666] The Renaissance saw the reinstatement of some of the pagan deities from the Classical world and pagan iconography crept back. The backlash was the witch-hunts. The Reformation took a similar approach, with Protestant Christianity denying the divine feminine and rejecting even the blameless Mary.

The theological ideas of Egypt which the 4th century Christians feared still had power in the 17th century. Giordano Bruno was burnt at the stake on 16th February 1600, a martyr for the Ancient Egyptian religion. He denied that Christianity was unique and said that the wisdom and magical religion of Ancient Egypt was equal to that of the

---

[663] *The Virgin of the World*, Kingsford & Maitland, 1885:30-31
[664] *The Secret Lore of Egypt: Its Impact on the West*, Hornung, 2001:85
[665] *Magic in Ancient Egypt*, Pinch, 2006:173
[666] *The Secret Lore of Egypt: Its Impact on the West*, Hornung, 2001:85

bible. For Bruno the best theology was that which had come from Ancient Egypt and he believed that the cross as a symbol was borrowed from the Egyptian *ankh*. At the same time that Bruno was murdered there were paintings of Isis in the Borgia apartments in the Vatican. In the 17th century the German Jesuit scholar Kircher said that Isis was the principal emanation of the Queen of Heaven and identified her with the moon.[667] A German miniature from an alchemical treatise says that Isis taught *"ploughing, planting, pressing wine and the Egyptian script"*.[668] Freemasonry adopted the rites of Isis and Osiris and Mozart's opera *Die Zauberflote* (1791) has strong masonic elements. Tamino and Papageno are led into the temple for initiation into the mysteries of Isis as the aria *"O Isis und Osiris"* is sung.

One unexpected consequence of the French Revolution was a revival of the Isis cult. They hoped to replace Christianity with a cult of the Goddess of Reason and Nature. It was said that Notre Dame in Paris was built on the foundations of an Isis temple. Dupois (1742-1809) wrote on the origins of religion claiming that they all began in Egypt. Napoleon I (1804-1814) held Isis as the tutelary Goddess of Paris. In 1793 the Fontaine de la Regeneration was dedicated to Isis. It was built on the ruins of the Bastille.[669] France reverted to Catholicism as soon as it was allowed and the revolutionary Isis cult soon disappeared.

The Revival of Paganism

"Isis and Nephthys have waited for you."[670]

The 18th century saw the development of romantic paganism, largely focused on Druid beliefs alongside a growing interest in and understanding of antiquities and archaeology. Nostalgia for the past and an appreciation of nature developed alongside this with the Romantic Poets focusing upon nature and classical paganism. Carpenter (1844-1929) accurately predicted *"the meaning of the old religions will come back...the worship of Astarte and of Diana, of Isis"*.[671]

---

[667] *Ancient Goddesses*, Goodison & Morris, 1998:99
[668] *Egyptian Magic*, Raven, 2012:185
[669] *The Secret Lore of Egypt: Its Impact on the West*, Hornung, 2001:133
[670] *The Ancient Egyptian Pyramid Texts*, Faulkner, 2007:120, Utterance 366
[671] *Civilisation: Its Cause and Cure*, Carpenter, 1906:46

The movement continued through the 19th and 20th centuries and now Paganism in all its forms is well established in many western countries. What is different now is the eclecticism of many groups. A few will focus solely on one pantheon but the rest will happily borrow from other pantheons as they see fit. Isis is well practised at this and accommodates all other Goddesses with ease. The Fellowship of Isis was founded in Ireland in 1976 by Olivia Robertson and Lawrence and Pamela Durdin-Robertson. Its underlying principle is to honour the Divine Feminine in all her forms. Isis is now associated with Goddesses such as Brigid from the Celtic lands and is worshiped according to the Western European Wheel of the Year cycle.

Isis Tomorrow

What if Isiacism had become the official religion of the Roman Empire and later of Europe? Alternate history is impossible to prove despite its appeal but it is probably valid to say that the Isis cult would have been used and misused, as all religions are, by those in power to enhance and justify their position and to keep the populace under control. Jesus preached peace and forgiveness but you couldn't have guessed this by studying the history of Christian countries. Goddesses have always been worshiped in India yet this has not had a positive impact on the way that women and girls are treated compared to other countries deprived of a Goddess.

It is accurate to say that Isis never entirely disappeared but it is also true to say that the unnumbered devotees of Mary did not believe that they were worshiping an Egyptian Goddess. With the freedom of religion that many people are able to enjoy today Isis devotees are able to worship Isis as they see fit. How close their Isis is to the Egyptian or Greco-Roman Isis varies and there are probably as many variations on the All-Goddess as she has followers. But that is what Isis excels at; being endlessly adaptable and able to metamorphose into the Goddess that each person needs. If we ever set up colonies in space or on other worlds I suspect that Isis Mistress of the Cosmos will be there as Isis *Extra-terrestrial*, always present on our journey.

CHAPTER 26

THE CONTINUING JOURNEY OF ISIS

"Isis, creator of the universe, Sovereign of the sky and the stars, Mistress of life, Regent of the Gods."[672]

The Return of the Great Mother?

In the beginning the Great Mother Goddess was worshiped by our Palaeolithic hunter-gatherer ancestors. She is our oldest deity and for a long time was the only one. The Mother of all living things, she birthed them and received them back into herself at death. She was both Nature as the source of life and the life-force itself. Settled lives and agriculture irrevocably changed society and with it the concepts and understanding of the Divine. The Bronze Age saw the emergence of warrior cultures and war as a 'noble art' and the Iron Age gave this further impetus. The impact on society was huge as warrior gods rose in importance and family ties were superseded by military alliances. All this undermined the role of women and the importance of the female divine power. The Great Mother Goddess declined in importance and began to splinter into a myriad of goddesses and gods. Gods became increasingly important and in many societies obliterated the Goddess.

Isis was never the Great Mother but has Isis of Ten Thousand names become the next Great Mother; being every Goddess who is

---

[672] *The Living Wisdom of Ancient Egypt*, Jacq, 1999:109

venerated under different names? We can certainly get a glimpse of the Great Mother Goddess as Isis reabsorbs the other goddesses into herself. The divine is not static and energy must flow and cycles never return to exactly the same place. If in Isis the Great Mother has found a way back into our psyche it is not in the form of Isis as the Sole Goddess but as Isis the All-embracing, All-accommodating Goddess.

Isis as the Web

How did Isis manage to assimilate so many different goddesses and then spread so easily throughout the Mediterranean world? Isis has the gift of universality. She is neither confined nor contained. Isis can respond to the various demands and expectations of each time and locality and can constantly be reinterpreted whilst retaining her important Egyptian soul and origins. Isis is infinitely adaptable; like a web of energy connecting many nodes she can embrace and encompass all, and each new addition strengthens and expands her web. This flexibility explains why Isis can adapt so well and be accepted by various cultures. Reaching out and establishing new connections is what Isis excels at. *"I am Isis: there is not another god or goddess who has done what I have done."*[673] Why is Isis so popular and enduring? I believe that it ultimately stems from her two fundamental characteristics; her great *heka* (magical power) and her unlimited supply of compassion and empathy. These two forces weave her fabric around us, whether as individuals, societies or the universe. *"She will never be distant from you."*[674]

And is Isis Still Isis?

The All-Goddess she may be but is she still Isis the Egyptian? Still the Isis whom Isidorus and Apuleius knew and worshiped? Isis has changed dramatically and continues to do so today but she has a strong and robust personality. As long as her original characteristics are not lost then I believe that everyone can see their 'own' Isis within her whole. *Una quae es Omnia Dea Isis. "You who are All, Goddess*

---

[673] *Imagining Isis*, Dousa, 1999:172
[674] *Traversing Eternity*, Smith, 2009:241

Isis."[675] For Isis is Isis *Unica,* Isis the Unique Goddess. She has begun to arise from the shadows of the Abrahamic faiths and another of her great cycles has commenced, regardless of our myriad perceptions and misconceptions. *"Endure' says Isis"*[676] and she will.

---

[675] *Imagining Isis,* Dousa, 1999:169
[676] *The Ancient Egyptian Pyramid Texts,* Faulkner, 2007:205 Utterance 536

APPENDICES

TEMPLES OF ISIS
IN EGYPT AND NUBIA

Temples within Egypt and Nubia

Most towns in the Fayum and the Delta had temples dedicated to Isis in the Greco-Roman Period. Cult centres of Isis also developed along the Nile valley. Many were simple chapels in the countryside with only a few priestesses or priests. Sometimes there was a single priestess or priest who owned their own small shrine to Isis.

– Abydos

Sety I (19th Dynasty) had three shrines dedicated to Isis, Osiris and Horus in his mortuary temple. The depictions of Isis are said to be amongst the finest of the Pharaonic Period. On a mound in the temple was a platform surrounded by water to form an island. Access was by stairs at the end of the platform. It was here that Isis and Nephthys were said to mourn the corpse of Osiris which lay on the bier, a scene which was replicated in many tomb illustrations.

– Alexandria

Isis *Pharia* or Isis *Pelagia* was the patron Goddess of the city of Alexandria. When the city was built Isis was already known in the Greek world, her worship introduced by Egyptian merchants. Alexander (356-323 BCE) dedicated a temple to Isis which was intended for use by the local Greek population rather than the Egyptians. He determined where the temples should be built *"both to the Greek Gods and to the Egyptian Isis*".[677] Isis had a number of temples in Alexandria. One was on the island of Pharos where she was Isis *Pharia* Protector of Seafarers and Mistress of Navigation. She was also Isis *Lochias* with a temple at the point of Cape Lochias.[678] A colossal statue of Isis, weighing 18 tons, was found in the bay of Alexandria.[679]

– Aswan

A sanctuary to Isis was built here by Ptolemy III (246-221 BCE) and Ptolemy IV (221-205 BCE).[680]

– Behbeit el-Hagar

This was a major cult centre for Isis in the northeastern Delta. It is mentioned in the *Pyramid Texts* (utterance 510) as providing the king with water possessing the breath of Isis the Great. No evidence of buildings dating to earlier than the 30th Dynasty have been found. The 30th Dynasty kings came from the eastern Delta and they were particularly devoted to Isis. Behbeit had the first temple dedicated specifically to Isis and became the main cult centre of Isis in the Delta. The Romans referred to it as the *Iseum*, the Greeks as *Isidopolis*. It was claimed to be her birthplace. The temple of Isis at Behbeit was started in the late 30th Dynasty and completed by Ptolemy III (246-221 BCE) over 100 years later, but there is a clear continuity in the decoration and design. Many Late Period temples were built partially of a hard stone but this temple of Isis appears to be unique in that it was built entirely of granite. The reliefs were of particularly fine craftsmanship. The Romans dismantled parts of the temple to be shipped back to Rome for display in her temples there. The remains of the temple can be seen. It is thought it collapsed during antiquity either from an earthquake or as a result of quarrying for stone when it was abandoned.

---

[677] *Ptolemaic Alexandria*, Fraser, 1972:193
[678] *Gods and Men in Egypt: 3000 BCE to 395 CE*, Dunand & Zivie-Coche, 2004:242
[679] *Isis in the Ancient World*, Witt, 1997:80 plate 13
[680] *Gods and Men in Egypt: 3000 BCE to 395 CE*, Dunand & Zivie-Coche, 2004:236

– Biggeh

There is no evidence for a temple or shrine to Isis here but there are references to one in hymns from Philae where she is called *"Isis, who dwells at Biggeh"*.[681]

– Buhen

By the 19th Dynasty Isis was called *"mistress of Nubia"* a title she shared with Hathor.[682] Buhen was an important frontier town and the site of a Middle Kingdom fortress guarding the Second Cataract. Amenhotep II (18th Dynasty) built a temple to Isis and Min, probably on the site of an earlier temple. It was removed to Khartoum in the 1960s.

– Busiris

This was a long established cult centre of Osiris and there was a temple to Isis nearby.

– Coptos (Koptos, Qift)

Coptos is at the entrance to the Wadi Hammamat which leads to the mines and quarries and is the route to the Red Sea. Min was worshiped here since early dynastic times. Isis became part of the local pantheon which included Min and Geb and from the Late Period she was worshiped as the divine wife of Min.[683] Ptolemy II (285-246 BCE) built a temple to Isis and Min. A trilingual inscription from the 1st century CE by Parthenios, a priest of Isis, records his involvement in building new temples at the site.[684] The hair of Isis, which she had cut off in mourning, was a sacred relic. It is mentioned by Plutarch and there are letters from people telling how they venerated the sacred hair and prayed for their relatives in the temple.[685] A Greco-Roman inscription tells how one of her devotees went to Coptos to *"glorify the great goddess daily"*.[686]

– Dakhla

A survey of Roman temples in the Dakhla area was carried out. Three temples in the area have Isis decorations; the temple of Isis and

---

[681] *Hymns to Isis in Her Temple at Philae*, Zabkar, 1988:84
[682] *The Great Goddesses of Egypt*, Lesko, 1999:169
[683] *Gods and Men in Egypt: 3000 BCE to 395 CE*, Dunand & Zivie-Coche, 2004:236
[684] *The Oxford Handbook of Roman Egypt*, Riggs, 2012:427
[685] *Egypt from Alexander to the Copts*, Bagnall & Rathbone, 2004:214
[686] *Isis in the Ancient World*, Witt, 1997:60

Osiris in Dush (Kharga Oasis), the *mammisi* of Tutu at Kellis and the temple of Amun-Re at Ain Birbiyeh. There is no reference to a temple of Isis at Dakhla but it appears that there was a cult of Isis attached to every temple. There is reference to the *pastophoros* of Isis at Deir el-Hagar. Isis was widely venerated in this area. She is depicted in every temple and there are a large number of personal names recorded which have an Isis component. In the formal temple decorations at Kellis and Deir el-Hagar Isis was added to the local triads. There are many votive images of Isis both in the temple at Kellis and in house decorations but none of the other goddesses of the area; Nut, Nephthys, Neith and Hathor.[687]

– Deir el-Shelwit

The temple at Deir el-Shelwit was referred to in one source as *"the temple of Isis at the south-western end of the lake"*.[688] A small temple to Isis was built here sometime between the end of the 1st century and early 2nd century CE. It was constructed in the traditional manner and it is likely that it was intended for use by Egyptians who celebrated the cult in their traditional manner.[689]

– Dendera

Dendera was the major cult centre of Hathor and Isis was present in her temple. Dendera claimed to be the birthplace of Isis in the Greco-Roman Period, as did a number of other places. To the south of Hathor's temple is the Iseum built to celebrate the birth of Isis. The building has a split plan, the main part faces east but the sanctuary faces north towards the main temple of Hathor. This may have been out of respect for Hathor. Within the rear walls of the sanctuary was a statue, now destroyed, of Osiris supported by the arms of Isis and Nephthys. On the walls are scenes showing the foundation of the temple with offerings by Cleopatra VII (51-30 BCE) and Caesarion (44-30 BCE) to Hathor and Isis.[690]

---

[687] *Isis in Roman Dakhleh: Goddess of the Village, the Province and the Country*, Kaper, 2010:179
[688] *The Oxford Handbook of Roman Egypt*, Riggs, 2012:427
[689] *Gods and Men in Egypt: 3000 BCE to 395 CE*, Dunand & Zivie-Coche, 2004:301
[690] *The Complete Temples of Ancient Egypt*, Wilkinson, 2000:151

– Dabod

South of the Aswan High Dam was a site of a small temple of Amun built by the Merotic kings in the early 3rd century BCE. Ptolemy VI (180-145 BCE), Ptolemy VIII (170-116 BCE) and Ptolemy XII (80-51 BCE) enlarged it and rededicated it to Isis and the associated gods, a way of showing her dominance over the older deities of the cataracts. Decorations were added in the time of Augustus (27 BCE -14 CE) and Tiberius (14 - 37 CE). In 1960 it was dismantled and taken to Madrid.[691]

– Gebel Abu-Dukhan

This was the settlement for the valuable Mons Porphyritis stone quarries. There was a temple to Serapis and two small temples to Isis.[692]

– Gebel el-Nour

Recent excavations found the remains of a temple dedicated to Isis built during the reign of Ptolemy II (285-246 BCE).[693]

– Giza

There is a temple of Isis as Mistress of the Pyramids in one of the three satellite pyramids of the queens.[694]

– Heliopolis

Little is known about the cult of Isis here. She was a member of the Ennead and in the chapel of Senusret Isis and Bastet are referred to as the two main deities of the Heliopolitan *nome*. An inventory tablet references her cult statue, which implies a temple or shrine, and she was called Isis of Hotep which was a district of Heliopolis. A hymn at Philae refers to her seat at Heliopolis which also indicates the presence of a temple.

– Hermopolis

There was a Ptolemaic temple dedicated to Isis at Hermopolis.[695]

---

[691] *The Complete Temples of Ancient Egypt,* Wilkinson, 2000:216
[692] *The Roman Remains in the Eastern Desert of Egypt,* Meredith, 1952:94-111
[693] *A New Ptolemaic Temple at Gebel el-Nour,* Boraik, 2015:45-56
[694] *The Routledge Dictionary of Egyptian Gods and Goddesses,* Hart, 2005:83
[695] *Gods and Men in Egypt: 3000 BCE to 395 CE,* Dunand & Zivie-Coche, 2004:236

– Kalabsha (Talmus)

The temple at Kalabsha was the largest free standing temple in Lower Nubia and was built between the end of the Ptolemaic Period and the reign of Augustus (27 BCE – 14 CE). It is thought there had been a temple on the site since the New Kingdom. The actual temple was relocated to save it from the waters of the Aswan dam. It is dedicated to Mandulis and Isis. There are also shrines for the cataract deities; Khnum, Satet and Anuket. It has a depiction of Augustus as an Egyptian king making offerings.[696]

– Kawa (Nubia)

From the mortuary temple of Taharqo (25th Dynasty) came an elegant bronze statue of Isis dating to the 25th or 26th Dynasty. The separate headdress has been lost. It was found amongst other bronzes in a layer of ash in the hypostyle hall, the temple was sacked and burnt in 3rd century CE.[697]

– el-Kharga

A brick temple dedicated to Isis and Serapis was built here in about 177 CE. Parts of the temple survive.[698]

– Luxor

There is a temple, built in the Greek style, dedicated to Isis.[699]

– Maharraqa (Hiera Sykaminos)

The temple is a mixture of Egyptian and Roman styles. It was moved about 50 km south in 1961 away from the rising waters of the Aswan dam. There is a full faced depiction of Isis seated under a sycamore tree wearing Roman dress. Horus, depicted as a young Roman boy, brings wine to her. Above her are Min, Isis and Serapis in Roman style. To the right of Isis is another depiction of her in the Egyptian style and on her right is Thoth, also in the Egyptian style.[700]

---

[696] *Egypt from Alexander to the Copts*, Bagnall & Rathbone, 2004:246
[697] *Ancient Egypt and Nubia*, Whitehouse, 2009:135
[698] *The Complete Temples of Ancient Egypt*, Wilkinson, 2000:238
[699] *Gods and Men in Egypt: 3000 BCE to 395 CE*, Dunand & Zivie-Coche, 2004:301
[700] *At Empire's Edge*, Jackson, 2002:142

– Medinet Madi (Narmouthis)

There is a small temple to Isis-Thermouthis here. Texts on the walls show that the temple was founded by Amenemhat III (12th Dynasty) and dedicated to Renenutet. On the stone wall of the temple were inscribed four hymns to Isis-Thermouthis. They were written in Greek by an Egyptian priest.[701] A 1st century BCE altar is decorated with a relief of a priest attending an altar garlanded with flowers, on which are placed incense and fruit offerings.[702]

– Menouthis

This Roman temple of Isis was an important cult centre renowned for oracles and healing. It survived the anti-pagan destruction and lasted until the middle of the 5th century where it gave way to a parallel Christian cult.[703]

– Memphis

There is a temple dedicated to Isis at Memphis. According to Herodotus it was *"Amasis who built the spacious and very remarkable temple to Isis at Memphis"*[704] in the 6th century BCE. (This was Ahmose II, 26th Dynasty). Memphis was an important pilgrimage site for the worshipers of Isis as well as a being a tourist attraction in general.

– Meroe (Nubia)

The cult of Isis spread south into Nubia and the Kushite kingdom of Meroe (now the Butana region of Sudan). Around Meroe there are a number of temples including some dedicated to Isis and Apedomak, the Merotic Lion God who was her consort in this region. There was a temple of Isis here from the Napaton Period (1,000 – 300 BCE). The first female ruler of Meroe was Queen Shanakdakhete around 2nd century BCE. In her funerary chapel she is depicted on her throne and protected by a winged Isis. [705] In a rear chapel of the Kushite pyramid tombs is a relief of the king being embraced by Isis as he offers a statue of Osiris to Osiris.[706]

---

[701] *Egypt from Alexander to the Copts*, Bagnall & Rathbone, 2004:143
[702] *The four Greek hymns of Isidorus and the cult of Isis*, Vanderlip, 1972:59
[703] *Egypt from Alexander to the Copts*, Bagnall & Rathbone, 2004:119
[704] *The Histories*, Herodotus & Selincourt, 2003:167
[705] *The British Museum Dictionary of Ancient Egypt*, Shaw & Nicholson, 2008:206-207
[706] *Meroe. The Last Outpost of Ancient Egypt*, Dodson, 2012:34-41

– Oxyrhynchus

There was a Ptolemaic temple dedicated to Isis at Oxyrhynchus.[707]

– Philae

Isis' best-known temple is at Philae and this is described in chapter 23.

– el-Qal'a

A small Ptolemaic temple was dedicated to Isis and Nephthys at el-Qal'a.[708]

– Ras el-Soda

A temple to Isis was built here in the 2nd century CE in the Greek style. It was probably designed for the Greeks and Romans in the area rather than the native Egyptians. A statue of Isis was found which was much larger than those of the other deities in the temple. It is suggested that this is of Isis *Canopica*, Isis of the Canopic branch of the Nile.[709]

– Samanud

There was a temple of Onuris-Shu (Onuris is a Warrior God often identified with Shu) at Samanud. A Greek story tells of how Isis appeared to Nectanebo II (30th Dynasty) in a dream and asked him to complete the decoration of the temple. The king hired a sculptor to work on the temple but he was distracted by beer and women. As the rest of the story is lost we will never know if the work was completed to Isis' satisfaction.[710]

– Saqqara

In the northern part of the site is a temple for Isis as Mother of the Apis Bull. A burial site for sacred cows, baboons and falcons was associated with the temple.

– Shanhur

A Greco-Roman temple is dedicated to Isis and Mut.[711]

---

[707] *Gods and Men in Egypt: 3000 BCE to 395 CE*, Dunand & Zivie-Coche, 2004:236
[708] *The Oxford Handbook of Roman Egypt*, Riggs, 2012:427
[709] *The Temple at Ras el-Soda*, Naerebout, 2006:50
[710] *An Epigraphic Survey of Samanud*, Spencer, 1999:55-83
[711] *The New Cultural Atlas of Egypt*, Gray, 2009:94

– Taposiris Magna

There was a temple of Isis here. Fragments of papyrus from Oxyrhynchus contain hymns to Isis of Taposiris.[712]

– Tebtunis (Umm el-Brigat)

A small temple to Isis-Thermouthis was located in the temple of Soknebtunis. It was originally built in the 3rd century BCE and was remodelled in the reign of Augustus (27 BCE – 14 CE).[713]

– Thebes

Ptolemy X dedicated several temples and an Iseum here.[714]

---

[712] *The Temple Treasures of Taposiris Magna*, Voros, 2010:15-17
[713] *Egypt from Alexander to the Copts*, Bagnall & Rathbone, 2004:143
[714] *A History of the Ptolemaic Empire*, Holbl, 2001:278

APPENDIX 2

EVIDENCE OF ISIS OUTSIDE EGYPT

This appendix lists all the places that I have found where there is evidence of a cult of Isis. The evidence varies from the identifiable remains of a temple to references in classical writing. I have excluded places referenced in the hymns as they may well be poetic licence, listing as many places as possible to highlight the importance of Isis rather than to give an accurate geographical summary of her cult centres.

Greece

– Aegira

Pausanias mentions a temple of Isis here.[715]

– Andros

An *aretalogy* to Isis was composed here.[716]

– Athens

"*Egypt has been dear to you as a place of residence; in Greece you have honoured above all Athens...there in fact for the first time you showed the fruits...distributed the seed among all the Greeks.*"[717] Isis was particularly popular in Athens and inscriptions suggest that there

---

[715] *Pausanias's Description of Greece Vol 1*, Pausanias & Frazer, 1898:369
[716] *Attic Grave Reliefs that Represent Women in the Dress of Isis*, Walters, 1988:1
[717] *The Hellenistic Face of Isis: Cosmic and Saviour Goddess*, Gasparro, 2006:42

was a cult here from the late 4th century BCE until the middle of the 3rd century CE. In Athens there are many grave reliefs showing women in the dress of Isis which reflects the popularity of her cult. The dress shown may have been used for ceremonial occasions. (Descriptions are given in chapter 3.) There is no evidence of the Iseum but a dedication tells how the temple was refurbished in 128 CE by a wealthy woman who served as a lamp bearer and dream interpreter.[718] A very finely carved colossal statue of Isis in Eleusinian limestone was found on the southern slopes of the acropolis and is believed to date to around 40 CE.[719]

– Beroea

Isis was merged with the local Artemis at Beroea.[720]

– Ceos (Kea in the Cyclades)

It is thought that the cult of Isis started on this island as a private cult brought back by someone who had been in the service of Ptolemy II (285-246 BCE).[721]

– Corinth

The earliest depiction of Isis in Corinth dates to the late 2nd century BCE. It is a statue depicting Isis as Mistress of the Sea, she has her arms set outward in the manner of the Greek rulers. One of her most popular epithets in Corinth was *"mistress of the open sea"*.[722] Pausanias says that *"on the way up the Acro-Corinth there is a precinct of the Marine Isis and another of the Egyptian Isis"*.[723] There was a cult of Isis at Kenchreai, the harbour of East Corinth. Pausanias mentions a sanctuary of Isis and of Asclepius here.[724]

– Delos

Delos is the island home of Artemis and Apollo. There was a temple to Isis here and over 200 inscriptions to Isis have been found. The earliest being the dedication of an altar by one of her

---

[718] *Attic Grave Reliefs that Represent Women in the Dress of Isis*, Walters, 1988:62-63
[719] *Isis in the Ancient World*, Witt, 1997:68
[720] *Isis in the Ancient World*, Witt, 1997:68
[721] *The four Greek hymns of Isidorus and the cult of Isis*, Vanderlip, 1972:78
[722] *Attic Grave Reliefs that Represent Women in the Dress of Isis*, Walters, 1988:15
[723] *Pausanias's Description of Greece Vol 1*, Pausanias & Frazer, 1898:77
[724] *Pausanias's Description of Greece Vol 1*, Pausanias & Frazer, 1898:73

priestesses.[725] There are fragments of a colossal statue of Isis dating to around 128 BCE. She is depicted in a similar form to Aphrodite.[726] The island was a possession of Athens from 166 BCE. The city of Athens provided new buildings and major dedications to the sanctuary at Delos. Athenians from the most important families who lived on Delos served as priests and officials and made costly gifts to the temple.[727]

– Delphi

An inscription mentions a young girl from Delphi who dedicated herself to Isis.[728]

– Demetrias

There is a reference to an Egyptian priest of Isis in Demetrias.[729]

– Eretria, Euboea

This was a cult centre of Artemis. There was a temple of Isis dating to the 2nd century BCE which was built in the Egyptian style. It contained representations of sphinx, crocodiles and ibises and marble statues of Isis-Cybele and Aphrodite-Adonis.[730]

– Gortyn, Crete

There was a large temple dedicated to Isis, Serapis and Hermes-Anubis.[731]

– Halicarnassus

There is mention of the cult of Isis here in the 3rd century BCE. In the 1st century BCE there is reference to a priest of Isis. She also appears on the coins of this period.[732]

– Hermion

There was a temple to Isis and Serapis here.[733]

---

[725] *Isis in the Ancient World*, Witt, 1997:68
[726] *Attic Grave Reliefs that Represent Women in the Dress of Isis*, Walters, 1988:15
[727] *Attic Grave Reliefs that Represent Women in the Dress of Isis*, Walters, 1988:61
[728] *Isis in the Ancient World*, Witt, 1997:66
[729] *Ptolemaic Alexandria*, Fraser, 1972:264
[730] *Isis in the Ancient World*, Witt, 1997:69
[731] *An Unexpected Turkish Delight*, Walker, 2009:36-37
[732] *The four Greek hymns of Isidorus and the cult of Isis*, Vanderlip, 1972:78
[733] *Pausanias's Description of Greece Vol 1*, Pausanias & Frazer, 1898:125

– Ios

An *aretalogy* to Isis came from Ios.[734] A *stele* invoking Isis was found in a church on Ios.[735]

– Kos

There are early depictions of Isis dating to the late 2nd century BCE.[736]

– Kyme

There was a temple to Isis in Kyme and the well-known *aretalogy* to Isis was written here.[737]

– Lesbos

There was a temple to Isis on Lesbos.[738]

– Megara

There was a temple of Isis located near to the temple of Artemis and Apollo.[739]

– Messene

There was sanctuary of Isis and Serapis here.[740]

– Methana

There was a sanctuary of Isis here.[741]

– Philippi

There was a sanctuary of Isis and Serapis here. Philippi was a Roman colony and they viewed Isis as the guardian of the city and the protector of the colony.[742]

---

[734] *Attic Grave Reliefs that Represent Women in the Dress of Isis*, Walters, 1988:1
[735] *Isis in the Ancient World*, Witt, 1997:275
[736] *Attic Grave Reliefs that Represent Women in the Dress of Isis*, Walters, 1988:14
[737] *Attic Grave Reliefs that Represent Women in the Dress of Isis*, Walters, 1988:1
[738] *The Secret Lore of Egypt: Its Impact on the West*, Hornung, 2001:67
[739] *Pausanias's Description of Greece Vol 1*, Pausanias & Frazer, 1898:62
[740] *Pausanias's Description of Greece Vol 1*, Pausanias & Frazer, 1898:228
[741] *Pausanias's Description of Greece Vol 1*, Pausanias & Frazer, 1898:124
[742] *Isis in the Ancient World*, Witt, 1997:192

– Phlius

There was a temple of Isis here.[743]

– Piraeus (harbour of Athens)

By the 4th century BCE Isis had a cult in Piraeus and a temple was founded by Egyptian traders.[744]

– Rhodes

The earliest known depiction of Isis in the Mediterranean is from the island of Rhodes. This is a statue dedicated to Isis and Osiris-Hapy which is believed to pre-date the Greek conquest of Egypt.[745] In 88 BCE Isis was said to have saved Rhodes by sabotaging the war machines of Mithridates Eupator who was laying siege to the city.[746]

– Samos

There was a temple of Isis on Samos.[747]

– Santorini (ancient Thera)

There was a sanctuary dedicated to Isis, Serapis and Anubis.[748]

– Thessalonica

An *aretalogy* to Isis comes from here.[749]

– Tithorea

There was a shrine to Isis at Tithorea.[750]

– Troezen

Pausanias mentions a temple of Isis where the *"image of Isis was dedicated by the people of Troezen"*.[751]

---

[743] *Pausanias's Description of Greece Vol 1*, Pausanias & Frazer, 1898:91
[744] *Isis as Saviour*, Bleeker, 1963:10
[745] *The four Greek hymns of Isidorus and the cult of Isis*, Vanderlip, 1972:77
[746] *Isis and Empires*, Bricault & Versluys, 2014:16
[747] *The Secret Lore of Egypt: Its Impact on the West*, Hornung, 2001:67
[748] *An Unexpected Turkish Delight*, Walker, 2009:36-37
[749] *Attic Grave Reliefs that Represent Women in the Dress of Isis*, Walters, 1988:1
[750] *Isis in the Ancient World*, Witt, 1997:66
[751] *Pausanias's Description of Greece Vol 1*, Pausanias & Frazer, 1898:122

Turkey

– Ephesus

Ephesus was the cult centre of Artemis and her temple was one of the wonders of the ancient world. There was a temple to Isis here.[752]

– Priene

There was a sanctuary of Isis at Priene.[753] An altar dating to the 3rd century BCE has an inscription to Isis, Serapis and Anubis. A text dating to around 200 BCE records some of the rituals carried out.[754]

– Soli

An Iseum and a sanctuary of Aphrodite were built next to each other.[755]

Italy

– Ariccia

There is a relief from Ariccia which depicts Isis.[756]

– Benevento (on the Appian Way)

A temple to Isis was either founded by or reconstructed by Domitian in 88 CE. Reliefs show Egyptian fauna and Isis in her barque.[757]

– Capua

There is an inscription dedicated to Isis at Capua.[758]

– Herculaneum

Frescos at Herculaneum show a cult service in progress.[759]

– Naples

A statue of Isis was found in Naples.[760]

---

[752] *Water in the Worship of Isis and Serapis*, Wild, 1981:23
[753] *Water in the Worship of Isis and Serapis*, Wild, 1981:21
[754] *An Unexpected Turkish Delight*, Walker, 2009:36-37
[755] *Water in the Worship of Isis and Sarapis*, Wild, 1981:14
[756] *The Flavians: Pharonic Kingship Between Egypt and Rome*, Vittozzi, 2014:254
[757] *Isis in the Ancient World*, Witt, 1997:86
[758] *The Secret Lore of Egypt: Its Impact on the West*, Hornung, 2001:65
[759] *The Legacy of Egypt*, Harris, 1971:plate 8

– Ostia (the port of Rome)

A priestess of Bastet dedicated an altar to Isis-Bubastis.[761]

– Pompeii

The best-preserved temple of Isis outside Egypt is at Pompeii. One estimate of her worshipers in the city is about two thousand. Here she was Isis *Panthea*, Mistress of All. See chapter 23 for details about the temple.

– Praeneste (modern Palestrina)

In Praeneste there are mosaics and bowls showing Isis wearing a winged sun disc on her forehead. The mosaic depicts the mountains of Sudan, the Nile inundation and a variety of Egyptian fauna.[762]

– Ravenna

An inscription on a woman's sarcophagus says she was initiated into the cult of Isis.[763]

– Rome

There was a temple to Isis at the Field of Mars which was a very prestigious site in the centre of the city. The *Iseum Campense* was of great importance to the cult. It was large with an open court 275m in length. The *Mensa Isiaca* (now in the Turin museum) is thought to have come from this temple. This table is a Greco-Roman reproduction of Egyptian art. Isis stands in the centre flanked by crowned serpents, the Apis bull and the baboon of Thoth. Isis is also present as Isis-Luna along with a winged solar disc, Ptah, Anubis, Bastet and various Egyptian creatures. From the temple there are four obelisks and basalt statues of lions, crocodiles and sphinxes and a portrait statue of a priestess of Isis.[764] In *The Golden Ass* Lucius returns to Rome and mentions his daily prayers to Isis. He says she was called Isis *Campensis* after the location of her temple.[765]

---

[760] *Attic Grave Reliefs that Represent Women in the Dress of Isis*, Walters, 1988:16
[761] *Isis in the Ancient World*, Witt, 1997:81
[762] *Isis in the Ancient World*, Witt, 1997:86
[763] *Attic Grave Reliefs that Represent Women in the Dress of Isis*, Walters, 1988:57
[764] *Isis in the Ancient World*, Witt, 1997:87
[765] *The Golden Ass*, Apuleius & Walsh, 1994:236

– Sicily

There are references to the cult of Isis and Serapis in Sicily from the 2nd century BCE[766] and there is a sanctuary of Isis and Serapis at Taormina.[767]

Austria

There was a temple of Isis at Frauenberg (Flavia Solva) in southern Austria. Here she was conflated with the local Celtic Goddess Noreia.[768]

England

– Dorchester

A statuette of Isis was found in Dorchester.[769]

– Exeter

Fragments of a faience *sistrum* were found in Exeter.[770]

– Gloucester

Fragments of an amulet of Isis were found here.[771]

– London

Details of the finds from London are given in chapter 24.

– Silchester

The bezel of a gold ring, thought to come from Silchester, depicts a goddess bearing fruits and corn which is believed to be Isis.[772]

– Thornborough (Buckinghamshire)

A bronze figurine of Isis was found near the Roman-Celtic site of Thornborough.[773]

– Welwyn (Hertfordshire)

A haematite amulet inscribed with Isis was found at a villa site near Welwyn.[774]

---

[766] *Apuleius of Madauros – The Isis Book*, Griffiths, 1975:151
[767] *The four Greek hymns of Isidorus and the cult of Isis*, Vanderlip, 1972:31
[768] *Isis and the Evolution of Religions*, Woolf, 2014:84
[769] *The Gods of Roman Britain*, Green, 2003:25
[770] *The Oriental Cults of Roman Britain*, Harris, 1965:90
[771] *The Oriental Cults of Roman Britain*, Harris, 1965:92
[772] *The Oriental Cults of Roman Britain*, Harris, 1965:81
[773] *The Gods of Roman Britain*, Green, 2003:25

– Wroxeter

A glass intaglio was found in Wroxeter. It shows Isis, or her priestess, with a *sistrum* and *situla*.[775]

– York

A bronze steelyard weight in the form of a bust of Isis is thought to have come from York.[776] The Legate of the VIth Victrix Legion built a temple of Serapis in York.[777]

France

– Arles

The amphitheatre at Arles had seats reserved for patrons of the various cults, including that of Isis.[778] There is reference to a *pausarri* of Isis at Arles.[779]

– Ehl

A small bronze figurine of Isis holding a cornucopia and a snake was found at Ehl, Alsace.[780]

– Lectoure

A votive altar to Isis was found here.[781]

– Nimes

An inscription references a temple to Isis and Serapis in Nimes.[782]

– Vaison-la-Romaine

There is a possible temple to Isis here.[783]

---

[774] *Women in Roman Britain,* Allason-Jones, 2005:155
[775] *The Oriental Cults of Roman Britain,* Harris, 1965:80
[776] *The Oriental Cults of Roman Britain,* Harris, 1965:80
[777] *Roman Towns in Britain,* Bedoyere, 2004:93
[778] *Roman France,* MacKendrick, 1971:61
[779] *Isis in the Ancient World,* Witt, 1997:182
[780] *Une Isis-Fortuna en Alsace,* Clerc, 1998:559
[781] *Isis and the Evolution of Religions,* Woolf, 2014:84
[782] *Roman Gaul and Germany,* King, 1990: 152
[783] *Roman France,* MacKendrick, 1971:112

Germany

– Cologne

A statue of Isis was found at the church of St Ursula near Cologne. It was inscribe *"Isidi Invicte"*, to the Unconquered Isis. The base of another statue was found with the inscription *"Isidi"* to Isis.[784] Fragments of a jug inscribed with her name have been found.[785]

– Mainz

In 1999 a temple dedicated to Isis *Panthea* and the Magna Mater was excavated. It is believed to have been founded in 71-80 CE.[786]

Hungary

In 188 CE an Iseum was built at Szombathely. It was enlarged in the 3rd century CE.[787]

Malta

There was a sanctuary of Isis and Serapis at Tas-Silg and an anchor stock inscribed with the names of Isis and Serapis was found offshore.[788]

Portugal

A curse tablet invoking Isis was found at Setabul.[789]

Romania

There is a reference to an Isis guild in Turda (ancient Potaissa, Dacia).[790]

---

[784] *The Romans in Cologne and Lower Germany*, Elbe, 1995:56
[785] *The Isiac Jug from Southwark*, Griffiths, 1973:233-236
[786] *The defixiones from the Sanctuary of Isis and Mater Magna in Mainz*, Blansdorf, 2010:141
[787] *A History of Pagan Europe*, Jones & Pennick, 1995:188
[788] *Serapis – Before and After the Ptolemies*, Mifsud & Farrugia, 2008:50-55
[789] *Cursing a Thief in Iberia and Britain*, Tomlin, 2010:260
[790] *The Isiac Jug from Southwark*, Griffiths, 1973:233-236

Spain

There is a report of an altar decorated with Anubis, ibis and a palm tree which was dedicated to Isis by her priestesses. It came from somewhere in Spain.[791]

– Cordova

A statuette of Isis as a River Goddess was found at nearby Pratum Novium. It was dedicated by the lamp-makers of her cult.[792]

– Emporiae

Fragments of a jug inscribed with the name of Isis were found here.[793]

– Valencia

An inscription refers to an Isiac association of slaves at Valencia.[794]

The Near East

– Antioch (near the modern city of Antakya)

The worship of Isis is first attested to in the reign of Antiochus II (261-246 BCE). Isis appears on coins from the reign of Antiochus IV (175-164 BCE).[795]

– Byblos

Plutarch refers to Isis in Byblos and says that *"even unto this day the people of Byblos venerate the wood lying in the holy place of Isis"*.[796] Isis appears on the coins of Byblos during the reign of Antiochus IV.[797]

– Petra

Hadrian established a temple for Isis in Petra.[798]

---

[791] *Isis in the Ancient World*, Witt, 1997:314 n32
[792] *The Isiac Jug from Southwark*, Griffiths, 1973:233-236
[793] *The Isiac Jug from Southwark*, Griffiths, 1973:233-236
[794] *The Isiac Jug from Southwark*, Griffiths, 1973:233-236
[795] *A History of Antioch in Syria: from Seleucus to the Arab Conquest*, Downey, 1961:91
[796] *Plutarch: Concerning the Mysteries of Isis and Osiris*, Mead, 2002:199
[797] *Isis and Empires*, Bricault & Versluys, 2014:16
[798] *Isis in the Ancient World*, Witt, 1997:236

North Africa

– Tunisia

At Carthage there was a temple to Isis as the Mother of Heaven.[799]

– Libya

There is reference to a sacred crocodile in an Iseum somewhere in Libya.[800]

– Cyrene

There are depictions of Isis dating to the late 2nd century BCE.[801] There was a small temple to Isis in the precinct of Apollo.[802]

– Leptis Magna

There is a temple of Isis here and a sanctuary of Serapis.[803]

---

[799] *A History of Pagan Europe*, Jones & Pennick, 1995:73
[800] *Isis in the Ancient World*, Witt, 1997:34
[801] *Attic Grave Reliefs that Represent Women in the Dress of Isis*, Walters, 1988:14
[802] *Water in the Worship of Isis and Serapis*, Wild, 1981:21
[803] *The Buried City: Excavations at Leptis Magna*, Caffarelli & Caputo, 1966:86 & 89

BIBLIOGRAPHY

Abt, T. & Hornung, E. (2003) *Knowledge for the Afterlife*. Zurich, Living Human Heritage Publications

Abt, T. & Hornung, E. (2007) *The Egyptian Amduat*. Zurich, Living Human Heritage Publications

Aelian & Scholfield A. F. (Trans.) (1958) *On the Characteristics of Animals Volume II*. London, William Heinemann Ltd

Alfoldi, A. (1937) *A Festival of Isis in Rome under the Christian Emperors of the IVth century*. Budapest, Pazmany University

Allason-Jones, L. (2005) *Women in Roman Britain*. York, CBA

Allen, T. A. (1974) *The Book of the Dead or Going Forth by Day*. Chicago, University of Chicago Press

Alvar, J. (2008) *Romanising Oriental Gods*. Leiden, Brill

Andrews, C. (1994) *Amulets of Ancient Egypt*. London, British Museum Press

Apuleius & Walsh, P. G. (trans.) (1994) *The Golden Ass*. Oxford, Oxford University Press

Assmann, J. (1992) W*hen Justice Fails: Jurisdiction and Imprecation in Ancient Egypt and the Near East*. In *Journal of Egyptian Archaeology*, Vol 78:149-162

Bagnall, R. S. & Rathbone, D. W. (2004) *Egypt from Alexander to the Copts*. London, British Museum Press

Bailey, D. M. (2007) *A Snake-Legged Dionysos from Egypt, and Other Divine Snakes*. In *Journal of Egyptian Archaeology*, Vol 93:263-270

Bailleul-LeSuer, R (Ed.) (2012) *Between Heaven & Earth. Birds in Ancient Egypt*, Chicago, Oriental Institute Museum Publications

Baring, A. & Cashford, J. (1993) *The Myth of the Goddess. Evolution of an Image*, London, Penguin Books

Bedoyere, G. (2002) *Gods with Thunderbolts: Religion in Roman Britain*. Stroud, Tempus Publishing Ltd

Bedoyere, G. (2004) *Roman Towns in Britain*. Stroud, Tempus Publishing Ltd

Bell, H. (1948) *Popular Religion in Graeco-Roman Egypt: I. The Pagan Period*. In *Journal of Egyptian Archaeology*, Vol 34:82-97

Bell, H. (1957) *Cults and Creeds in Graeco-Roman Egypt*. Liverpool, Liverpool University Press

Betz, H. D. (Ed.) (1996) *The Greek Magical Papyri in Translation. Volume I: Texts*. Chicago, University of Chicago Press

Bianchi, A. (1987) *Remarks on Beings Called mrwty or mrwryt in the Coffin Texts*. In *Journal of Egyptian Archaeology*, Vol 73:206-207

Bird, J. G. (1986) *An Inscribed Mirror in Athens*. In *Journal of Egyptian Archaeology*, Vol 72:187-189

Blackman, A. M. & Fairman, H. W. (1943) *The Myth of Horus at Edfu: II. C. The Triumph of Horus over His Enemies a Sacred Drama (Continued).* In *Journal of Egyptian Archaeology,* Vol 29:2-36

Blackman, A. M. & Fairman, H. W. (1944) *The Myth of Horus at Edfu: II. C. The Triumph of Horus over His Enemies a Sacred Drama (Concluded).* In *Journal of Egyptian Archaeology,* Vol 30:5-22

Blackman, A. M. & Fairman, H. W. (1949) *The Significance of the Ceremony Hwt Bhsw in the Temple of Horus at Edfu.* In *Journal of Egyptian Archaeology,* Vol 35:98-112

Blansdorf, J. (2010) *The defixiones from the Sanctuary of Isis and Mater Magna in Mainz.* In Gordon, R. L. & Simon, F. M. (eds.) (2010) *Magical Practice in the Latin West: Papers from the International Conference Held at the University of Zaragoza 2005.* Leiden, E J Brill.

Bleeker, C. J. (1963) *Isis as Saviour.* In Brandon, S. G. F. (Ed.) (1963) *The Saviour God.* Manchester, Manchester University Press

Bleeker, C. J. (1963) *The Sacred Bridge.* Leiden, E J Brill

Bleeker, C. J. (1973) *Hathor and Thoth: Two Key Figures of the Ancient Egyptian Religion.* Leiden, E J Brill

Bleeker, C. J. (1975) *The Rainbow.* Leiden, E J Brill

Bleiberg, E., Barbash, Y. & Bruno, L. (2013) *Soulful Creatures. Animal Mummies in Ancient Egypt.* New York, Giles

Bomhard, A. S. (1999) *The Egyptian Calendar: A Work For Eternity.* London, Periplus Publishing

Boraik, M. (2015) *A New Ptolemaic Temple at Gebel el-Nour.* In *Egyptian Archaeology* Vol 46:45-56

Borghouts, J. F. (1978) *Ancient Egyptian Magical Texts.* Leiden, E J Brill

Bourriau, J. D. & Ray, J. D. (1975) *Two Further Decree-Cases of S3k.* In *Journal of Egyptian Archaeology,* Vol 61:257-258

Bowman, A. K. (1986) *Egypt After the Pharaohs.* London, British Museum Publications

Bricault, L. & Versluys, M. J. (2014) *Isis and Empires.* In Bricault, L. & Veymiers, R. (2014) *Power, Politics and the Cults of Isis: Proceedings of the Vth International Conference of Isis Studies,* Leiden, E J Brill.

Bricault, L. & Veymiers, R. (2006) *Isis in Corinth: the Numismatic Evidence. City, Image and Religion.* In Bricault, L., Versluys, M. J. & Meyboom, P. G. P. (Ed.) (2006) *Nile into Tiber: Egypt in the Roman World: Proceedings of the III*rd *International Conference of Isis Studies.* Leiden, E J Brill.

Buck, A. (1949) *The Earliest Version of Book of the Dead 78.* In *Journal of Egyptian Archaeology,* Vol 35:87-97

Budge, E.A.W. (1969) *The Gods of the Egyptians Volume One.* New York, Dover Publications

Burket, W. (1987) *Ancient Mystery Cults.* Massachusetts, Harvard University Press

Caffarelli, E. V. & Caputo, G. (1966) *The Buried City: Excavations at Leptis Magna.* Praeger, New York

Caminos, R. A. (1972) *Another Hieratic Manuscript from the Library of Pwerem Son of Kiki (Pap. B.M. 10288).* In *Journal of Egyptian Archaeology,* Vol 58:205-224

Carpenter, E. (1906) *Civilisation: Its Cause and Cure.* London, Swan Sonnenschein

Casson, L. (1994) *Ships and Seafaring in Ancient Times.* London. British Museum Press

Clark, R. T. (1978) *Myth and Symbol in Ancient Egypt.* London, Thames & Hudson

Clerc, G. (1998) *Une Isis-Fortuna en Alsace.* In Clarysse, W., Schoors, A. & Willems, H. (Eds.) (1998) *Egyptian Religion. The Last Thousand Years. Part I.* Leuven, Peeters Publishers

David, R. (2002) *Religion and Magic in Ancient Egypt.* London, Penguin Books

Davis, S. (1998) *Uncharted Saqqara: A Postscript.* In *Journal of Egyptian Archaeology*, Vol 84:45-56

Delia, D. (1998) *Isis, or the Moon.* In Clarysse, W., Schoors, A. & Willems, H. (Eds.) (1998) *Egyptian Religion. The Last Thousand Years. Part I.* Leuven, Peeters Publishers

Diodorus Siculus & Murphy, E. (1990) *The Antiquities of Egypt. A translation with notes of book 1 of the Library of History of Diodorus Siculus.* London, Transaction Publishers

Dodson, A. (2012) *Meroe. The Last Outpost of Ancient Egypt.* In *Ancient Egypt* Vol 71:34-41

Dousa, T. (1999) *Imagining Isis.* In Ryholt, K (Ed.) (1999) *Acts of the Seventh International Conference of Demotic Studies.* Copenhagen, Museum Tusculanum Press

Downey, G. (1961) *A History of Antioch in Syria: from Seleucus to the Arab Conquest.* Princeton, Princeton University Press

Dunand, F. & Zivie-Coche, C. (2004) *Gods and Men in Egypt: 3000 BCE to 395 CE.* Ithaca, Cornell University Press

el-Khachab, A. (1963) *A Collection of Gems from Egypt in Private Collections.* In *Journal of Egyptian Archaeology*, Vol 49:147-156

el-Khouly, A. (1973) *Excavations East of the Serapeum at Saqqara.* In *Journal of Egyptian Archaeology*, Vol 59:151-155

el-Sabban (2000) *Temple Festival Calendars of Ancient Egypt.* Liverpool, Liverpool University Press

Emery, W. B. (1971) *Preliminary Report on the Excavations at North Saqqara, 1969-70.* In *Journal of Egyptian Archaeology*, Vol 57:3-13

Fairman, H. W. (1935) *The Myth of Horus at Edfu: I.* In *Journal of Egyptian Archaeology*, Vol 21:26-36

Fairman, H. W. (1974) *The Triumph of Horus.* London, Batsford

Faulkner, R. O. (1936) *The Bremner-Rhind Papyrus: I. A. The Songs of Isis and Nephthys.* In *Journal of Egyptian Archaeology*, Vol 22:121-140

Faulkner, R. O. (1938) *The Bremner-Rhind Papyrus: IV.* In *Journal of Egyptian Archaeology*, Vol 24:41-53

Faulkner, R. O. (1958) *An Ancient Egyptian Book of Hours.* Oxford, Griffith Institute

Faulkner, R. O. (1968) *The Pregnancy of Isis.* In *Journal of Egyptian Archaeology*, Vol 54:40-44

Faulkner, R. O. (1989) *The Ancient Egyptian Book of the Dead.* London, British Museum Publications

Faulkner, R. O. (2007) *The Ancient Egyptian Coffin Texts.* Oxford, Aris & Phillips

Faulkner, R. O. (2007) *The Ancient Egyptian Pyramid Texts.* Kansas, Digireads.com Publishing

Fletcher, J. (1999) *Oils and Perfumes of Ancient Egypt.* New York, Harry N Abrams Inc.

Foster, J. L. (1992) *Echoes of Egyptian Voices.* Oklahoma City, University of Oklahoma Press

Foster, J. L. (1995) *Hymns, Prayers and Songs.* Atlanta, Scholars Press

Fowden, G. (1986) *The Egyptian Hermes.* New Jersey, Princeton University Press

Fraser, P. M. (1972) *Ptolemaic Alexandria.* Oxford, Clarendon Press

Friedman, F. D. (Ed.) (1998) *Gifts of the Nile: Ancient Egyptian Faience.* London, Thames & Hudson

Gardiner, A. H. (1938) *The House of Life.* In *Journal of Egyptian Archaeology,* Vol 24:157-179

Gardiner, A. H. (1944) *Horus the Behdetite.* In *Journal of Egyptian Archaeology,* Vol 30:23-60

Gardiner, A. H. (1953) *The Coronation of King Haremhab.* In *Journal of Egyptian Archaeology,* Vol 39:13-31

Gardiner, A. H. (1957) *The So-Called Tomb of Queen Tiye.* In *Journal of Egyptian Archaeology,* Vol 43:10-25

Gasparro, G. S. (2006) *The Hellenistic Face of Isis: Cosmic and Saviour Goddess.* In Bricault, L., Versluys, M. J. & Meyboom, P. G. P. (Ed.) (2006) *Nile into Tiber: Egypt in the Roman World: Proceedings of the 3rd International Conference of Isis Studies.* Leiden, E J Brill.

Gilula, M. (1982) *An Egyptian Etymology of the Name of Horus.* In *Journal of Egyptian Archaeology,* Vol 68:259-265

Goodison, L. & Morris, C. (eds.) (1998) *Ancient Goddesses.* Madison, University of Wisconsin Press

Grant, F. C. (1953) *Hellenistic Religions: The Age of Syncretism.* In Kraemer, R. S. (Ed.) (2004) *Women's Religion in the Greco-Roman World. A Sourcebook.* Oxford University Press.

Gray, L. (Ed.) (2009) *The New Cultural Atlas of Egypt.* London, Brown Reference Group

Green, M. J. (2003) *The Gods of Roman Britain.* Shire Publications, Princes Risborough

Grenfels, B. P. & Hunt, A. S. (1974) *The Oxyrhynchus Papyri.* In Kraemer, R. S. (Ed.) (2004) *Women's Religion in the Greco-Roman World. A Sourcebook.* Oxford University Press.

Griffith, F. L. & Thompson, H. (1974) *The Leyden Papyrus.* New York, Dover Publications

Griffiths, J. G. (1973) *The Isiac Jug from Southwark.* In *Journal of Egyptian Archaeology,* Vol 59:233-236

Griffiths, J. G. (1975) *Apuleius of Madauros – The Isis Book.* Leiden, E J Brill

Griffiths, J. G. (1982) *Eight Funerary Paintings with Judgement Scenes in the Swansea Wellcome Museum.* In *Journal of Egyptian Archaeology,* Vol 68:228-252

Harris, E. & J. R. (1965) *The Oriental Cults of Roman Britain.* Leiden, Brill.

Harris, J. R. (1971) *The Legacy of Egypt.* Oxford, Oxford University Press

Hart, G. (2005) *The Routledge Dictionary of Egyptian Gods and Goddesses.* Abingdon, Routledge

Haycock, B. G. (1972) *Landmarks in Cushite History.* In *Journal of Egyptian Archaeology,* Vol 58:225-244

Herodotus & Selincourt, A. (Trans.) (2003) *The Histories.* London, Penguin Books

Hill, M. (Ed.) (2007) *Gifts for the Gods: Images from Egyptian Temples.* New York, Metropolitan Museum of Art

Holbl, G. (2001) *A History of the Ptolemaic Empire.* London, Routledge

Hornung, E. & Bryan, B. M. (Eds.) (2002) *The Quest for Immortality: Treasures of Ancient Egypt.* London, Prestel Publishers

Hornung, E. (1996) *Conceptions of God in Ancient Egypt.* Ithaca, Cornell University Press

Hornung, E. (2001) *The Secret Lore of Egypt: Its Impact on the West.* Ithaca, Cornell University Press

Houlihan, P. F. (1996) *The Animal World of the Pharaohs.* London, Thames & Hudson

Hutton, R. (1993) *The Pagan Religions of the Ancient British Isles.* London, Wiley

Jackson, R. B. (2002) *At Empire's Edge.* New Haven, Yale University Press

Jacq, C. (1998) *Magic and Mystery in Ancient Egypt.* London, Souvenir Press

Jacq, C. (1999) *The Living Wisdom of Ancient Egypt.* London, Simon & Schuster

Jones, C. (1996) *The Jewellery of Roman Britain.* London, UCL Press

Jones, P. & Pennick, N. (1995) *A History of Pagan Europe.* London, Routledge

Kakosy, L. (1982) *The Nile, Euthenia and the Nymphs.* In *Journal of Egyptian Archaeology,* Vol 68:290-298

Kaper, O. E. (2010) *Isis in Roman Dakhleh: Goddess of the Village, the Province and the Country.* In Bricault, L. & Versluys, M. J. (Ed.) (2010) *Isis on the Nile. Egyptian Gods in Hellenistic and Roman Egypt: Proceedings of the IVth International Conference of Isis Studies.* Leiden, E J Brill.

Kaster, J. (1993) *The Wisdom of Ancient Egypt.* New York, Barnes & Noble Books

Kemp, B. (2007) *How to Read the Egyptian Book of the Dead.* London, Granta Books

King, A. (1990) *Roman Gaul and Germany.* San Francisco, University of California Press.

Kingsford, A. & Maitland, E. (1885) *The Virgin of the World,* London, George Redway

Kitchen, K. A. (1974) *Nakht-Thuty: Servitor of Sacred Barques and Golden Portals.* In *Journal of Egyptian Archaeology,* Vol 60:168-174

Kockelmann, H. (2008) *Praising the Goddess.* Berlin, Walter de Gruyter

Kozloff, A. P. (2012) *Pharaoh Was a Good Egg, but Whose Egg Was He?* In Bailleul-LeSuer, R (Ed.) (2012) *Between Heaven & Earth. Birds in Ancient Egypt,* Chicago, Oriental Institute Museum Publications

Kurth, D. (2004) *The Temple of Edfu.* Cairo, The American University in Cairo Press

Lee, A. D. (2000) *Pagans and Christians in Late Antiquity.* London, Routledge

Lesko, B. S. (1999) *The Great Goddesses of Egypt.* Norman, University of Oklahoma Press

Lichtheim, M. (2006) *Ancient Egyptian Literature Volume I.* California, University of California Press

Lichtheim, M. (2006) *Ancient Egyptian Literature Volume III.* California, University of California Press

Lindsay, J. (1962) *Apuleius: The Golden Ass.* In Meyer, M. W. (1987) *The Ancient Mysteries. A Sourcebook of Sacred Texts.* Philadelphia, University of Pennsylvania Press

Lindsay, J. (1963) *Daily Life in Roman Egypt.* London, Frederick Muller

Lindsay, J. (1968) *Men and Gods on the Roman Nile*. London, Frederick Muller

MacKendrick, P (1971) *Roman France*. London, G Bell and Sons

Manuelian, P. & Loeben, C. E. (1993) *New Light on the Recarved Sarcophagus of Hatshepsut and Thutmose in the Museum of Fine Arts, Boston*. In *Journal of Egyptian Archaeology*, Vol 79:121-155

Markowitz, Y. J. & Doxey, D. M. (2014) *Jewels of Ancient Nubia*. Boston, MFA Publications

Martin, G. T. (1973) *Excavations in the Sacred Animal Necropolis at North Saqqâra, 1971-2: Preliminary Report* In *Journal of Egyptian Archaeology*, Vol 59:5-15

Martin, G. T. (2012) *The Tomb of Maya and Meryt I: The Reliefs, Inscriptions, and Commentary*. London, Egypt Exploration Society

Mead, G. R. S. (2002) *Plutarch: Concerning the Mysteries of Isis and Osiris*. Montana, Kessinger Publishing (Reprints)

Meredith, D. (1952) *The Roman Remains in the Eastern Desert of Egypt*. In *Journal of Egyptian Archaeology*, Vol 38:94-111

Mifsud, A. & Farrugia, M. (2008) *Serapis - Before and After the Ptolemies*. In *Ancient Egypt* Vol 50:50-55

Mojsov, B. (2005) *Osiris. Death and Afterlife of a God*. Oxford, Blackwell Publishing

Morenz, S. (1992) *Egyptian Religion*. Ithaca, Cornell University Press

Muller, H. W. & Thiem, E. (1999) *The Royal Gold of Ancient Egypt*. London, I. B. Tauris

Naerebout, F. G. (2006) *The Temple at Ras el-Soda*. In Bricault, L., Versluys, M. J. & Meyboom, P. G. P. (Ed.) (2006) *Nile into Tiber: Egypt in the Roman World: Proceedings of the 3rd International Conference of Isis Studies*. Leiden, E J Brill.

Naerebout, F. G. (2010) *How Do You Want Your Goddess?* In Bricault, L. & Versluys, M. J. (Ed.) (2010) *Isis on the Nile. Egyptian Gods in Hellenistic and Roman Egypt: Proceedings of the IVth International Conference of Isis Studies*. Leiden, E J Brill.

Noble, V. (2003) *The Double Goddess*. Vermont, Bear & Co.

O'Connell, R. H. (1983) *The Emergence of Horus. An Analysis of Coffin Text Spell 148*. In *Journal of Egyptian Archaeology*, Vol 69:66-87

Oakes, L. & Gahlin, L. (2004) *Ancient Egypt*. London, Hermes House

Ovid & Green, P. (1982) *Ovid – The Erotic Poems*. London, Penguin Books

Parkinson, R. (1991) *Voices from Ancient Egypt*. London, British Museum Press

Pausanias & Frazer, J. G. (1898) *Pausanias's Description of Greece*. London, Macmillon & Company

Peck, W. H. (1978) *Egyptian Drawings*. New York, E. P. Dutton

Pinch, G. (2002) *Egyptian Mythology*. Oxford, Oxford University Press

Pinch, G. (2006) *Magic in Ancient Egypt*. London, The British Museum Press

Pliny & Rackham, H. (Trans.) (1940) *Natural History Volume III*. London, Heinemann Ltd. 940)

Poo, M. (1995) *Wine and Wine Offering in the Religion of Ancient Egypt*. London, Kegan Paul International

Raven, M. (2012) *Egyptian Magic*. Cairo, American University in Cairo Press

Ray, D. J. (1987) *A Pious Soldier: Stele Aswan 1057*. In *Journal of Egyptian Archaeology*, Vol 73:169-180

Raynor, D. (2004) *The Homeric Hymns.* Los Angeles, University of California Press

Riggs, C. (Ed.) (2012) *The Oxford Handbook of Roman Egypt.* Oxford, Oxford University Press

Roberts, P. (2013) *Life and Death in Pompeii and Herculaneum.* London, British Museum Press

Sayell, L. S. (2012) *Servants of Heket.* In *Ancient Egypt* Vol 75:10-15

Schweizer, A. (2010) *The Sungod's Journey Through the Netherworld.* Ithaca, Cornell University Press

Scott, N. E. (1951) *The Metternich Stele.* In *The Metropolitan Museum of Art Bulletin,* Vol 9:201-217

Shafer, B. E. (Ed.) (2005) *Temples of Ancient Egypt.* London, I. B. Tauris

Shaw, G. J. (2014) *The Egyptian Myths.* London, Thames & Hudson

Shaw, I. & Nicholson, P. (2008) *The British Museum Dictionary of Ancient Egypt.* London, British Museum Press

Shonkwiler, R. (2012) *Sheltering Wings: Birds as Symbols of Protection in Ancient Egypt.* In Bailleul-LeSuer, R (Ed.) (2012) *Between Heaven & Earth. Birds in Ancient Egypt,* Chicago, Oriental Institute Museum Publications

Shorter, A. W. (1935) *Notes on Some Funerary Amulets.* In *Journal of Egyptian Archaeology,* Vol 21:171-176

Smith, H. S. (1976) *Preliminary Report on Excavations in the Sacred Animal Necropolis, Season 1974-1975.* In *Journal of Egyptian Archaeology,* Vol 62:14-17

Smith, M. (1993) *The Liturgy of Opening the Mouth for Breathing.* Oxford, Griffith Institute

Smith, M. (2009) *Traversing Eternity.* Oxford, Oxford University Press

Solmsen, F. (1979) *Isis Among the Greeks and Romans.* Massachusetts, Harvard University Press

Spencer, N. A. (1999) *An Epigraphic Survey of Samanud.* In *Journal of Egyptian Archaeology,* Vol 85:55-83

Stevens, A. (2006) *Private Religion at Amarna: the Material Evidence.* Oxford, Archeaopress

Szpakowska, K. (Ed.) (2006) *Through a Glass Darkly.* Swansea, The Classical Press of Wales

Szpakowska, K. (2008) *Daily Life in Ancient Egypt.* Oxford, Blackwell Publishing

Taylor, J. H. (Ed.) (2010) *Journey Through the Afterlife: Ancient Egyptian Book of the Dead.* London, British Museum Press.

Teeter, E. (2011) *Religion and Ritual in Ancient Egypt.* Cambridge, Cambridge University Press

Thomas, E. (1956) *Solar Barks Prow to Prow.* In *Journal of Egyptian Archaeology,* Vol 42:65-79

Thomas, S. (1999) *A Saite Figure of Isis in the Petrie Museum.* In *Journal of Egyptian Archaeology,* Vol 85:232-235

Thomas, S. (2011) *An Unnamed Statue of a Late Middle Kingdom Vizier.* In *Ancient Egypt* Vol. 69:10-14

Tibullus, Dennis, R. & Putman, M. (2012) *The Complete Poems of Tibullus.* Oakland, University of California Press

Tomlin, R. (2010) *Cursing a Thief in Iberia and Britain.* In Gordon, R. L. & Simon, F. M. (eds.) (2010) *Magical Practice in the Latin West: Papers from the International Conference Held at the University of Zaragoza 2005.* Leiden, E J Brill.

Troy, L. (1986) *Patterns of Queenship in Ancient Egyptian Myth and History*. Uppsala, Stockholm University Press

Tyldesley, J (2010) *Myths & Legends of Ancient Egypt*. London, Allen Lane

van Elbe, J. (1995) *The Romans in Cologne and Lower Germany*. Mainz, Ursula Preis Verlag

Vanderlip, V. F. (1972) *The four Greek hymns of Isidorus and the cult of Isis*. Toronto, Hakkert

Venit, M. S. (2010) *Referencing Isis in Tombs of Greco-Roman Egypt*. In Bricault, L. & Versluys, M. J. (Ed.) (2010) *Isis on the Nile. Egyptian Gods in Hellenistic and Roman Egypt: Proceedings of the IVth International Conference of Isis Studies*. Leiden, E J Brill.

Vittozzi, G. C. (2014) *The Flavians: Pharaonic Kingship Between Egypt and Rome*. In Bricault, L. & Versluys, M. J. (Ed.) (2014) *Power, Politics and the Cults of Isis: Proceedings of the Vth International Conference of Isis Studies*. Leiden, E J Brill.

Voros, G. (2010) *The Temple Treasures of Taposiris Magna*. In *Egyptian Archaeology* Vol 36:15-17

Walker, M. (2009) *An Unexpected Turkish Delight*. In *Ancient Egypt* Vol 56:36-37

Walker, M. (2013) *The Temple of Isis at Pompeii*. In *Ancient Egypt* Vol 80:33-47

Walters, E. J. (1988) *Attic Grave Reliefs that Represent Women in the Dress of Isis*. New Jersey, American School of Classical Studies at Athens

Watterson, B. (2003) *Gods of Ancient Egypt*. Stroud, Sutton Publishing Ltd

Wente, E. (1990) *Letters from Ancient Egypt*. Atlanta, Scholars Press

Wente, E. F. (2003) *The Contendings of Horus and Seth*. In Simpson, W. K., Ritner, R. K., Tobin, V.A. & Wente, E. F. (2003) *The Literature of Ancient Egypt*. London, Yale University Press

Whitehouse, H. (2009) *Ancient Egypt and Nubia*. Oxford, Ashmolean Museum

Wild, R. A. (1981) *Water in the Worship of Isis and Sarapis*. Leiden, Brill

Wilkinson, R. H. (1994) *Symbol & Magic in Egyptian Art*. London, Thames & Hudson

Wilkinson, R. H. (2000) *The Complete Temples of Ancient Egypt*. London, Thames & Hudson

Wilkinson, R. H. (2003) *The Complete Gods and Goddesses of Ancient Egypt*. London, Thames & Hudson

Wilkinson, R. H. (2008) *Egyptian Scarabs*. Oxford, Shire Publications

Wilkinson, R. H. (2011) *Reading Egyptian Art*. London, Thames & Hudson

Wilkinson, T. (2003) *Genesis of the Pharaohs*. London, Thames & Hudson

Witt, R. E. (1997) *Isis in the Ancient World*. Baltimore, The John Hopkins University Press

Woolf, G. (2014) *Isis and the Evolution of Religions*. In Bricault, L. & Versluys, M. J. (Ed.) (2014) *Power, Politics and the Cults of Isis: Proceedings of the Vth International Conference of Isis Studies*. Leiden, E J Brill.

Xenophon of Ephesus & Anderson, G. (1986) *Ephesian Tale of Anthia and Habrocomes*. In Kraemer, R. S. (Ed.) (2004) *Women's Religion in the Greco-Roman World. A Sourcebook*. Oxford University Press.

Zabkar, L. V. (1988) *Hymns to Isis in Her Temple at Philae*. Hanover, University Press of New England

INDEX

Published by Avalonia
www.avaloniabooks.co.uk

Made in the USA
Charleston, SC
24 August 2014